LEON H. GINSBERG was the West Virginia Social Worker of the Year in 1978; the Chairman of the Public Policy Committee of the Child Welfare League of America; and is currently the President of the American Public Welfare Association. He is the editor of *Social Work in Rural Communities*, co-author, with Anita Harbert, of *Human Services for Older Adults*, and with Nancy Datan, of *Life Span Developmental Psychology: Theoretical and Applied Perspectives*. He is the current Commissioner of Welfare for the State of West Virginia.

The Practice of
Social Work
in Public Welfare

Fields of Practice Series

Francis J. Turner and Herbert S. Strean, Editors

The Practice of Social Work in Public Welfare

Leon H. Ginsberg

THE FREE PRESS
A Division of Macmillan Publishing Co., Inc.
NEW YORK

Collier Macmillan Publishers
LONDON

The Free Press
A Division of Macmillan Publishing Co., Inc.
866 Third Avenue, New York, N.Y. 10022

Collier Macmillan Canada, Inc.

Library of Congress Catalog Card Number: 82–71888

Printed in the United States of America

printing number

1 2 3 4 5 6 7 8 9 10

Library of Congress Cataloging in Publication Data

Ginsberg, Leon H.
  The practice of social work in public welfare.

  (Fields of practice series)
  Bibliography: p.
  Includes index.
  1. Public welfare—United States.   2. Social service—United States.   3. Social case work.   I. Title.
II. Series.
HV91.G47   1983   361.3'0973   82–71888
ISBN 0–02–911760–7

Contents

Foreword

In 1978 The Free Press published the first of a series of books each of which addresses a particular theoretical approach of significance in the helping professions. Once this series was well underway it became evident that a second series was needed, one that differentially examines practice from the dimension of specific fields of practice.

Every profession has to face the complex question of specialization versus generalization. In this regard it has to come to terms with issues related to training and practice, and to make decisions about the relative emphasis given to those matters that are common to all areas of the profession's various fields of practice and those that are specific to each area.

There are of course dangers in emphasizing either extreme. If the generic is overemphasized there is a risk that important aspects of practice will be dealt with at a level of abstraction that bears little immediate relevance to what the worker actually does. If the emphasis is on the particular there is the danger of fragmentation and neglect of the need to search for commonalities and interconnections. Obviously, a balance between these two extremes is desirable.

Many of the human services, and social work in particular, have tended to overemphasize the generic to the detriment of the specific needs of clients with highly specialized needs. The majority of social work literature over the past three decades has focused either on modalities of practice as a single entity or on a specific theoretical basis of practice. This is not to say that there are not practitioners who are highly skilled in working effectively with specialized groups of clients. What is lacking is an organized compilation of the particular practice components of each of these specialized areas of practice in a way that is readily accessible to other practitioners in these areas.

Certainly within the periodical literature of social work there is a rich array of individual articles addressing specific components of practice involving work with particular client target groups. But such articles are scattered and not written from a common perspective and thus are of varying utility to practitioners.

It is the purpose of this new series to move in the direction of tapping this rich wealth of practice wisdom in a way that makes it readily available on a broad basis. To this end a series of specific fields of practice has been identified and known experts in each field have been asked to write about practice in their specialty from a common framework.

The goal of each book is to address not only the therapeutic aspects of practice in these fields but also the range of sociological, policy, administration, and research areas so as to present the reader with an overview of the specific field of practice as well as the specifics about therapy. In addition to helping the individual worker to learn more about a specific field of practice, the series as a whole, it is hoped, will provide an opportunity to make comparisons among fields of practice and thus facilitate the ongoing expansion of general knowledge.

Certainly there is growing awareness of the need for addressing the specific training and practice needs of each field of practice. Many schools of social work now arrange their curricula along the line of fields of practice. The NASW has utilized the notion of fields of practice to relate systematically to how some social workers are employed and to prescribe the roles most appropriate for them.

The fields selected for coverage in this series may or may not represent clearly defined areas of specialization in social work. Rather they are identifiable human needs or problem populations or even settings for which a discrete and identifiable cluster of attitudes, skills, and knowledge is thought to be needed in order to intervene effectively.

We are delighted to welcome Commissioner Leon Ginsberg's book to our series. Dr. Ginsberg comes to his task well-equipped—he has been a practitioner, academician, and administrator—and he fulfills his task extremely well. Not only does his book describe the public welfare system accurately and comprehensively, but also the practitioner, student, teacher, supervisor, and administrator can learn from Dr. Ginsberg just what are the necessary skills, attitudes, and knowledge that are necessary to help clients in the welfare system.

In contrast to other books on public welfare, Dr. Ginsberg is neither defensive nor hypercritical. He pinpoints some of the limitations of the public welfare system as they now exist, and he helps the reader come to grips with what he or she can and cannot do within it.

The book describes the philosophy, history, and methods of social

work so that the reader never loses sight of the social worker's responsibilities as he or she negotiates the complex public welfare system. Dr.
Ginsberg also discusses the social worker's role as he or she relates to
government officials and members of other disciplines.

This book will be of particular interest to any helping professional in
the public welfare system and to all social workers who care about
meeting with Charlotte Towle called the "common human needs."

FRANCIS J. TURNER
HERBERT S. STREAN

Preface

PUBLIC WELFARE IS by far the largest social welfare system in the United States. Its programs of financial assistance, medical assistance, food stamps, social services, and purchases of various services from private and other public social welfare programs make it the nation's largest influence on social welfare and, therefore, social work.

Social workers are employed in every element of the vast public welfare field. Those in public welfare include heads of state and local departments, occupants of other high level administrative posts, as well as the most direct providers of client services. Although professionally educated social workers in most departments are concentrated in jobs associated with the planning and delivery of social services such as foster care, adoption, child protection, probation services, and social aid to the elderly and disabled, significant numbers also serve as researchers, hearings officers, public assistance specialists, fraud investigators, and fiscal planners and managers. Public welfare employees include people educated in many disciplines, but social work is the single most commonly represented profession.

This text briefly describes the public welfare field and the range of services it offers. The various administrative arrangements under which it operates in federal, state, and local government units are examined. The major focus of the text, however, is on the ways in which social work knowledge, particularly knowledge of the practice methods, is applied in the public welfare field.

The book deals generally with the structure and functions of public welfare agencies because those agencies vary dramatically from jurisdiction to jurisdiction. Whereas one state may include only cash assistance and child welfare in its public welfare department, another may include those plus dozens of other services such as correctional and mental institutions and vocational rehabilitation services. These patterns of organization frequently change within each state. The jurisdictional arrangements of public welfare also vary from state to state. Some states have centralized, state-administered public welfare programs while others have local administration with state supervision. Those who need specific, current information may consult the annuai directories of public welfare which are published each year and are widely available in libraries and social agencies.

The book assumes some knowledge or parallel study of other elements in the social work curriculum. For example, it is expected that most readers will have knowledge of concepts such as the culture of poverty, variations in socio-economic status among ethnic minorities, the special problems of families sufficiently impoverished to receive public assistance, family dynamics, and various other information ordinarily included in courses in the human behavior and social environment sequences of social work programs. Similarly, the text avoids instructing the reader on how to conduct research, inasmuch as students learn the skills of research in the larger curriculum. Instead, the book identifies research strategies in the field of public welfare and raises some research questions that may be pursued.

The social welfare policy and services issues such as the strong differences of opinion on public welfare policies are not covered in detail. Many other texts are devoted solely to those issues (Dobelstein, 1980; Greenblatt, 1979). However, the role of the social work practitioner in developing and applying public welfare policy is discussed in Chapter 11.

Essentially, the focus of the text is on the application of social work methods to the public welfare field. Those methods are broadly defined and include not only the traditional intervention strategies of social casework, social group work, and community organization, but also the use of administrative, research, adjudication, and investigation methods in the field. But, again, it is assumed that the student will obtain detailed knowledge about and assistance in developing methodological skills in other classroom and field experiences.

Students interested in learning more about the practice of social work in public welfare are the primary audience for the text. Many of them will be students in practice or methods courses on that subject. Others may have field instruction placements in public welfare agencies. Students in related fields such as public administration, counseling, economics, and sociology, may also find this book useful. Employees in public welfare departments who are continuing their professional studies are also part of this text's audience.

This book is designed to fill an unmet need in social work education.

Through the 1960s and the 1970s social work education on public welfare was centered on social welfare policy issues. The emphasis was on matters such as the organization of welfare rights movements and legal decisions affecting fair hearings, eligibility regulations, and benefit levels. But little has been published in recent years on the specific roles played by professional social workers in public welfare. Consequently, many professional social workers have been educated without formally learning about the functions of their profession in the public welfare field. Many find themselves employed in public welfare upon graduation from social work programs and discover that they have little specific preparation for some of the complex and demanding responsibilities they are expected to perform. This text is designed to help fill the gap and correct the lack of attention to this subject in social work education programs.

The citations located throughout the text refer the reader to sources listed in the bibliography. Some of these sources are the basis of the statements they follow in the text. In other cases they simply suggest readings which further explain or expand upon the content of this book.

Much of the content is based upon the author's work as the head of a state public welfare agency and as an officer of several national organizations involved in public welfare services. Some of the concepts and methods have not previously been reported in the literature of social work.

I am grateful to Governor John D. Rockefeller IV of West Virginia for giving me the opportunity to learn firsthand about the fascinating and diverse field of public welfare. My thanks also to the West Virginia Legislature which has allowed me to direct public welfare in my state without severing my ties to the academic world.

Special thanks for editorial and manuscript assistance go to Elaine K. Ginsberg, Michael H. Ginsberg, Mary Lou Webb, and to Joy B. Jones for bibliographical help, as well as to Laura Wolff and Robert Harrington of The Free Press.

In addition, I am grateful to the editors of this series, Dr. Herbert S. Strean and Dr. Francis J. Turner, for conceiving the idea for this book and for their guidance, encouragement, and support during its preparation.

LEON H. GINSBERG

PART I

INTRODUCTION

Part I introduces the three major components of public welfare, which are discussed and described for the purpose of helping the reader develop some understanding of and skill in the practice of social work in public welfare. Those three fundamental components are public welfare agencies, public welfare employees, and public welfare clients.

Chapter 1 provides a brief overview of the public welfare field, its origins, its functions, and its contemporary concerns. Chapter 2 identifies and discusses the social workers who comprise a large part of the employees of the public welfare programs. Part I ends with Chapter 3 which describes the clients of public welfare services.

Subsequent chapters in Parts II and III, which comprise the bulk of the text, analyze the ways in which public welfare agencies and their employees help clients overcome their personal and social problems through the application of social service programs and social work methods. But this initial part of the text provides information that lays the groundwork for understanding the practice of social work in public welfare agencies.

For those who are familiar with public welfare through previous study or employment, some of the information in this part of the text will be repetitive. For those who are newcomers to the systematic study of public welfare, these chapters may provide shocking contradictions to ideas the reader may have held for a long time. As Chapter 2 points out, for example, most of the people who provide services in public welfare departments are not professionally educated in social work. Although social work is the profession most commonly found in public welfare, most employees, including those who carry the civil service title of social worker, have not studied social work in a college or university.

The information in Chapter 3 on public welfare's clients may also contradict stereotypes long held by the reader. Chapter 3 describes the actual recipients of public welfare. Despite widely held public stereotypes, most of those who receive public welfare are not unemployed or malingering males. Instead, they are typically women with young children, the fathers of whom refuse to support them.

Part I points out the diversity of public welfare's clientele, which includes people from all age groups, professions, ethnic groups, and regions of the United States. Public welfare, its employees, and its clients, are described in this text as normal and critical parts of the societies in which these programs operate.

CHAPTER 1

The Public Welfare Field

WELFARE, a term which combines the words "fare" and "well" to mean, simply, doing well, exists wherever and however people live. Charity, benevolence, and mutual aid are found in the histories of all peoples in every part of the world. Welfare is the word used to include all these activities, which have taken different forms in different civilizations. Public welfare is welfare that is organized, directed, and financed by government, rather than by voluntary contributions or activities.

Early Forms of Welfare

Helping the disadvantaged is a natural social function and, therefore, welfare is one of the things all peoples create as part of their culture along with providing for the education of the young, developing rules for family life, obtaining food, and worshipping. Certainly the welfare created varies with geography, life style, and era. In the unmechanized agricultural villages of Africa, Asia, and Latin America, welfare may be simply sharing food and taking in orphans and widows. For some desert societies, in which family life is all-pervasive, welfare may include an unmarried man marrying his deceased brother's widow. In the early years of America, rural villagers assisted one another with the construction of houses. Burial societies and insurance for widows and orphans are also early examples. All of these services and activities and more, as varied as the problems humans encounter, constitute welfare (Federico, 1980).

3

Welfare and the Industrial Society

With the evolution of the industrial society, people faced new kinds of problems. The industrial society focuses less on agriculture and other forms of food production for its own community and more on the production of goods and services for others who are totally removed from it. Citizens of industrial societies produce very little food or other goods and services for their personal use. Instead, they are employees, who produce for a broad regional, national, or international market. They earn wages for their work and with those wages they purchase the things they need for their own sustenance. Citizens of industrial societies do not live in isolated villages and grow their own food on their own land. Instead, they live close together in towns, cities, and metropolitan areas, near the mines, factories, and offices where their labor is needed—where there are jobs. They have access to little or no land or building materials or livestock. But they purchase food, shelter, and clothing with the wages they earn. In other words, the industrial state is a money-centered, complex society in which people exchange their labor for the products of the labor of others, through the medium of wages (Trattner, 1979; Wilensky and Lebeaux, 1958).

The people of industrial societies are highly dependent on one another but their interdependence is impersonal. One cannot obtain the necessities without someone else producing and distributing them. One cannot have the resources to obtain them without work and wages. But only rarely does one know the producer of the goods one buys or the purchaser of the products one produces. Each may be thousands of miles away.

Although the simple exchange of aid is often still sufficient welfare in nonindustrial societies, it is not adequate in industrial societies where:

1. *Products and services are not exchanged directly—the economy is based upon cash.*
2. *One may or may not be near families and friends who feel an obligation to help in time of need.*
3. *Disadvantage may strike everyone at once so that few are able to help either themselves or others.*

Nongovernmental Welfare

Governmental participation in welfare is a relatively recent development in much of the world. In pre-industrial states, in which many people still live, sharing meets many welfare needs. In the early industrial societies welfare began with families, self-help groups, and churches. For example, many of the fraternal and civic groups, which continue to serve the needy today, began as mutual aid organizations. Groups such as the Masonic lodges, the Knights of Columbus, B'nai B'rith, and many others began as associations of men with similar occupational or religious backgrounds who banded together for the purposes of protecting one another and one another's families from the disasters of the industrial society through early forms of life insurance. Philanthropists often established orphanages for homeless children or homes that could provide shelter and care for widows and their children. Churches provided relief for the poor through contributions from church members. All of these services remain in existence today but they serve different people with different needs. The fraternal and civic organizations sponsor hospitals and special care for people with special problems. Or they sponsor programs of religious and cultural development for youth, recreation and nutrition for the aged, or rehabilitation of the handicapped. The former orphanages provide care for children who cannot live with their own families for various social or psychological reasons. The churches often provide assistance to victims of emergencies such as fires.

LOCAL WELFARE

In addition to the nongovernmental charity which met most of the industrial society's welfare needs, many local governments—counties and cities—operated some welfare services, too. These included housing for the disadvantaged in the form of poor farms and homes for children, and some cash assistance, food, and other benefits that could allow a family to remain in its own home. Again, the services were directed to the aged, young children, widows, and the handicapped.

Throughout most of the history of industrial nations, voluntary charity and local welfare sufficed to meet the needs of most people who were disadvantaged (Brieland et al., 1980).

ECONOMIC DISASTER AND THE INDUSTRIAL STATE

As the industrial state became more pervasive, voluntary and local welfare became less able to meet the needs of the disadvantaged. From time to time, whole communities experienced economic collapses that threw the total work force into unemployment (Wilensky and Lebeaux, 1958). Individuals could not help one another or themselves. No one could pay taxes so the local governments were unable to assist those in need. Few had funds with which to make contributions, so churches and voluntary groups could not help either. It was clear that help was needed from outside the community. Therefore the federal government became involved in human services.

The experience of the United States was typical of that of many other industrial nations. When the economy collapsed in 1929 because of the unfortunate convergence of a number of factors, the nation found it necessary to either tolerate the suffering of a third of its people or make major changes in the ways it provided assistance to its disadvantaged. Some believed that the United States population was on the verge of revolting against its government because so many were unemployed and unable to support themselves or their families.

Public Welfare Through Social Security

In the United States, the answer to widespread poverty and potential social chaos was the Social Security Act of 1935, part of the program of President Franklin D. Roosevelt, who was elected in 1932, in the middle of the worst depression in United States history. Roosevelt's program, called the New Deal, was not unlike the antidepression programs of many other Western industrial states. Parts of his new Federal welfare program were based upon programs he had sponsored as governor of New York and which were administered by his close friend and aide Harry Hopkins, who also helped design his federal programs (May, 1980).

Many of the measures taken to end the Depression were not considered public welfare services. Some reformed the ways in which government was financed. Others provided work on public projects for the unemployed. Of course, programs of economic reform and public works play major roles in improving the conditions of disadvantaged citizens (Macarov, 1980). But the public welfare services—the first truly public, national program in the nation—were embodied in the Social Security Act.

That Act, which has been changed regularly and dramatically to reflect changing social conditions and changing beliefs about human need, remains the basis for United States public welfare in much the same way the Constitution is the basic document of the United States government.

As originally passed, the Social Security Act provided for three primary means of helping people prevent or cope with social and economic disadvantage (Leiby, 1978).

First, it created a national social insurance program which required participation by most people employed in business and industry. Annual premiums were shared by employers and employees. When the family breadwinner died, the program provided benefits to dependent children until they reached eighteen years of age. Widows were assisted by their husband's benefits. The retired, disabled, and blind benefited from monthly pensions.

For those in need who were already disabled, orphaned, widowed, or too old to be employed, the Act established a public program under which states could receive federal funds to provide cash assistance to the impoverished aged, blind, disabled, and families with dependent children.

The Act also provided for services to rural infants and children through a program of child welfare assistance. The Act has always included some social as well as economic assistance to its beneficiaries.

Of course, the Social Security Act is now quite different than it was in 1935, just as the social conditions which led to its passage have changed. Now almost all employed and self-employed people must participate in the social insurance program. The aged, blind, and disabled poor are now covered through a federal program of Supplemental Security Income, rather than through state programs.

The child welfare services have been expanded to cover urban as well as rural families. Medical payments for the aged and disadvantaged have been added.

But public welfare in the United States is still, fundamentally, the programs and services which fall under the provisions of the Social Security Act. Although the focus of this text is on public welfare in the United States, most of the services described are similar in Canada and most of Western Europe. Public welfare services differ in most of Eastern Europe, Asia, Africa, and Latin America, for economic, cultural, and political reasons, but many of the economic and social services are available to some extent and in some form everywhere in the world. These are described more completely in Chapter 18.

These comprehensive welfare services, which are supported by public funds, have supplanted the local and voluntary charitable efforts that were once the basis of welfare in the United States.

Organization of Public Welfare in the United States

Each of the states and commonwealths has a public welfare program, although the name of the agency which houses the program varies from state to state. Some agencies are known as departments of human resources, others as departments of human services, still others as departments of social services and some retain the more traditional title of department of welfare or department of public welfare. A listing of all the state agencies may be found in Appendix 1.

These state agencies vary, too, in the ways they are organized. In some states, the department is a single organization and provides all of the public welfare services throughout the state. In other states, the services are organized and delivered by the counties, cities, or towns while the state only provides guidance, supervision, and some funds to the local agencies.

The federal government provides funding to the state according to a series of complex matching formulas, based upon the state's per capita income and the state government's appropriations for public welfare. The funding of public welfare is discussed in greater detail in Part III.

Public welfare services are not the same in all states. In some states the public welfare department provides not only cash assistance for the disadvantaged but also social services, juvenile corrections programs, mental health services, vocational rehabilitation, hospitals and homes for the aged, employment services, maternal and child health programs, and public health. In some cases the agencies that organize and deliver these services are called "super agencies" and combine once separate governmental departments. They represent attempts to coordinate those services throughout large, umbrella-like structures. The precise definition of public welfare's services varies from state to state. Appendix 2 shows the range and variations of the organization and delivery of public welfare.

The sizes of assistance grants also vary from state to state. For example, Texas paid a maximum grant of $140 per month for a family in 1981, while Hawaii granted $546 per month for a similar family. Payment levels are not statistically related to the state's cost of living or wealth. Instead, the most important criterion is the amount of money the state government chooses to appropriate for assisting the poor. Of course, many other social, political, and economic factors affect that decision.

THE SCOPE OF PUBLIC WELFARE

Public welfare in the 1980s is one of the largest industries in the United States. Each year, local, state, and federal governments spend nearly $100 billion on public assistance for some eleven million people. An estimated 200,000 people from virtually every imaginable professional and occupational group in the United States were employed in public welfare in 1981 (Street et al., 1979; U. S. Department of Health and Human Services, 1980).

In addition to the direct expenditure of funds for public welfare, large sums are expended each year by private and voluntary social welfare agencies which, through contracts for purchases of services, continue to provide large quantities of help in cooperation with public welfare. In addition, billions are expended on social services for the disadvantaged by government agencies.

As later chapters demonstrate, the scope of public welfare in the United States has moved far beyond its original clientele of disabled, aged, or handicapped people, and families with dependent children. Today's programs of public welfare provide such a wide range of services that almost all citizens, at some time in their lives, benefit from it.

SOME UNRESOLVED ISSUES

During the years of public welfare's development, several issues have arisen that remain sources of public controversy and that lead some to criticize public welfare programs. These are issues that are not easily settled. Although the goals of this text are to help readers effectively understand employment in public welfare, it is useful to be aware of some of the fundamental conflicts about welfare in the United States (Morris, 1979).

1. Should public welfare's economic assistance be national or should it continue to vary state by state? Some plans for reforming welfare (President Richard M. Nixon's Family Assistance Program and President Jimmy Carter's Better Jobs and Income Program of 1977) place all economic aid under the Social Security program. President Reagan proposed that all economic assistance be a state responsibility.

2. What level of benefits will assist families in achieving economic independence without making them dependent on public help for the rest of their lives? Should public assistance be a program of last resort for the most needy or should it also supplement the working poor?

3. Should the requirements that clients accept work or work training apply equally to men and women? When might it be wiser to leave single women at home to care for their children, thus maintaining some family integrity and avoiding the cost of day care?

4. Are public welfare services best delivered as a single program of one agency of state government or is there special value to the super or umbrella agency approach?

Conclusion

Public welfare is one of the world's largest, most complex, and least understood industries. It evolved in the pre-World War II years from a network of voluntary and religious charities and services which could no longer cope with the economic dislocations of industrial society. Although every nation of the world has some sort of public welfare system, the philosophies that underlie them and the services they offer differ dramatically from nation to nation.

In the United States, after nearly fifty years of history, the scope and nature of public welfare continues to be a source of unresolved public conflicts over who should be helped, how they should be served, how generous those services should be, and how they should be organized and delivered.

CHAPTER 2

The Social Work Profession in Public Welfare

THE PROFESSION of social work and the field of public welfare have experienced long and intertwined histories. The effects of public welfare on professional social work have been inestimable and the impact of social work on the field has been as significant as any other force affecting public welfare. The relationship between the two has changed often—from cooperation at some times to conflict at other times.

The contradictions, conflicts, and shared history are not unusual because fields of practice such as public welfare and professions such as social work are different in their objectives and priorities. At times their concerns merge while at others they diverge.

There are many examples of these surprising confusions and contradictions between the field of public welfare and the profession of social work. For one, a large proportion of all social workers have, at one time or another, been employed by or been connected through their employment with public welfare agencies. It is likely that as many as half of all the social workers holding master's degrees have either had part or all of their educations financed by public welfare agencies, participated in public welfare field experiences, or worked in agencies that were at least partially funded by contracts with public welfare departments. Some of those individuals have become disenchanted with public welfare and are likely to express their discontent even though they are or have been firmly rooted in the field.

No matter what disagreements they may have, almost any social worker in any agency will at least occasionally call upon public welfare departments for help with clients. Public welfare is so much larger than any other social work field and its services are so fundamental to meeting the needs of people who have social or economic problems that one cannot effectively serve clients without calling upon public welfare for help. But the cooperation public welfare departments provide to other agencies varies from locality to locality and, at times, from worker to worker. This may lead to conflicts between public welfare agencies and professional social workers who serve in other agencies. Perhaps the most glaring contradictions between the profession and the field are conflicts over policy issues between professionally educated social workers who are employees of public welfare agencies and the official positions of professional social work organizations. It is not unusual to find a professional social work organization whose members are largely public welfare employees condemning a public welfare department for a specific policy.

But in reality the conflicts between public welfare departments and professional social workers often have the tone of friendly disagreements rather than conflicts between permanent adversaries. By and large the profession of social work and the field of public welfare agree. The differences are almost always over levels of assistance and program formats rather than over more fundamental matters. In the final analysis, social work is central to public welfare and public welfare is central to social work.

Definitions of Social Work and Social Workers

Just what is social work and who are social work professionals (Briar, 1981)? Those would seem to be relatively easily answered questions but, in fact, the definitions of both social work as a profession and social workers as a professional group are dynamic and are subject to both debate and frequent change. That is because the social welfare industry has expanded so much over recent years and because the title of social worker is used in a variety of ways by various organizations and individuals. Only a few states have laws to protect the term social worker from being used by people who have not completed social work degrees or who have not otherwise associated themselves with the profession.

But there are some qualities that characterize professions and professionals (Etzioni, 1964). These are some of the fundamental characteristics of professions and professionals.

1. Professions have codes of ethics and members of professions subscribe to those codes.
2. Professions are generally organized and professionals tend to affiliate with professional organizations. The professional organizations serving social workers are discussed in Chapter 15.
3. Professionals have a body of knowledge that they use in carrying
   out their work.
4. Professionals are trained in that body of knowledge, usually in
   professional educational programs. Social work's professional education programs are discussed later in this chapter.

Some social scientists, such as Amitai Etzioni (1964), distinguish between professionals and semi-professionals in terms of the length of
their training. Etzioni describes social work as a "semi-profession" because, in most cases, the training is not as long as he expects for a full
profession. Etzioni also suggests that full professions deal with matters
of life and death and although it is true that some social workers are
involved in life and death matters, most are not. Etzioni also says that
full professionals are self-directed and likely to consult with their peers
for guidance, rather than being formally supervised on their day to day
activities. Most social workers, including those in public welfare, are
closely supervised and only a tiny fraction are engaged in private
practice.

The reality of social work practice in public welfare is that some social
workers practice as if they were professionals while others practice as if
they were semi-professionals, by Etzioni's definitions. In any case, competent social workers do have specific training and do subscribe to and
follow a code of ethics (Steiner and Gross, 1981; Reamer, 1979, 1980).

The ethics that are most commonly accepted for social work may be
summarized as follows:

1. Social workers believe in self-determination for all people. That is,
they generally oppose compelling people who are not harming others to
change their behavior. Instead, they believe that people should be given
choices, options, and opportunities to become what they would like to
be.

2. Social workers tend to have a passion for equality. That is, members of the profession generally believe that all human beings are entitled to at least a minimal level of health care, food, nutrition, and
housing but also, and even more important, opportunities for self-im-
provement through education and work so that the humblest citizens
may have access to the highest stations in life.

3. Similarly, social workers tend to be outraged by discrimination
and inequality. Watch a group of ten people visiting an important historical monument. The one who is paying less attention to the monument

and more to the beggar standing beside it is probably the social worker in the group.

4. Members of the profession tend to believe in democratic processes and democratic government.

5. Social workers tend to believe that everyone who is sick, in trouble, or poor ought to have a chance to be rehabilitated to the highest possible level and to the point that the person reaches his or her maximum level of functioning. The older cancer victim should never, social workers believe, be left alone to simply die peacefully. Instead, the person ought to be rehabilitated to the maximum level of functioning. For some, maximum functioning may mean a well paying professional job. For others it may mean the ability to dress oneself without help. Either is acceptable, depending upon the needs and capacities of the client. But giving up on any client is always unacceptable.

Social workers vary in their beliefs and values. There are politically liberal and politically conservative social workers. There are social workers who are leaders in all religious groups and a special association of evangelical social workers. There are social workers who are dedicated socialists and social workers who have strong convictions about the importance of free enterprise. One should never assume that there is only one kind or even one dozen kinds of social workers.

Social workers come from a variety of backgrounds. Many of those most influential in the field have not been professionally educated in social work.

Harry Hopkins, perhaps the primary architect of the New Deal, was not a professionally educated social worker, although he devoted his life to social work programs. Wilbur Cohen, Secretary of Health, Education, and Welfare under President Lyndon B. Johnson, was one of the developers of the Social Security Act and one of its main defenders and interpreters for decades. He has held prominent positions in many of the professional social work organizations, although he was not professionally educated in social work.

As a profession, social work has always attracted social reformers and others anxious to bring about change in the lives of people (Greenstone, 1979). The early social work pioneers such as Edith Abbott (1940), Jane Addams, (1910), and Mary Richmond (1917) were crusaders for the development of a better life for people who were socio-economically deprived in the United States, including migrants and the native poor (Greenstone, 1979).

Later social workers such as Dr. Whitney Young, who was president of the Urban League, continued that tradition. Dean Elizabeth Wisner and her colleague Florence Sytz of the Tulane University School of Social Work were strong advocates of equal rights for blacks in New Orleans well before equality was a reality anywhere in the American South.

Social workers such as Jane Addams fought for peace in the early twentieth century (Davis and McCree, 1969). Social workers were feminists almost a century ago and helped secure passage of the nineteenth amendment to the Constitution, which permitted women to vote. And social workers crusaded for the rights of gay people before that movement became popular and acceptable. So the profession has always been social reform oriented and directed toward change that would better the lives of individuals.

Professional Social Workers in Public Welfare

It is not known precisely how many professionally educated and identified social workers work in public welfare, but an estimated one-third of those who belong to the 90,000 member National Association of Social Workers, the largest of all the social work organizations and the only one that involves the whole spectrum of social work practitioners, are employed in public welfare agencies.

Most statistics on social workers in public welfare positions demonstrate that they constitute a small but significant minority of all the employees working in the field (Gummer, 1979). The Child Welfare League of America has found that fewer than 9 percent of the public welfare child welfare workers hold Master of Social Work degrees. Increasingly more hold bachelor's degrees in social work and many of those who do not hold specific social work degrees have had some course work or continuing education in professional social work education programs. In addition, many of those who work as social work aides or assistants in public welfare have had specialized social work training in community colleges or four-year colleges as preparation for their work.

However, available figures do not always indicate the realities of public welfare employee identification with the social work profession. Many professionally educated social workers do not belong to the National Association of Social Workers. But the National Association of Social Workers enrolls employees of social agencies, including public welfare, who do not have formal educations in social work.

Even though the last National Association of Social Workers study showed that less than ten percent of its members were employed in public welfare, the number who called themselves caseworkers, family service workers, and child welfare workers indicates some crossover between these definitions.

No matter how they are defined, however, most of the people who are employed in public welfare think of themselves as social workers, are called social workers by the general public, or carry government job titles of social worker or derivatives of the title such as "caseworker," "economic service worker," "eligibility worker," or "social services worker." Many professionally educated social workers are upset when those without formal preparation in the field identify themselves as social workers, and question their right to call themselves social workers. In some states social workers must be licensed and anyone who wants to practice or be called a social worker must meet certain educational requirements and pass a written licensing examination.

Social workers in public welfare participate in a variety of tasks, some of which are only rarely taught by social work education programs and are seldom included in most traditional definitions of the practice of social work. Public welfare social worker responsibilities are as common to social work as family counseling, client interviewing, and group services to people with social problems. But they are also as unrelated to direct service roles as locating absent parents, developing and administering programs for people encountering a variety of socio-economic difficulties, conducting research, educating others to meet their responsibilities, and investigating fraud and abuse. The various roles social workers play in public welfare and the ways in which they play them are the subject of most of the subsequent chapters of this text.

Goals for Public Welfare

The social work profession's objectives for public welfare change from time to time but remain somewhat consistently focused upon the following (Turner, 1978):

1. Social work professionals want to promote universalization of social services. Social workers and the profession as a whole generally believe strongly in the values of social work services. They believe those services ought to be made widely available to the total population as part of society's efforts to deal with social problems such as poor health, mental illness, and developmental disabilities, and as a means of improving society through better and more extensive social welfare programs. A general attitude among social workers is that social services are not for the poor and the disadvantaged alone, as public welfare services are, but for everyone. Therefore, public welfare's assistance with social and economic problems ought to be expanded and made available in the whole population.

2. The social work profession has generally battled to insure that public welfare services are performed by professional social workers who are identified with the profession. They believe that services will improve if better prepared people deliver them. They also are concerned

that services be delivered by people with an ethical commitment to helping others, rather than by people who simply do what they are told. In other words, the social work profession's hope is that the professional and ethical commitments of social workers will permeate the delivery of all public welfare services. When it became clear in the second half of the twentieth century that public welfare departments would never realize social work's goal of hiring all or almost all professional social workers, the National Association of Social Workers changed its definitions to allow public welfare employees to affiliate with NASW, even though they may never have studied social work.

3. The social work profession generally supports major reforms of public assistance. Programs such as guaranteed minimum incomes, objective and simplified methods of determining eligibility, and other forms of more humane and less law-enforcement-like public assistance appeal to and have been supported by professional social workers.

4. Short of major reforms, social work supports improving the level of public assistance and other public welfare benefits so that fewer people will be poor and so that there will be a general minimal level standard of living for all citizens, no matter what their station in life, whether or not they are able to be employed.

5. The profession of social work also endorses programs of national health insurance and other benefits for all citizens, no matter what their social or economic status.

6. The profession has been influenced in recent years by some of the theories of Dr. Abraham Maslow who has developed a concept of a hierarchy of needs. In Dr. Maslow's hierarchy people are viewed as first needing to satisfy basic minimal needs such as food, shelter, and clothing. After satisfying these, they may move to higher order needs, the highest of which is self-actualization (Maslow, 1971). Public welfare programs by and large deal with the fundamental needs of people for food, clothing, shelter, and security. It is only after they resolve these kinds of needs that some of the higher order of needs come into play. Social workers in fields other than public welfare are more likely to assist clients in their movement toward self-actualization, while the public welfare social worker is most likely to help a client or group of clients with the fundamental elements of survival.

From time to time the policy positions of the professional social workers and social work organizations conflict with those supported by leaders of public welfare departments. As already mentioned, these conflicts are usually over the degree of support proposed for a client or group of clients rather than real conflicts over fundamentals. The professional social work organizations operate voluntarily and participation in them by professional social workers is a reflection of the right of those social workers to express themselves on public issues, as people are entitled to do under constitutional guarantees of the right of free speech. Staff members of public welfare departments, on the other hand, are public employees who must carry out the objectives and the mandates of various elected public officials. They cannot refuse to do the things they are required to do by their job definitions and by their supervisors.

Perhaps it is most important for social workers in public welfare and those who draft policies about public welfare programs to recognize that public welfare is part of government and that it and its employees are always bound to carry out the will of the elected officials who ultimately represent the people.

Education for Public Welfare Social Work

Since early in the twentieth century, the United States and most other nations have prepared social workers for public welfare and other professional practice through colleges, universities, and government training institutes.

Social work education typically includes both classroom and practical work with clients so that students can both understand and apply social work knowledge about clients, programs, and methods of helping people. Student practicum placements often include various units of public welfare departments.

Social workers with baccalaureate, master's, and doctoral degrees all work in public welfare agencies. Many agencies provide scholarships to employees who agree to pursue social work degrees and subsequently work for the agency.

Many public welfare departments make special efforts to recruit and retain employees with public welfare degrees, although, as mentioned earlier in this chapter, those employed in public welfare who have social work degrees are a minority of all those who are employed in public welfare.

Conclusion

Professional social work is a significant factor in public welfare. Although it is by no means the only profession represented in the field, it is the single largest and is probably the greatest influence on the way public welfare departments play out their responsibilities.

Professional social work is defined in a variety of ways based upon the professional tasks one performs, the education one has completed, and the ways in which one views the world ethically and philosophically.

Social work education is a major factor in the operation of public welfare departments and social work education is offered, in various forms, throughout the world.

CHAPTER 3

Public Welfare Clients

THE PUBLIC WELFARE industry is so large and pervasive that it affects almost every citizen in some way. This chapter defines the client groups served by public welfare programs, specifies the ways in which they are helped, and explains how assistance provided directly to clients in need often indirectly helps groups of people who, although they are not direct recipients of public welfare, are also beneficiaries.

Low Income Families with Dependent Children

The most typical welfare recipient is the family with low income that cannot meet its basic survival needs without the help of cash assistance. In the United States, the public welfare cash assistance program for families is called Aid to Families with Dependent Children (AFDC). The program provides monthly checks to dependent children and the families who care for those children, in an amount that is based upon each state's appropriation.

No individual adults are clients of AFDC, as it is commonly called. Aged, blind, and disabled adults who need financial help may qualify for the federal Supplemental Security Income program. Only adults who have or care for children qualify for AFDC, which varies from state to state with a low payment in 1981 of $120 per month in Mississippi to a high of $546 in Hawaii for families of four people. The federal government, as discussed in other sections of this book, matches the state's appropriations with federal funds. The formula for federal matching is based upon the state's per capita income and is modified every two years. However, no state paid more than 50 percent of the cost of its public assistance grants as the program operated in 1982.

But who are the clients of public assistance? Those who receive public assistance are only poorly understood and there are strongly held myths among American citizens about these families.

The overwhelming majority of the families receiving public assistance, or AFDC, are women with young children who are not supported, for one reason or another, by the fathers of those children.

In 85 percent of AFDC families, the father is absent. In 1977, half of all children receiving AFDC had parents who were divorced or separated. Another 34 percent had parents who were not married to each other. Eighty-five percent of all AFDC families have no father in the home.

Most AFDC families are small. In 1977, the United States government found that 40.3 percent of all AFDC families had one child, 27.3 percent had two children, 16.1 percent had three children, and 8.2 percent had four children. Only 1.6 percent of all AFDC families had seven or more children.

The federal government studies public assistance clients regularly and publishes information about their characteristics. The latest study of Aid to Families with Dependent Children recipients was in 1977 (U.S. Department of Health and Human Services, 1977). At that time—and over the years the changes in the overall characteristics of clients are very small—the typical AFDC family was white and included 3.2 people, two of whom were children.

Eighty percent of the households were headed by women who were the biological, adoptive, or stepmothers of the AFDC children. At the same time, among all families in the United States only 13.6 percent were headed by women. Fifteen percent of the AFDC children lived with their grandparents, 8 percent with brothers or sisters, and 15 percent with other relatives. But of all the families, four-fifths of the households were headed by females.

Most recipients of public assistance are residents of big cities. Seventy-seven percent live in metropolitan areas and 20 percent of all the AFDC families in the United States live in the six largest cities—Chicago, Detroit, Houston, Los Angeles, New York, and Philadelphia.

Ethnically, approximately one percent of the AFDC recipient families were American Indians, less than half of one percent were of Asian origin, 43 percent were black, and of the 52.6 percent who were white, 12.2 percent were of Spanish origin.

Over 90 percent of the children receiving assistance who were of school age were in school. One out of every four of the mothers was employed, actively seeking work, or laid off from a job.

Most of the mothers were young—over half under age thirty, and one-third under age twenty-five. Over half of the mothers had completed some high school and one-third of them were high-school graduates.

Either the biological or adoptive father was present in 10 percent of the AFDC families. Most of them were also young— 26.5 percent were under thirty. Over half the fathers were disabled and 46 percent were unemployed. However, their educational attainment was much lower than the women's. Seventeen percent were high school graduates but over two-thirds had not completed the eighth grade.

As for the kind of work AFDC families did, the mothers were typically in service positions such as waitresses or beauticians. Over half the employed fathers were "blue-collar workers" such as craftsmen or laborers. Almost all the fathers were working or had worked at some time.

There are several widely held stereotypes of families that receive public assistance, many of which are largely invalid (Morgan, 1979). There is, for example, an assumption that illegitimate birth is often the reason families depend upon public aid. Although it is true that many of the children whose families receive public assistance were born out of wedlock, illegitimacy alone is not a legal reason for receiving assistance and is often not the cause of need. Many children who are born out of wedlock are fully supported by their fathers, mothers, or other relatives. Many others are relinquished by their parents for adoption. The fundamental reason families with children born out of wedlock need help is that those who might have supported the children are either unwilling or unable to do so.

Another widely held American belief is that women who receive public assistance continue to add children to their families as a means of increasing their welfare grants. Such behavior is widely discussed and widely believed among the nonrecipient population. However, there appears to be little evidence to support this conclusion. That is because, among other reasons, it does not work. Although in some states cash assistance increases slightly with family size, many states have a maximum grant that is available for a family of four, five, or six. And the additional increments do not add very much to the monthly check. Therefore, although some public assistance recipients add to their families, most do not do so to increase their assistance.

For the most part, public assistance to low income families is quite mundane. The families do not exhibit exotic family characteristics, unusual sexual behavior, or rich and complex fantasy lives. By and large, public assistance is the program which serves women who have become pregnant and delivered children they cannot support on their own. That problem, which is fundamentally economic in nature, is as old and as common to human experience as any in the history of civilization.

The AFDC program provides assistance to men, under some circumstances, too. In some states, a separate category, Aid to Families with Dependent Children—Unemployed, provides assistance to families in which need is based upon the wage earner's unemployment. In most cases, that wage earner is a man. In some other cases, male members of households receive support because they are disabled, too elderly to be employed, or for other reasons eligible for assistance.

Although all states will include men in the grant if they are incapable of working, only half the states have assistance for families in which the wage earner is in need because of his or her inability to find work. Subsequent chapters will discuss the social worker's responsibilities for determining who is and who is not eligible for cash assistance, and investigations of applicants and recipients both to verify eligibility and to identify and reduce fraud and abuse.

Nutritionally Needy

Many clients who do not need or who do not qualify for AFDC or who receive assistance from other government programs qualify for public welfare's food stamp program, which is operated in conjunction with the United States Department of Agriculture. Federal funding provides food stamps to eligible applicants on the basis of family size and income (MacDonald, 1977). The food stamp program, which began in 1961, provides nutritional assistance to over 20 million Americans.

In 1981 the U. S. Department of Agriculture reported that the average income of food stamp households was $3,900 per year. However, half of all food stamp recipient households have gross incomes of less than $3,600 per year. Less than 2 percent of the food stamp population live in households that have incomes of over $9,000 a year. In total, almost 90 percent of all the households served by the food stamp program are far below the federally defined poverty level. Over half the families who receive food stamps have no liquid assets such as savings, real estate other than a home, life insurance policies with cash value, or other items that are readily convertible to cash. And families who received food stamps were far below the U. S. average of 67 percent in home ownership. Fewer than 30 percent of food stamp households own their own homes. And two-thirds of all those receiving food stamps own no car or other vehicle at all (Fersh, 1981).

In the past, some college students were able to obtain food stamps. Now, however, only two-tenths of one percent of all food stamp users are students and even they must qualify by being disabled, having dependents, or participating in work-study programs. Prior to 1981, persons on strike could receive food stamps. Beginning in 1981, however, strikers were excluded from food stamp eligibility (Fersh, 1981).

Medically Indigent

Public assistance provides cash grants to people who would otherwise not be able to obtain food, clothing, and shelter. Food stamps provide assistance so that low income people can increase the adequacy of their diets. Public welfare also pays for medical services through the Medicaid program under Title XIX of the Social Security Act. This program provides payments for hospital care, nursing home care, physician's visits, prescription drugs, payments to other providers, some home health care for those who cannot care for themselves but who are not so ill that they need institutional placement, as well as surgery and some rehabilitation. The Medicaid program, which is provided in most states but which varies in scope and levels of payment from state to state, serves three general categories of people. These are recipients of public assistance, recipients of Supplemental Security Income, and other members of the population whose incomes are not sufficiently high to provide them with either health insurance or with enough resources to attain treatment for health problems they encounter. These medically needy clients are ill enough so that paying for their own medical care would reduce their assets and income to that of one who would be a recipient of public assistance or Supplemental Security Income.

Medicaid programs also provide, however, for special services to low income children—those whose families are supported or partially supported by public assistance funds. These children are provided with free health screening and treatment of any identified health problems as a means of preventing their becoming disabled or ill in the future.

Emergency and Other Kinds of Need

Cash assistance, food stamps, and medical care are the three most common kinds of assistance offered by public welfare. But a variety of other kinds of aid is also offered to people who face social and economic problems.

One of the most common forms of assistance is emergency help for those who have suffered disasters, suddenly find themselves out of work, need some small amounts of money to help them through crises in their lives, or who otherwise find themselves suddenly in need. Most public welfare programs have or have access to emergency funds that can help people in these difficult circumstances. When public welfare itself does not sponsor these programs, it often helps clients obtain emergency relief funds maintained by churches, settlement houses, and other community groups that want to help people. Some federal funding is available for emergencies in cases when families who might otherwise be eligible for public assistance seek emergency help with their difficulties.

Another form of aid that has been significant in recent years is federal energy assistance. The United States government, at the time petroleum prices caused the cost of home heating to increase dramatically, began a program of assistance to low income people so they could more readily pay their utility bills.

General Assistance

The assistance most difficult to describe but often the most important of the economic programs is general assistance. General assistance is usually provided to people who need help without regard to the category of poverty into which they fall. Although the criteria for eligibility vary throughout the nation, most clients only have to prove their need to receive the assistance. Because there is no federal financial participation in general assistance programs, they are highly limited. Many states have no general assistance at all.

The criteria for qualifying as eligible for most social welfare programs are so strictly defined that they exclude many people who, although they are clearly ineligible, may also clearly be in need. General assistance programs assist those who do not fit into welfare's public assistance program, Supplemental Secruity Income, or other federally funded cash assistance. But millions of people do not qualify for public help where they live. Women whose children are grown, who are too young and healthy for SSI, and unqualified for anything else, are a good example of people who often still must rely on their families or non-public aid for help. The following is a case example:

Mildred Brown had reached age 59. Her husband had died the year before and Mildred had suffered a serious depression upon her loss. She spent all of the modest insurance policy he left her on treatment for her depression. She had two children but they, too, were short of funds. They lived in distant cities, had adequate jobs, but little money to help her with more than an occasional birthday or holiday gift. Mrs. Brown was trying to receive Social Security payments. Her children were too old to receive such payments. She had no work skills. Her low income qualified her for food stamps and her health problems as well as low income provided her with some medical assistance. She earned the balance of her support by working part time in a local department store until she reached age 62, when she could draw Social Security.

Social Services Clients

In addition to the economic assistance recipients described in this chapter, public welfare clients also include people whose economic needs are being met, including some who may have all the money they need, but who still need the assistance of public welfare for help in overcoming social, emotional, or personal problems.

NEGLECTED OR ABUSED CHILDREN

Children who need protection are the most typical social services clients of public welfare. These are children whose parents or guardians are unable or unwilling to care for them properly. As a result, children in need of protective services may become ill, may suffer from emotional problems, may fail to succeed in school, or, in extreme cases, may be murdered by the adults who are responsible for them. Protective services are a part of the whole child welfare field, which is discussed in Chapter 4. It is critical to note that although the primary clients of protective services are children, in most cases the public welfare agency attempts to work not only with the child but also with the parents or guardians to overcome the neglect or abuse that has been identified. Thus the parents or guardians are also clients. When social casework or other forms of assistance to the family do not suffice to end the abuse or neglect, the department may have to turn to other solutions which remove the child from the home. Some of these are emergency shelter care, foster care with a family, group care in a residential children's facility, or termination of the rights of the parents or guardians so the child is in the permanent custody of the agency or is adopted. In some ways, all of these individuals and groups are clients of the public welfare program—the child, the parents or guardians, the foster parents, emergency care shelters, and adoptive parents.

Children and their families also frequently need other forms of services such as day care, homemaker services, family planning, and health screening, in order for the family to function adequately. These are discussed in Part II.

DISABLED ADULTS

Many adults need social services too. Public welfare departments typically provide services to adults who are in need of protection from abuse or neglect as well as services to help them function adequately in their own homes. The elderly, the mentally ill, and the mentally retarded, for example, are often exploited by neighbors or their own relatives.

Public welfare departments can often help older adults avoid the exploitation of their wealth and property when they are unable to resist efforts to separate them from their resources.

Other kinds of services often make it possible for adults to remain in their own homes, rather than face institutional care. Home health services, homemaker and chore services, and telephone reassurance programs are among the ways in which social workers help aged clients remain successfully in their own homes.

INDIRECT BENEFICIARIES

This chapter has identified the individuals who receive direct assistance in the forms of cash, coupons (such as food stamps), or services from public welfare departments. But there are equally large numbers of people who are indirect beneficaries of the services public welfare departments provide to the disadvantaged in the United States.

For example, vendors of goods and services are major beneficiaries of public welfare programs. These are the individuals and corporations who rent office space for public welfare agencies, who sell office equipment and supplies, and who perform the medical services for Medicaid patients. Prior to the creation of the Medicaid program, many medical services were donated to patients by health care providers. Medicaid (and its counterpart program, Medicare, for the aged) began paying for services that had once gone uncompensated. Health care providers currently receive the largest proportion of the money spent by public welfare.

Employers may also benefit from public welfare because of its work, training, and placement efforts (Garvin *et al.*, 1979). Most public welfare departments have programs of work and placement for able-bodied men and women who need financial help. Whether these activities are carried out through the federally funded Work Incentive Program or simply by the direct efforts of the public welfare program, hundreds of thousands of low income people are placed in jobs. In many circumstances employers receive special incentives, such as tax advantages, for accepting public welfare clients in their work forces. Thus although the public welfare department's efforts are being enhanced by the employer, the employer is also being rewarded by the welfare department and becomes a recipient, too, of public welfare's services.

Family members also benefit from some of the programs of public welfare that are directed toward assisting their relatives. Children of aged people who receive food stamps, general assistance, Medicaid, or social services often find that public welfare is paying for services to their relatives that under other circumstances either would not be provided or would be paid for by the family. The financial savings and the

emotional savings experienced by the family members constitute a benefit to those people, as they are for the client, who is the direct recipient of
public aid.

Government officials sometimes benefit from public welfare programs. Elected officials find, when they are running for office, that the
assistance provided to some of their constituents or to the relatives of
some of their constituents gives voters good feelings toward incum-
bents. And when a constituent telephones a member of Congress, senator, or state legislator to ask for help, that representative can frequently
satisfy the constituent by asking the department to provide services to
the constituent. Usually the department would provide the services under any circumstances but the representative's intervention often helps
in the election.

MISCELLANEOUS BENEFICIARIES

Depending upon the organization, any number of other popular and
valuable services may be of benefit to large numbers of citizens, directly
or indirectly. In some states, the school hot lunch program is provided
through the welfare department.

Other welfare departments provide services to handicapped children, to handicapped adults who need vocational rehabilitation, and
direct hospitals for physically and mentally handicapped people who
have long-term or terminal illnesses.

Public welfare departments are so large and so diverse that large
portions of the population benefit directly or indirectly from welfare
programs. Many people believe that welfare departments serve only a
small, specialized population but, in reality, every citizen is a potential
client of public welfare and many people benefit directly or otherwise
have contact with departments.

It is reasonable to assert, in fact, that every citizen of the United
States benefits from public welfare programs to some extent. Merchants
and bankers receive money from welfare clients; retail grocers, farmers,
and wholesalers of food benefit from the food stamp program. Hospitals, pharmacies, and physicians are paid through the Medicaid program for services they might otherwise provide without charge.

Just as citizens benefit from the economic activity of public welfare,
they also all benefit from the social order which results from public
welfare programs. Many believe that civil strife and disorder would be
greater if there were no public welfare programs (Piven and Cloward,
1971). Most citizens benefit from public welfare programs because they
provide a safer environment and a population that is better-treated than
it would be if public welfare programs did not exist. And public welfare

programs remain available for those who may need them in times of social and economic difficulty.

Conclusion

Public welfare serves the disadvantaged who include those who need money for basic needs, those who need nutritional assistance, people whose health problems could not be treated were it not for welfare's Medicaid program, children who are disadvantaged by the abuse or neglect they suffer in their families, adults who are in danger of being exploited, abused, or neglected, and people who temporarily need public help because of emergency situations. In addition to those who are direct beneficiaries of services, family members of direct recipients, vendors of services to public welfare agencies, and vendors of services to clients on behalf of public welfare agencies also benefit from the existence of public welfare. Public welfare is, in many ways, a universal program that affects most citizens directly or indirectly. And it has the potential for affecting every individual at some time in his or her life.

PART II

THE SOCIAL WORK PRÀCTICE METHODS: THEIR APPLICATIONS IN PUBLIC WELFARE

AT THE CORE of all social work practice are the methods—the means by which social workers carry out their responsibilities to clients. Because social work is a profession that is always engaged in doing something with and for others, the means of helping are bound to be central to the profession's concerns. It is this orientation toward doing, rather than toward understanding or studying alone, that sets social workers apart from social scientists. Another unique approach to helping overcome problems also sets social work apart from other helping professions such as counseling, nursing, and teaching. That orientation is toward the use of a variety of methods in overcoming problems—not just the one method that is most understood or favored by the worker serving the client.

Social work has traditionally used methods that affect clients through interventions into the lives of individuals and families, through working with groups of clients, and through providing services designed to resolve problems in the total community. These methods—social casework, social group work, and community organization—are the fundamental approaches to helping people. Chapters on each of these methods are included in this part of the text. In addition, there are supportive methods that social workers use to make the applications of the fundamental methods possible and effective. These supportive methods are discussed in Part III.

Education and scholarship in social work, when dealing with the practice of the profession, have tended to focus on the three practice methods. However, during the past decades many social work educators and scholars have been dissatisfied with the traditional organization of helping methods. The focus of a profession dedicated to helping people overcome their problems ought to be on the clients' needs, not the social worker's methodological preferences. Therefore, many social work practice texts and curricula designs have focused on practice with specific client groups, rather than the general methods of helping all clients. For example, some schools of social work abandoned teaching social casework, social group work, and community organization as methods, and turned instead to teaching about services to the aging, the mentally disabled, the urban poor, and other groups encountering social problems. For each group any number of methods, including the three traditional approaches, could be applicable and their applicability might be taught. Other educational models focused on different combinations such as sequences of social work practice courses that divided the content between social strategies and social treatment. Still other models divided courses into those on serving individuals, families, and groups, and those on working with institutions and communities.

These chapters are not entries into the theoretical debates on the organization of social work practice methods teaching. In fact, the material presented here ought to be compatible with any format for teaching about services to clients—whether those clients are individuals, groups, families, or communities. The material offered here is organized traditionally in the belief that no matter how the content is taught or studied, those who want to practice social work will continue to want to master and use the skills that have traditionally been called social casework, social group work, and community organization. More important, it is clear that all these methods are currently used by social workers in public welfare. Knowing about them and knowing when and how to use them are essential for those who work or aspire to work in public welfare agencies.

CHAPTER 4

Social Casework in Public Welfare: Economic Assistance and Child Welfare

CENTRAL TO MOST of the services provided to public welfare clients is social casework, the method that has traditionally been the specialization of most social workers. The practice of social casework in public welfare agencies is the subject of this and the following two chapters because so much of the work in public welfare is, by necessity, casework. However, social group work and community organization, the other methods social workers use in serving clients, also have significant usage in public welfare. They are discussed in subsequent chapters.

Describing social casework practices in public welfare is simpler than defining the method because it has changed so much since it was first developed by the pioneer social worker, Mary Richmond (1917, 1922), at the beginning of this century.

Today, the term means many different things to different groups of social workers (Meyer, 1979). For many, social casework is identified with psychoanalytic theory and ego psychology (Strean, 1979). Some view it as a problem-solving process through which a worker helps a client understand and act to overcome a personal or social problem (Reid and Epstein, 1977, 1978). The worker assists the client using agency resources to resolve the problem. For still others, social casework follows a "functional" approach that emphasizes the client's ability to grow with the help of the worker and through the creative use of the agency's purpose or function, from which the name of this orientation comes. Still other social workers follow a psychosocial approach and some others subscribe to behavior modification as an orientation to the practice of social casework. And small groups of social workers have developed and followed off-shoots of these and yet other approaches that are based on diverse religions, philosophies, and the social and behavioral sciences.

Those who are interested in pursuing the subject of social casework methodology and all its variations may benefit by consulting some of the readings suggested in the bibliography.

Although any number of approaches to working with people are currently being taught and used in social work, some common themes run through all of them. For example, it seems clear that no method designed to change human behavior works very well unless those who are the subjects of the service are motivated to change. That is, when people do not want to change, no method works very well. On the other hand, when people are motivated to modify their behavior or their attitudes, many of the methods seem to work. For that reason, every approach to social work practice has its strong adherents who can document the successful application of their approach. But every approach to providing services also has its detractors who can cite evidence of the approach having failed with a client or client system.

There are some special characteristics of social casework in public welfare which distinguish it, no matter what the theoretical or philosophical orientation of the worker, from practice in other settings.

Public welfare social workers who practice social casework share the following characteristics (Abbott, 1940; Dobelstein, 1980; Doscher, 1980; Greenblatt, 1979).

1. They are in positions of authority. They collect information from the client and other sources that determines whether or not the applicant will receive economic assistance; they make home visits to determine whether or not a client is being abused, neglected, or exploited; they serve as probation or parole officers for persons accused or convicted of crimes.

2. They serve large case loads. Funding for public services is traditionally such that most workers serve very large numbers of clients—as many as several hundred, depending on the worker's assignment.

3. They see most of their clients only once or twice or, if for longer periods, only infrequently. Weekly visits with all clients are not possible for most public welfare social workers. In many situations they are unnecessary. Therefore, the worker spends the most time with the clients who need it most and the least with those who function well without it.

4. They work in clearly defined situations with specific goals—to determine eligibility for assistance; place a child in a satisfactory adoptive or foster home; monitor an adult or child abuse or neglect case to determine whether or not the problem will be resolved without police or court action.

The worker's theoretical orientation to social casework, along with agency training and supervision, have impact on *how* the public welfare social worker serves the client in carrying out these responsibilities.

Fundamental Skills in Social Casework

The basic requirements for social work and, in particular, social casework, transcend all theoretical orientations, agencies, and programs within agencies. These include:

1. A positive relationship with the client should be developed by establishing positive rapport. It is unlikely that the client will be helped by a worker who does not seem interested in the client's problems or needs. Competent social casework requires an ability to help the client understand that one is concerned about the problem, wants to help, and believes the client can help himself or herself. In other words, one must convey respect for the client and the client's situation. This can be conveyed by listening with interest, establishing and maintaining eye contact with the client, hearing and using the client's name with the client, working to insure the client's comfort in the interview situation, avoiding seeming rushed, preoccupied, or bored by the client, and clearly explaining one's own and the agency's function.

2. Effective communication must be established. Too often, social workers in public welfare become so well trained in their own technical language they forget that most people cannot understand them without detailed explanations. Terms such as "AFDC," "eligibility determination," "re-certification," and "policy manual," simply do not mean anything to most people who do not work in public welfare. Therefore, using clear, everyday language with clients is a fundamental rule of good communication. Of course, one communicates with more than words; eye contact, concern for the client's comfort, and the worker's posture often say a good deal more than words alone will.

3. One must listen carefully. Listening is another part of communication—the other side of talking. And effective listening can be even more important to the client than what one says. Hearing what the client says and discerning what the client really means is an essential part of communicating. One also listens well by observing the client carefully for signs of discomfort, depression, fond memories, or anxiety. Relating the client's behavior to the client's words increases the effectiveness of the listening.

4. Confidentiality of sensitive information must be maintained. By necessity, the public welfare social worker learns a good deal about clients' personal lives that they would not want shared with others. A competent social worker tells no one about this information unless it is needed to serve the client. A client's personal information is not appropriate subject matter for gossip or party jokes.

5. Information must be carefully recorded. Each agency maintains its own system for keeping records on clients. A qualified social worker accurately and carefully records that information so it can be used for the benefit of the client.

6. The client must be helped to break the problem into small, manageable components, which social workers call "partializing." Most clients come to public welfare agencies in some distress. They are in need of financial assistance because of desertion, unemployment, or illness. Or they can no longer cope with a child or an aging parent. The world seems to be descending in one heap on the client's shoulders. Good casework usually means helping the client identify and partialize the problems into smaller, manageable pieces. With some, the welfare department can help resolve them. For others, the worker can suggest other agencies that may be able to assist.

Serving Clients Through Social Casework

Most social workers in public welfare are involved in the two core groups of services provided by welfare agencies. These are the provision of economic assistance to people who are in need and the provision of social services to adults, children, and families. Although these two primary classifications of service differ significantly from one another in many cases, the skills of social casework which are used in providing them remain constant.

PROVIDING ECONOMIC ASSISTANCE TO THE DISADVANTAGED

The most common reason clients come to welfare offices is economic disadvantage. Therefore, the most frequent problem with which public welfare employees work is economic disadvantage. Whether the problem that has caused the client to come to the office is long term or short term, whether it is chronic or situational, virtually all workers in public welfare must be familiar with and capable of helping resolve the economic problems that their clients face. Even social services workers who do not directly arrange for economic assistance services to clients often find that the root of the social problem faced by their clients is lack of money. Helping their clients resolve those problems often means helping them locate and obtain economic assistance (Spindler, 1979).

THE RELATIONSHIP OF SOCIAL SERVICES TO PUBLIC
ASSISTANCE

Public welfare departments have followed a number of patterns in providing economic help to their clients (Trattner, 1979). For much of the history of public welfare programs, all employees who worked directly with applicants for aid also offered them social services to help them overcome their need for economic assistance when these services appeared necessary or warranted. The agencies believed that many people who needed economic assistance required it because of social and psychological problems that inhibited their capacity to be self-supporting. Some experiments showed that if well-educated social workers worked intensively with clients, those clients had relatively good prospects for becoming independent of the public welfare program through reconciliation with a spouse, employment, or through some other means of nonpublic support (Cohen and Ball, 1962). For a time the United States government required public welfare departments to educate and employ professionally-educated social workers to take applications for cash assistance and, more importantly, to provide social assistance to families so they could become independent. The conviction was that high quality social work services provided by well-prepared social workers would rehabilitate clients, alleviate poverty, and reduce public expenditures for public welfare. For several reasons, however, this approach, embodied in the 1962 amendments to the Social Security Act, did not have the predicted results. In fact, coincidentally, with the use of more social services for recipients of public assistance, the caseloads began to increase dramatically.

Many factors led to the increase. Some people blamed the social workers themselves and said that those workers, in cooperation with organizations such as the National Welfare Rights Organization which were pursuing better benefits and better treatment of the poor in America, were burdening the system so that it would be overloaded and would eventually reveal how inadequate American public welfare really was in dealing with the deep poverty experienced by many Americans. Others suggested that the research leading to the requirements for more social services was faulty. A professional social worker who spent many hours every month with one family could help that family but, some suggested, the families chosen were those that would have succeeded anyway.

Others blamed the implementation of the projects. Whereas in the successful projects one social worker served very few cases and visited with those families regularly, the national implementation was such that public welfare programs did not provide intensive social work. The standard was that each of sixty families would see one social worker four times each year (Benton, 1980).

Later analysts described the situation as more complex and suggested many reasons why adding special social workers did not reduce caseloads.

1. The research projects which led to the 1962 Social Security changes may have only proven something that observers of public assistance clients had known for a long time—that most people use public welfare economic assistance for only a few months and few use it for periods of years.

2. The studies may have been conducted in a period of high employment and a growing economy. When there are plenty of jobs it is not difficult to place someone who might otherwise be unemployable in a job. The better the times, the better the chance for job placements for welfare recipients and the more likely welfare recipients are to be employed.

3. Several court decisions beginning in the early 1960s and extending through the 1970s made it easier for clients to become and to remain public assistance recipients. (*Goldberg* v. *Kelly*, 397 U.S., 254-1970; *Shapiro* v. *Thompson*, 394 U.S. 618-1969 are examples.) These court decisions were aided, in no small way, by the activities of public interest lawyers who were funded, for the first time, by the United States government to help the poor obtain their rights. Among the court decisions were those requiring fair hearings for people denied assistance or removed from the assistance rolls; the striking down of residence requirements, which made all citizens of the United States eligible for public assistance wherever they lived, without a waiting period; and a requirement that agencies reach out to find clients eligible for food stamps and other forms of assistance.

4. There was a growing awareness among low income people of the availability of public aid and a growing willingness to use it.

In any case, the requirement that professionally educated social workers be employed in increasing numbers by public welfare departments to interview and provide assistance to applicants was stricken from the books and replaced by a different requirement—that social services and economic assistance be separated from one another (Benton, 1980).

SEPARATION OF SOCIAL AND ECONOMIC SERVICES

It became the view of the United States government as well as many states that professionally educated social workers were not needed to take applications from public assistance clients. That was considered a clerical function that could be handled by someone with a high school education. Government officials now believed that most clients needed little more than a monthly check to solve their problems, and it would be wasteful to use professionally educated people when those with high school educations and administrative training would suffice. Better to save the professional social workers, it was concluded, for intensive social services for those whose problems went beyond the need for money, medical care, or food stamps. Thus state departments were required for a time to separate their social services social workers from their economic assistance social workers. States could pay different salaries, could experiment with handling applications by mail, and could otherwise simplify, routinize, and decrease the cost of determining eligibility for economic assistance (McDonald and Piliavin, 1980).

Still later in the evolution of economic assistance programs for low income United States citizens, all specifications about the education of social workers were dropped, as was the requirement for separation. As an alternative, presidents began proposing simplifications of welfare programs through the development of national standards, federal administration, and simplification. These ideas were proposed in President Richard M. Nixon's Family Assistance Plan and later in President Jimmy Carter's 1977 Better Jobs and Income Act, neither of which was passed.

This constant manipulation of the public assistance eligibility determination process reflects the widespread discontent with that system. The discontent often appears to be shared by administrators, the workers who meet and serve the clients, legislators, executive branch officials, the courts, and the clients themselves. Many people believe that cheating in the program is rampant, that more people receive assistance than should, that public assistance provides disincentives to people who ought to be working instead of receiving public aid, and that the whole program costs too much to administer, and these widely shared beliefs contribute to the national unpopularity of public welfare programs (Anderson, 1978).

The Social Worker's Role

Despite the controversy over public assistance and the frequent shifts in administrative attitudes about who should see the clients and how the service should be organized and provided, the role of the practitioner who interviews clients and works with them on their applications for assistance does not change very much. The worker must follow certain principles of social work and must work effectively to take the client's application and complete the steps of determining whether or not the client is eligible for assistance (Street *et al.*, 1979). At the same time, the worker must determine whether or not the client could usefully consult with a social services staff member. And the worker must follow up on the application by verifying the information provided by the client and must also insure that the client is checked upon periodically to determine whether or not the family has needs that are not being met and to determine that the client is eligible for continuing assistance under the program.

The worker's main objectives in determining eligibility for economic assistance are:

1. To the best of the worker's ability to insure that people who are ineligible for assistance do not receive it.
2. To insure that those applicants who are eligible for assistance receive it in the amount to which they are entitled.
3. To follow all established agency procedures and policies in dealing with the application.
4. To understand the client's needs and to help the client obtain the assistance and services necessary to help the client and the family function adequately.

The effective worker begins by understanding the client and the distress that client is experiencing from being in need of economic assistance (Perlman, 1979). Economic independence is so highly valued in most Western cultures that requiring the public assistance often proves demeaning to the applicant, no matter how he or she may be treated by the agency's representatives. The public assistance applicant is almost always under stress for two reasons—first, the economic problems that caused the need for assistance to begin with, and second, the distress of needing help from someone else. Because of that great distress and because the client ascribes great power to the worker over the client's ultimate economic situation, workers are often viewed as people of great significance by clients ('Vyers, 1980). Some very young, very poorly paid economic assistance workers are amazed to discover that their clients perceive them as powerful authorities, similar to the way automobile drivers perceive highway police. The worker's first task is to understand the client's feelings about needing assistance, about asking for assistance, and about revealing personal information to a public employee.

A second function of the worker is to behave in a way that will put the client at ease. The worker can accomplish this by explaining the policies of the agency to the client, by outlining the regulations governing eligibility for assistance, and by letting the client know that he or she is respected by the worker and by the agency as a citizen with a right to apply for help and a right to receive it if determined eligible. Some reassurance that it is all right to be in need may also make a difference in preserving an applicant's self-esteem (Seabury, 1980).

A third activity of the effective worker is to arrange the physical situation in a way that helps the client feel comfortable and helps the agency communicate its concern for the client and his or her needs. That means the worker may want to use a private interviewing room when the client's problems may be embarrassing. It means speaking to the client in friendly and concerned tones without being or appearing to be judgmental about the person who needs help.

It means not interrupting the interview, which may be one of the more important events in the client's life, for gossip with colleagues or other avoidable interruptions. The client must believe that his or her family's economic need is the most important thing in the world at that moment to the worker, just as it is to the applicant. Small but meaningful matters such as referring to the client as Mr., Miss, Mrs., or Ms. rather than by a first name or nickname, or avoiding loud statements which may embarrass the client or violate client confidentiality, are all part of the sensitivity that an effective worker shows to a public assistance applicant.

SKILL IN REFERRING CLIENTS

The worker's task does not end with a positive or negative action on an application. In addition, the worker must be able to refer the client for services to other units of the public welfare department, when that is indicated, or to other social work or health agencies, when other social and health needs are identified (Austin, 1980).

Within the department, for example, the worker may realize that the client's primary need is for the father of her children to pay support. If that is the case, a referral to the child support enforcement unit can solve the problem for the client as well as resolving society's basic problem, which is that it is paying for the care of children whose father may be quite capable of supporting them but who is too irresponsible to do so.

Or the worker may make an effective referral to an employment services unit or work incentive unit for a client to receive training or job placement that may lead to economic independence.

Or the client may be having difficulty in caring appropriately for children, which may warrant a referral to the child welfare services unit (Costin, 1979).

Or the client may exhibit clear indications of emotional problems which ought to lead the worker to make a referral to a community mental health clinic. Members of the family may have health problems but may not have been able to find any resources for treating those problems. In such a case, the worker may be able to make a referral to a primary care clinic, a physician's office, or a hospital emergency room. The family may be encountering economic difficulty because of lack of budgeting and, in such cases, they may be effectively referred to a consumer counseling service.

Perhaps the client is applying for food stamps in addition to or instead of cash assistance. It is often useful to refer a food stamp client for nutritional education (Fersh, 1981).

In other words, an effective economic assistance worker is ideally more than an application taker. The worker is also an interpreter of agency policies, a counselor, even if that counseling is only designed to help the client accept the need for assistance, an educator, and one who makes referrals for collateral help that may make a large difference in an applicant's well-being.

Public Welfare's Social Services

The most intensive use of social casework methods in public welfare is in the provision of social services which are now commonly offered separately from the economic assistance just described. Traditionally, public social services have been child welfare services—assistance to children and their families who are facing personal, social, and economic problems. Economic assistance, which was originally considered the most important of the child welfare services, may still be the most significant. The cash grants provided to families with dependent children play a dramatic role in keeping families together and in making it possible for parents to care more adequately for their children than they could if no aid were available. Some families function quite well with cash assistance alone. Others need more direct help with the nonmonetary, personal, and social problems they face. Still other families, with adequate earned income, require public social services (Kamerman and Kahn, 1976).

Protective Services for Abused and Neglected Children

Investigation of and the provision of service to families that are neglecting, exploiting, or abusing their children is the most common child welfare service offered by public welfare agencies (Shyne, 1979). In most states, the welfare department is charged with the responsibility of investigating and dealing with abuse and neglect complaints that come to the attention of the department, schools, other social agencies, law enforcement agencies, and health care providers. This is often called child protective services (Garbarino and Stocking, 1980).

Child neglect is by far the most common complaint (Polansky, 1972). It includes such poor practices as leaving young children at home alone, allowing children to leave their houses without proper clothing, failure to provide an adequate diet, failing to seek or use medical care when it is needed, allowing a child to be truant from school, permitting delinquent behavior, and leaving children untended in automobiles.

Ignorance is often the cause of neglect. Some parents simply do not know how to care for children properly. Lack of resources or poor management of the resources the family has may also be the cause of neglect. In some cases, the poor health of the parents or their mental disability cause the neglect.

In the United States, the range of family standards for child care is so broad that situations which appear neglectful to some may not appear to be problems at all to others (Hartman, 1981). The social worker attempts to determine if the neglect is harmful to the life, health, or emotional development of the child. Neglect that is harmful—not failure to conform to someone else's standards for child care—should be the concern of the public. Therefore, social casework in child neglect requires the social worker to avoid imposing arbitrary standards on the family (Puryear, 1980).

Abuse is less ambiguous in most cases. It consists of treatment that is harmful to the health and safety of the child (Fontana, 1973; Folks, 1978). Examples include beatings with heavy objects, burning a child with cigarettes, both homosexual and heterosexual rape, chaining children to their beds, hurling children from windows, scalding in hot bathtubs, and every other bizarre form of torture and sadism one may imagine. The problem is not small—hundreds of children die each year from abuse (Gerbner et al., 1980). Law enforcement agencies and the courts arrest, prosecute, and convict parents and others who abuse children each year (Goldstein, 1979).

Public intervention into child abuse and neglect has become controversial in recent years and there is some opposition to government's investigation of and assistance to families where abuse is encountered (Murdach, 1980; Getzel, 1981). Resistance to these child welfare services has arisen, in part, from poor social casework in which social workers have been more authoritarian than the circumstances would justify in cases of questionable neglect or abuse.

THE PROTECTIVE SERVICES CASEWORKER'S TASKS

Once a complaint is received that a child is being abused or neglected, a worker is assigned to investigate it (Costin, 1979). Although the laws vary, the response of the welfare department follows a pattern that is rather consistent throughout the United States. First, the investigation is made quickly—within a day of the report, or immediately if the report indicates the child is in imminent danger. The worker may or may not notify the family in advance of a visit, depending upon the circumstances. The family, including the child, are interviewed and confronted directly with the issues that are the basis of the report. When cooperation is not offered by the family, law enforcement personnel and court orders may be necessary for the complaint to be investigated.

In most cases, the investigation and discussion between the protective services social worker and the family is all that is needed. The family is told about the danger to the children from the neglect or the abuse and is made aware of the concern their behavior has caused to the community (Giovannoni and Becerra, 1979). The worker does not reveal the source of the complaint, which remains confidential. The family is urged to forget about revenge and, instead, to resolve the problems that are the cause of concern. In the case of an unjustified complaint or an attempt at harrassment by neighbors or relatives, the worker confirms that and ends the investigation (Sussman and Cohen, 1975).

When some action is indicated, beyond simply visiting, most problems are resolvable without dramatic interventions such as removing children from the home (Jones and McNeely, 1980). The worker, in conversation with the family and, many times, with a supervisor of protective services, recommends services such as mental health counseling from an appropriate agency, parental participation in parent education classes, the use of day care for the children, help in the home from a homemaker who can help educate the family about better homemaking practices, or the enrollment of the children in leisure time programs such as scouting or recreation centers. Often the worker arranges to visit with the family again to monitor their situation (Maybanks and Bryce, 1979). In some cases, the worker arranges to visit weekly until the family seems to have overcome the difficulty that led to the abuse or neglect.

In a small fraction of cases the children are in such danger that they cannot remain with the family. Under those circumstances the worker and law enforcement officials, operating with a court order or under emergency custody powers specified by law, remove the children from the home and place them in temporary shelters until they can return to their homes or until some more permanent arrangements may be made. Frequently, no matter how severe the danger faced by children, they want to stay with their parents. The fear of the unknown coupled at times with their unawareness that their parents' behavior is unusual and inappropriate, often cause them severe emotional trauma. That is why social workers and courts use removal of children from their parents as only a last resort. In addition to the obvious concern of and imposition on the rights of parents, the trauma of removal is severe for the children as well.

Protective services are also provided to parents other than those who are reported for abuse and neglect. Many single parents find that they cannot care for children and also meet their other social and occupational goals. Many find the difficulty of child-rearing so demanding they fear they will abuse their children. Therefore, many cases are referred directly to protective services workers in welfare departments by parents themselves, who are visited by workers and who, in some cases, temporarily or permanently relinquish their children to social agencies.

SUBSTITUTE CARE FOR CHILDREN

Those children who cannot be cared for by their own families and who for that reason are placed in the temporary or permanent custody of welfare agencies (which can only occur voluntarily or by involvement in a court action), need alternative living arrangements (Kadushin, 1970). Most public welfare departments have a range of residential services for children which they operate themselves or which they obtain by contracting with individuals and institutions. Whenever it seems possible and warranted, the social worker attempts to keep the family and the child in contact with one another because, in most cases, the objective is for the child and the family to be reunited (White, 1981). It is the general consensus of social workers, policy makers, and researchers, that children are better off in their own homes, except when the family problems are extreme, than they are in any substitute care arrangement.

Emergency shelters are either private residences or group homes operated by public welfare agencies or other organizations. They are available for child placements at any hour of any day. Normally children remain in them for thirty days or less, until they can return home or until some longer term care facility is available. Emergency shelter is particularly important because so many abuse and neglect cases arise on weekends, in the middle of the night, and on holidays, when school is out, and when the usual arrangements of family life are interrupted. Weekends, nights, and holidays are also when families tend to overuse alcohol, which is implicated heavily in child abuse and neglect, just as it is in every other social problem.

When necessary, foster homes are used for children who are abused and neglected (Combs, 1979). They are also used for children who need temporary living arrangements because their parents are ill, imprisoned, or deceased. Foster parents are recruited, supervised, and trained by social workers in public welfare, often by protective services staff members. They are people who take children into their homes and raise them as if they were family members, even though the initial placement of the child may be temporary. The family receives a monthly stipend, the amount of which is based upon the child's age, health condition, and any special needs the child may have.

Many children in foster care are physically ill, developmentally disabled, emotionally disturbed, or behaviorally difficult. In some cases, these problems result from abuse or neglect (Russell and Silberman, 1979). In others, the children have been relinquished because the family cannot handle their special problems. Children with such problems are hard to place permanently with families as adoptive children. The special costs of caring for such children are recognized in the amount of the stipend provided to foster parents. In addition, the child's medical care and some other special expenses are paid by the public welfare department.

Some foster care is arranged on a contractual basis. The department pays a voluntary agency to recruit and supervise foster parents who take responsibility for wards of the agency.

Permanent foster care is an increasingly common trend in public welfare. In circumstances when children cannot be adopted for legal reasons, the agency agrees that the child will be in a single foster home until reaching his or her maturity.

Recruiting, supervising, and training foster parents are among the main responsibilities of social workers in public welfare. Many agencies have special promotional campaigns for recruiting foster homes and training curricula, including some developed by organizations such as the Child Welfare League of America, for preparing the homes to accept children. Among the criteria used in selecting foster homes are the demonstrated concern for and capacity to handle children, the physical condition of the home, the reputations and behavior of the parents, and the willingness of the foster parents to cooperate with the agency. Although homes are sought from the whole range of socio-economic classes, an effort is made to avoid choosing families who are interested in serving children primarily because of the stipend paid to them (Wiltse, 1979).

Because most foster care is temporary, foster families must be oriented to the fact that a child placed with them may leave. When circumstances require it, families are also informed of the need for the foster child to visit with the natural parents. On the other hand, foster families that have children for long periods of time are often afforded legal protection against having foster children removed without valid cause and without notice. Many foster parents ultimately adopt their foster children.

GROUP CARE FOR CHILDREN

Children who cannot be served in their own homes or in foster care may be placed in group facilities such as small group homes or larger children's homes. Children who are placed in these larger, institutional settings, are often members of sibling groups that do not want to be separated but which cannot readily be placed in foster care. Others may be adolescents who find it more acceptable to be part of a group of children, rather than new children in established families. Still others have special health, emotional, or behavioral problems which make it difficult for them to adjust to substitute families (Buckholdt and Gubrium, 1979).

Group care facilities usually are divided into two classifications— small group homes of four to ten children, and group care agencies which may house several dozen children in several cottages. Modern group care facilities, no matter how large, attempt to create and maintain a home-like atmosphere. They are staffed by houseparents, who live with the children in cottages that are as comparable to homes as possible. Meals are prepared in cottage kitchens and eaten in cottage dining rooms, rather than large dining halls, whenever possible. The children attend public schools, participate in community groups, and are generally cared for in the same way they would be were they living with their parents.

ADOPTION

Children who are permanent wards of welfare departments because their biological parents have died, relinquished them, or had the children involuntarily and permanently removed from them by court order, may be eligible for adoption. In adoption a child becomes a permanent family member of adoptive parents. Public welfare departments place a large proportion of the children eligible for adoption in adoptive homes. However, public welfare agencies are not the only organizations which arrange for adoptions (Ward, 1979). Privately sponsored family and child welfare agencies also place children who are in their custody. In addition, many states permit private adoptions in which biological parents turn their children over to adoptive parents, with physicians, attorneys, nurses, or family members serving as intermediaries and sanctioned by a court.

Social workers generally agree that all adoptions ought to be arranged through social agencies such as welfare departments. When they are not, children may virtually be sold, which can conflict with the interests of those children. Because of private adoptions, many potential adoptive parents who request children from social agencies must wait extraordinary lengths of time because children who would be available to them are siphoned off by private adoptions.

Public welfare social workers screen applicants for adoptive children, make adoptive placements, and visit with the adopting family during the period of temporary custody before a court makes the adoption final. In some states public welfare workers investigate and participate in private adoptions, as well, by making reports to judges who must decide on the adoption.

Social workers also work as caseworkers with men and women who are considering relinquishing their children for adoption. In many states the law requires that the biological father as well as the mother be given the opportunity to keep the child, even when the parents are not married or living together. It often falls upon the public welfare social worker to properly notify the father of his rights or to attempt to do so by means specified in law. In most states the law now also requires a woman to have a specified waiting period, after the birth of a child, before she can legally relinquish that child for adoption. These laws responded to the circumstances of many women who believed they were pressured by parents and others to give up their children prior to the child's birth, even though they might have acted differently once the child had been born.

After every effort made to restore the child and the parents to one another has failed, steps are taken to place the child in the care of a permanent family. Subsidized adoption is one means used to arrange for the permanent placement of children (U.S. Department of Health, Education, and Welfare, 1976). In subsidized adoption, families legally adopt children under contracts that provide for continued subsidies to the families so they can afford the children they have adopted.

Subsidized adoption is increasingly used to provide permanent homes to foster children and to locate adoptive homes for other children who are difficult to place because they are older, have physical or emotional handicaps, or are members of minority groups.

Summary—Children's Welfare Services

The issues surrounding care for children who cannot live with their own parents are highly complicated and, to an extent, controversial. The objective of the public welfare agency and generally of government is to keep children with their parents whenever that is possible. When it is not possible, however, social work values support making permanent plans for the child as rapidly as possible. It is healthier for a child to be placed permanently with an adoptive family or in the foster care of a single foster family than to be in limbo or to be shifted between a number of foster homes over his or her early years.

Child welfare services are complex and critical in public welfare. It should be realized that the place of family life in United States society is held so sacred that many legal protections forbid intervention into families, except under unusual circumstances when the life or death of a child might be involved. The balance between society's protection and promotion of family life and its desire to protect vulnerable people such as children is one of the many difficult issues faced by social workers in public welfare.

Conclusion

Social casework is the method most commonly used in serving public welfare clients in providing them with both economic and social assistance. It includes a heavy emphasis on child welfare services, particularly protective services for abused and neglected children. The following chapters describe social casework with other client groups and offer examples of services provided through the social casework method.

CHAPTER 5

Social Casework Methods: Services to Meet Special Needs

As the preceding chapter makes clear, much of the effort of social workers in public welfare is directed toward assisting children and their families. However, children in need of improved family lives, protection against abuse and neglect, foster care, or adoption are not the sole objects of social services in public welfare.

Youngsters in Conflict with the Law

A major category of clients in many welfare departments is children who are in conflict with the law. Welfare agencies often provide the probation officers who supervise children placed on probation in lieu of being incarcerated in institutions for juveniles, operate correctional institutions for young offenders, and provide parole supervision for youngsters after they are released from these institutions. Although some view the services provided youngsters who are in difficulty with the law as part of the public corrections or law enforcement system, social workers view these services as part of the overall child welfare system (Martin and Fitzpatrick, 1965; Silberman, 1978; Gottesman, 1981). Children in trouble with the law are, in the minds of most social workers, a special client group in the overall child welfare system.

Few areas of social services have changed as much in recent years as services to juvenile offenders. The history of the juvenile court system and the services it has provided reflect a swing from treating children as people with problems to treating them as young criminals, and then swinging back again. For many years, children who appeared before juvenile judges were treated as if they were being cared for in a social agency. The court did what it considered best for the child, in relation to the child's needs and circumstances. There was little formality, the court's sessions were secret, lawyers did not always appear on behalf of the child, there were no witnesses—the child was viewed as a troubled person and the court viewed its role as one of helping, not judging, the child (Murray and Cox, 1979).

Some began to notice, however, that the benevolence of the court could work against the desires of the child, even if the interests of the child, as the court defined them, were pursued. Children who had committed crimes that would have led to no punishment at all, or small fines at the most, had they been adults, were incarcerated in correctional institutions for years. Some youngsters who had not committed crimes at all were sent to institutions.

After a series of state and federal court decisions—most notably the *In Re Gault* case which was decided by the U. S. Supreme Court in 1967—as well as actions by the United States Congress and many state legislatures, these practices were changed. Currently many states handle juveniles in accordance with the following principles:

1. A child accused of a crime is entitled to all the constitutional guarantees an adult would have, such as an opportunity to face one's accusers, representation by legal counsel, a public trial, and a sentence no greater than an adult would face for a similar offense.

2. Some "status" offenses such as truancy, using alcohol, and promiscuity have been decriminalized. While children may be required to use social or mental health services as well as child protective services, they may not be incarcerated as law violators for these offenses alone.

3. Youngsters in trouble with the law can be diverted from the law enforcement and judicial systems into social service agencies such as foster homes, group child care facilities, special education programs, and recreational activities.

The changes have been so dramatic that some states have almost totally abandoned their juvenile correctional centers. The burden of caring for youngsters in this category now falls most heavily on social workers in public welfare programs.

SOCIAL SERVICES FOR YOUTHFUL OFFENDERS

Children who are arrested for suspected violations of the law are often held first in detention centers, which are short-term, secure holding facilities that are used while more permanent arrangements are made for the child. These have increasingly replaced the jails and special juvenile cells within jails that had been used for youngsters who were arrested. The use of jails for the incarceration of children has been abandoned because of the likely development of criminal attitudes by children housed with adult offenders, the high rate of suicides among juveniles housed in jails, and the belief that children ought to be considered legally incapable of committing crimes.

Adequate programs of education, social casework, and recreation are ideally provided in juvenile detention centers, which are often directed and staffed by social workers. And they are used to house only children who are likely to run away from less secure environments or to harm others or themselves, if allowed to remain free. Under the best circumstances, children who pose no special problems to themselves or the community remain in detention centers for only a few days.

AVOIDING INTERRUPTIONS IN THE CHILD'S LIFE

The short-term use of detention centers and the removal of children to their own homes whenever possible are based upon a desire to help the child avoid interruptions in his or her life. Children have a better chance for success and avoidance of crime as adults when they have completed their educations and when they have the support and care of their parents. Therefore, the welfare department's objective for the child who is suspected of violating the law is to prevent future violations but also to help the child continue receiving family and community support that will avoid future difficulties. That is why, under most circumstances, such children are returned to their parents.

When their parents cannot care for them or when they seem unwilling to help their children avoid trouble, other arrangements are made such as temporary residence with a neighbor or relative. Foster care, emergency shelter care, and other forms of group residential services are used for many children. However, strong efforts are made to help the child continue in school without interruption.

The basic concept used in dealing with children who are in conflict with the law is *the least restrictive alternative.* That is, a child who can be safe and from whom the community faces no danger can be in the custody of his or her parents. A child who may continue to commit crimes may require placement in a foster home. The child who commits serious crimes and who may commit them again may require incarceration in a secure children's correctional institution. The following is a case example:

Deborah Wearden, a twelve-year-old girl, was arrested for auto theft on several occasions. Her action would have been criminal if she had been an adult and she posed a clear danger to the community. A court in her community placed her in the custody of her mother. The child stole another automobile. She was arrested and appeared before the juvenile judge once again. He ordered her placed in the custody of her aunt. Deborah ran away, returned to her mother's house and stole another car. This time the judge ordered her placed in the state correctional center for girls. Her attorney insisted that she did not need such secure detention and, on an appeal, she was released again to the custody of her aunt, with the provision that a juvenile probation officer from the welfare agency continue providing services to the child and her family.

Deborah's case was not unusual. Only in the most difficult and dangerous situations may children, in most states, be held in correctional centers. Whereas for adults the key concept is fitting the punishment to the crime, in juvenile matters the law does not ordinarily assume that a crime has been committed. Instead, an act of delinquency has been committed and, the law orders, corrective action must be taken. But punishment is not an acceptable form of corrective action. The action must meet the needs of the child and must be the least restrictive action that will meet those needs.

ALTERNATIVE SERVICES

Because they recognize that children who are in conflict with the law need special kinds of help, a variety of special services for youthful offenders have been created by communities (Whittaker, 1979). The following services are resources where children may be diverted from the judicial and correctional systems:

1. Alternative schools tolerate behavior that may lead to expulsion from some public schools, and offer curricula and teaching methods designed to hold the attention of children who might be truants from more traditional programs. Truancy and delinquency are closely related.

2. Employment training and work experience programs are often made available for children who cannot succeed in school. These programs often prevent adolescent offenders against the law from becoming adult criminals.

3. Special leisure time and recreation programs are provided for some youngsters who, in an earlier time, might have been placed in correctional institutions. These programs include wilderness camps, weekend ranch experiences, and training in seamanship. Such programs often coexist with public education. Youngsters attend school from Monday through Friday and participate in these programs on weekends and during vacations, when they are most likely to be in trouble.

Services for youthful offenders often require the skills of social group work and community organization, which are discussed in subsequent chapters.

SOCIAL CASEWORK WITH JUVENILE DELINQUENTS AND THEIR FAMILIES

Among the most important services afforded youngsters in difficulty with the law and their families are social casework provided by public welfare social workers. Many times the family problems that led to the child's delinquent behavior can be resolved through the efforts of the social worker with the family. Under some circumstances, the worker will refer the family to family service agencies and community mental health programs for more intensive social casework or other services.

The objectives of casework with the youth and the family are often to help them understand the reasons for the child's offenses against the law and to take action to remove those factors from the family's behavior. In other cases, the worker helps the family change its ways of dealing with the child in the hope that the family will give higher priority to the child's attendance at school, his or her maintenance of more regular hours, the encouragement of part-time employment, and otherwise setting limits for the youngster. Other families may need guidance in granting the child more freedom to spend time with friends. In still others, parents may need to learn to love the child, even when successes in school are limited. In some cases the public welfare social worker may help the family talk with the child's teachers so that the home and the school may work together on behalf of the child. All the skills and all the possible forms of helping families through clarification of feelings, change in family environment, and referral to other agencies may come into play when a worker assists a child who is in conflict with the law.

SERVICES FOR "STATUS OFFENDERS"

Reforms in the laws governing juveniles have led to the creation of a new category of offenses which are known as "status offenses." A status offense is one that would not be punished or even come to the attention of law enforcement authorities if the person committing it were not a child. Status offenses include:

1. Smoking tobacco cigarettes and drinking alcoholic beverages.
2. Engaging in sexual intercourse.
3. Violating a community's juvenile curfew laws.
4. Failing to attend school.

These offenses, which are based on the juvenile status of the perpetrator rather than the behavior itself, were once treated as if they were crimes. Correctional institutions throughout the United States were filled with adolescents who had been truant, girls who had become sexually active, and children who had been arrested for being out after specified hours and therefore in violation of curfew laws.

When state and federal court decisions and legislation began to distinguish between criminal and status offenses, the treatment of status offenders changed dramatically. They were no longer held in correctional institutions, could not be detained in detention centers, and were not always subject to the decisions of juvenile courts (Teitelbaum and Gough, 1977; Polivka *et al.*, 1979).

Despite the constitutional guarantees afforded them, status offenders still seemed to be *persons in need of supervision,* which is the term used in some states to designate youths who are in trouble but who have not committed adult crimes.

Social Casework Services for Adults

Children are not the only concern of public welfare agencies. Many adults also need help for problems they are facing. Some of those problems are comparable to those faced by children (Harbert and Ginsberg, 1979; Getzel, 1981; Hickey and Douglass, 1981).

THE ABUSED, EXPLOITED, OR NEGLECTED ADULT

Older, mentally disabled, and handicapped adults are often subject to abuse, exploitation, or neglect by their families, neighbors, and others (Weiner and Brok, 1978). Their Social Security or Supplemental Security Income checks may be taken from them, their possessions stolen, and they may be denied adequate quarters in their own homes. They may be denied food and medical care, they may be sexually abused—in short, a large number of adults are in danger from others because they cannot adequately defend or care for themselves. Public welfare departments receive referrals about such situations from the victims themselves, from neighbors, and from health providers (United States Senate, 1977).

When reports are received, social workers investigate to determine what, if anything, should be done to protect the older or disabled person (Hall and Mathiasen, 1968, 1973). In many states the successful intervention of the public welfare agency depends upon the worker's skill in obtaining voluntary cooperation of the victim and the family inasmuch as most state laws do not permit positive intervention of the kind used when children are involved (Lehmann and Mathiasen, 1963). In most cases, the investigations lead to actions similar to those resulting from investigations of child abuse and neglect—the associated social casework leads to the problems being resolved and the endangered adult receiving better care. In a very small percentage of situations, almost always with the cooperation of the adult or a person representing the interests of the adult, placement is made in a group home, nursing facility, or other appropriate facility. In unusual cases, the cooperative efforts of police departments may be required. Social workers from the welfare agency also follow up on the adults who need help by arranging for the provision of additional services offered by the agency or by other community services programs such as homemakers, home health aides, community mental health services, medical care, participation in senior citizen center programs, participation in nutrition programs or home delivered meals, and other appropriate services that will enable the client to regain some degree of independence (Nelson, 1980; Nardone, 1980).

SERVICES TO THE INSTITUTIONALIZED MENTALLY
DISABLED

Increasingly, public welfare agencies are providing special help for the institutionalized mentally disabled client, the majority of whom are adults.

Although care of people defined as mentally ill or retarded in mental hospitals or other institutions is not a responsibility of most public welfare departments, public welfare social workers are increasingly becoming involved in providing some services to the mentally disabled and their families (Safford, 1980):

1. They help mentally disabled people obtain alternative placements such as adult foster homes or institutional care when the disabled person can no longer live in the community. For example, mentally retarded adults, long cared for at home by their parents, may have to be placed in institutions when the last parent in the home dies or the remaining parent is no longer sufficiently healthy to care for them.

2. They arrange for services that will relieve the mentally disabled adult's family from some of the burden of caring for this person. This includes arranging for temporary care elsewhere or arranging for the mentally disabled adult to attend an adult day care center or sheltered workshop. Counseling and other services may be provided to assist the family in coping with caring for a mentally disabled person, thus avoiding inappropriate or premature placement of the mentally disabled adult in an institution.

3. They help a hospitalized mentally disabled person and that person's family maintain contact with one another. The public welfare worker may be called upon to help arrange for transportation between

the family's community and the institution. The worker may assist the family in arranging the mechanics as well as the emotional elements of a visit home by an institutionalized person.

4. They help mentally ill or mentally retarded people arrange for community living outside institutions. Public welfare social workers may participate in training for basic community living skills such as using public transportation systems, participating in day hospital or day recreation programs, instruction on obtaining and using medicine, and otherwise surviving without the constant supervision of institutional attendants.

5. They coordinate group discussions with patients in institutions about their return to the community, the problems they are likely to face, and the means they might employ for coping with those problems.

6. Organizing and conducting training sessions for family members so they will have a clearer understanding of some of the problems those returning from institutions for the mentally disabled may face upon return to the community.

Collaboration with Others. In situations when the community placement of a mentally disabled client is both desired and possible, the public welfare social worker often plays a major role.

As in most public welfare social work practice, the social worker serving the mentally disabled in institutions may find that his or her most important responsibility is collaborating with other social workers, particularly those employed full time in institutions, or the state mental health department, or in a community mental health center which serves the community or region from which the patient came and will return. The public welfare social worker's goal may be to help obtain the services of mental health programs for the client, in collaboration with the mental health social worker.

As has been mentioned, the public welfare social worker has special skills and resources for serving the mentally disabled person and the family. These are often in the social and economic components of the family's life. For example, the worker can assist the family in overcoming the social and economic barriers they may face in re-integrating the family member into the community. These efforts may range from locating suitable living quarters to helping the client obtain cash assistance for which he or she is eligible. They may include obtaining special transportation services, arranging for vocational or rehabilitation evaluations, or expediting the enrollment of the disabled person in special recreation or adult day care programs.

On some occasions it may be necessary for the public welfare social worker to play the same role as the mental health worker—to assist the client and the family in evaluating their feelings about the disabled person moving back to the community or—when institutional place-ment appears to be least restrictive—to an institution. Such work, which is more commonly associated with the skills of the psychiatric social worker, may fall upon the public welfare worker when no one else more specially qualified is available to deal with some of the emotional compo-nents of the family's situation.

SUMMARY OF WORK WITH THE MENTALLY DISABLED

On behalf of the mentally disabled, the public welfare social worker serves as an identifier and mobilizer of resources whose efforts are di-rected toward connecting the client with those resources, as a means for meeting the client's needs. In addition, the worker collaborates with other social workers in institutions and community mental health pro-grams to provide services to the client. The worker must also, at times, be an interpreter to the community of the needs of mentally disabled people so that appropriate community resources may be created and operated. The worker must also be a family counselor, helping the fami-ly of the mentally disabled client reach decisions about the care of that client, in consonance, too, with the wishes of the disabled person.

Conclusion

This chapter has covered the social casework services provided to three special categories of clients served by public welfare—children who are in trouble with the law, adults who are abused, neglected or exploited, and the institutionalized mentally handicapped.

Although these individuals are not all normally recipients of public assistance from welfare departments, they often require social services provided by public welfare agencies. Therefore, the social casework methods used in public welfare agencies are made available to them when deemed necessary by the courts, law enforcement authorities, family members, and the clients themselves. Social casework is the most common approach to working with such cases because they require investigation of the clients' situations and action to overcome their prob-lems. But social group work and community organization efforts, which are covered in subsequent chapters, are also useful in resolving the difficulties faced by public welfare clients.

CHAPTER 6

Additional Social Casework Services and Case Examples

IN THE COURSE of providing help to people with social and economic problems, welfare department social workers provide a variety of services that are included in the general category of social casework. Social workers in public welfare deliver some of these services directly. In other cases, they bring the services to the attention of clients and help those clients make use of the assistance.

Day Care for Children

One of the largest expenditures in public welfare is for day care for preschool children (Rhodes, 1979; Belsky, 1980; Slavin, 1979). Day care is provided in two basic forms: in centers, where children are taken for day-long attention by staff members; and in private homes, where children receive similar care provided by people in their own houses, which is called family day care. In some communities, children are placed in federally funded Head Start day care programs, which have purposes beyond day care but which serve similar purposes for clients.

The purposes of day care are several and they vary with the families who receive it.

1. In cases of child abuse and neglect, day care provides parents with opportunities to be separated from their children long enough to

pursue activities other than child care, such as participation in parent education courses, employment, and psychiatric care. Children from these families are given opportunities for learning experiences and social activities with other children. Observations of their health and development are made by day care providers.

2. For the majority of public assistance recipients who are women, day care for their children frees them for employment training and employment itself, leading to their becoming self-supporting.

3. Day care helps socialize children for public education and, in the cases of children with special needs, may provide them with sufficient self-confidence and learning skills to perform adequately in school.

4. Some day care serves school age children by providing them with a safe and secure place to go after school while their parents are unavailable to care for them at home.

Public welfare departments themselves rarely provide day care. Instead they contract either with private day care providers who operate centers as businesses, or with nonprofit day care centers that offer day care as a community service. For family day care, welfare departments recruit providers and pay them a fee for serving children in their homes. Many are current or former clients themselves. The department sets standards for day care, licenses centers and family providers, provides training and supervision to them, and consults with them on their programs. Many social workers in public welfare are responsible for organizing and supervising their department's day care service program.

Employment Training and Placement

Most welfare departments provide opportunities for their clients to be trained for work and to be placed on jobs. This is discussed in detail in Chapter 9. Often this activity is carried out jointly with the state's employment service agency. Many workers in public welfare are responsible for locating employment and training opportunities for their clients, arranging for their participation in them, and monitoring their participation. Because work is the most sought-after alternative to public assistance, a large proportion of staff time is devoted to this development of work opportunities.

There is a social casework component to this training and work placement. Most clients need other supportive services if they are to succeed in employment. These services include day care, of course, along with transportation assistance, help in purchasing tools and uniforms, advice on budgeting, insurance, and taxes, and credit counseling. All of these may be made available by public welfare agencies, either on their own or through contracts for services with other organizations.

Family Planning

Public welfare agencies are required to offer family planning services to their clients who need and want them (Gould, 1979). Most agencies contract for the provision of these services with clinics and health departments, rather than providing the services themselves. Family planning services include providing information about the whole range of contraceptive devices, counseling on means for avoiding or spacing the conception of children, payment for voluntary sterilization of both men and women, and, in some states, abortions.

In addition to direct social casework with clients on family planning matters, public welfare social workers often refer clients to various kinds of services. In some cases, clients are directly referred to family planning clinics that may be sponsored by privately funded social welfare agencies or local health departments. Family planning aids provided by these clinics may include specialized social casework provided by social workers, psychological testing and counseling, education on contraceptive drugs and devices designed to prevent pregnancy, referral information for those in need of prenatal care or arrangements for childbirth, and abortion services.

In addition, many family planning clinics also offer fertility services—medical, educational, and social services—that assist women who have been unable to conceive to become pregnant. Couples may be informed on means for becoming pregnant by choosing the proper times and positions for intercourse. Or they may be referred to physicians or other specialists for fertility testing and, in some cases, surgical procedures or prescriptions that might improve the possibility of pregnancy.

Homemaker, Chore, and Home Health Services

Many families that are clients of public welfare need the assistance of service providers who come into their homes and provide them with guidance on home management as well as actual assistance with home management work and health care (Maybanks and Bryce, 1979; Stempler and Stempler, 1981). Public welfare agencies often employ staff members who provide these services, but most use a combination of employees and contracted services from voluntary agencies or profit-making firms.

Homemakers assist with the care of the home but, more significantly, assist family members in learning how to prepare meals, clean properly, use their money prudently, and care for their children. Homemakers are usually not social workers but they are often assigned to serve families by social workers and are also often supervised by them.

Chore services providers shop, clean, prepare meals, and otherwise assist people who can remain in their homes and stay out of institutions if they are assisted with some of those practical problems of household operation. Many of those who receive these chore services are aged and disabled adults. Services are provided by a broad range of people, some of whom have been or remain public welfare clients themselves. The service providers are paid an hourly wage.

Home health care is, as the term implies, the provision of health services such as the administration of medicines, monitoring health conditions, dressing wounds, assisting people who are bedridden with changing their linens and clothing, and otherwise aiding in treating health problems. Most of the care in home health services is provided by licensed practical nurses or others trained in home health care under contract with departments of welfare.

Vendor Payments

Some families that are demonstrably incapable of using their cash assistance grants require arrangements for their money to be spent for them on rent, food, utilities, and other necessities (Casey and Freedman, 1979). In most circumstances, the clients whose bills are paid for them by the public welfare agency suffer from some disabling emotional or mental handicap such as alcoholism, mental retardation, or drug addiction. In these cases, social workers assist the client by arranging payments to those who are owed funds from the client's resources.

Telephone Reassurance

In some communities, people who are aged or ill are called periodically—in most cases daily—by telephone. That service helps build clients' feelings of security because they know someone will be trying to reach them before long. People who live alone are frequently concerned that they will become ill and need medical attention but will be unable to secure it. Visits are made to the homes of telephone reassurance clients if they do not answer repeated calls.

Purchases of Services

It is well to pause in this listing of social services used by welfare departments to describe how services are purchased and how contracts are executed to obtain these services for clients. Both federal and state funds may be used to purchase services for eligible clients from community welfare agencies, other agencies of local or state government, and profit-making organizations. Many social workers in public welfare arrange for and monitor these contracts (U.S. Department of Health, Education, and Welfare, 1979).

Although agency policies differ from locality to locality, generally the public welfare department may contract for any service it wants to provide, including all of those described in these chapters on social casework. There is some controversy in social work over how many of the services ought to be delivered directly and how many may be delivered under contract with others. There is little controversy over the wisdom of departments contracting for activities they traditionally have not carried on and do not have the resources to initiate, such as health care, day care, and mental health services. In programs such as these, the department is merely buying a part of the organization's services, which are provided to many people, for some of its clients. However in the case of services that are the core responsibility of public welfare, such as child abuse investigation and adoption, there is often opposition to the agency relinquishing its direct provision of the service. Some small agencies, which come into existence almost exclusively to serve the welfare agency's needs, become dependent on annual contracts from the department. In effect, critics suggest, the department is contracting for services that it could provide itself and, in the process, it must pay for both its own costs of arranging and monitoring a contract and the administrative costs of operating the contracting organization. Some have observed that contracting agencies begin to count upon the department's funds and use political pressure, rather than the quality of their services, to guarantee continued receipt of contracts.

Domestic Violence Assistance

Many welfare agencies participate in financing and operating domestic violence shelters for abused family members. Such shelters, which are located throughout North America, offer temporary housing for adults and their children who are in danger of being abused by someone else in the home. In most cases these shelters serve women and their children, although some men are also victims of domestic violence (Bass and Rice, 1979; Cantoni, 1981; Chapman and Gates, 1978; Langley and Levy, 1977).

Domestic violence victims need housing where they cannot readily be found by the spouse who endangers them. Many are unwilling, or believe it is unsafe, to stay with relatives or friends, because an angry spouse will be able to locate them. Others find themselves alone in communities, without relatives or close friends and they are in particular need of domestic violence shelter care.

In addition to the living environment, domestic violence victims also need services such as employment training and placement, so they can become independent of the abusing spouse, day care for their children, mental health services and, in some cases, economic assistance.

Welfare Departments and Disaster Victims

Public welfare social workers must often perform special services for victims of disasters such as floods, earthquakes, and fires. Although the American National Red Cross in the United States and its counterparts throughout the world usually play the major coordinating role in the social services needed for disaster victims, public welfare workers are often the individuals who carry out the casework services to those victims. The Federal Disaster Assistance Administration supplies some services, including funds for helping the lowest income people obtain the help they need in recovering from a disaster.

The services provided often include emergency financial aid and food stamps, loans from federal assistance programs, temporary housing programs, the provision of emergency shelters, food and clothing assistance, and social casework help with the emotional problems engendered by the disaster.

EXAMPLES OF DISASTER

Public welfare social workers become engaged in services to disaster victims in many circumstances. Fires, accidents which injure large numbers of people, floods, and other natural disasters lead to emergencies for many people who are or who become clients of public welfare.

The social worker who works with the victims of a disaster needs special skill in understanding and dealing with people who are in the midst of crises. Crisis services require workers with special skill in helping people with intense, short-term problems. The skills involved in crisis services and intervention into crisis situations are described in detail by many authors (e.g. Puryear, 1980).

Effective social work with people who are victims of disasters requires attention to both their socio-economic and emotional needs. Because so many crises involve the death or disappearance of family members, the sense of loss and often the sense of failure that result from disasters may even require a referral for mental health services in addition to the social casework that may be provided by the public welfare social worker.

Information and Referral Services

Although public welfare departments do many things, they do not do everything. Therefore, one of their most important services is the provision of information about and referral to community resources needed by clients. Such services are often provided under contract with community agencies that not only offer information by telephone and to drop-ins about assistance available to meet the needs they face, but also identify gaps in services. These gaps may indicate that significant problems are not being addressed in the community. Therefore, the information and referral service assists in the community's planning of services so that, to the extent possible, the most critical needs are met (Austin, 1980).

Advocacy on behalf of clients is another social service that is often related to information and referral. The concept of advocacy dictates that the social worker not only inform a client of the availability of a service but that the worker also serve as the client's advocate, by helping secure the service for the client. The advocacy concept developed out of the experiences many workers in public welfare and other agencies shared. They found that their most needy clients were not served because they or their problems were either unattractive or too difficult to serve. In some cases welfare departments themselves were slow in providing services to clients. Social workers from other agencies began serving as advocates with welfare departments to insure that clients received the help to which they were entitled.

Referral of clients is a typical role of the public welfare social worker, as has been made clear throughout this text. But referral is best supplemented with advocacy by the worker on behalf of the client, to be certain that the referral is effected and that the client receives the assistance to which he or she is entitled.

Case Examples

The following case materials illustrate the various ways social casework is used in public welfare agencies on behalf of clients.

Carla Huston

When she was 17, with another year to go before she finished high school, Carla Huston discovered that she was pregnant. She had broken up with her boyfriend three weeks earlier because of his chronic abuse of alcohol, which prevented his finding or keeping a job despite his skill as a refrigeration technician, a trade he had learned at the vocational-technical school in their community. But Carla had no desire to see him again and certainly no desire to marry him, despite her pregnancy.

At the suggestion of her school counselor, Carla visited the local public welfare department and spoke to a social worker who specialized in services to young people. The worker spoke with Carla and helped her clarify her feelings about her situation. Carla did not want to marry the boyfriend; she had not yet finished school and, therefore, could not support herself and had little hope of being able to support herself and her child; her family doctor had diagnosed the pregnancy but Carla had not yet told her parents. Carla and the social worker, Pat Riffle, discussed abortion as an alternative. Carla thought she could obtain the small amount of dollars she would need for an abortion but rejected terminating the pregnancy because she thought it would be wrong to do so.

Ms. Riffle referred her to a maternal and child health clinic operated by the local health department, which arranged for Carla to have prenatal care and delivery of the child, since she could not afford to pay for the care herself and did not want to disclose her condition to her parents right away. Over the months that passed, Carla resolved many of the conflicts she was facing. She told her parents of her pregnancy when they began asking if she was ill on the several days her morning sickness kept her from going to school on time. Although they were upset initially, they ultimately understood their daughter's predicament and agreed to help her with some of her medical bills and with the child, if she decided to keep it.

Shortly before she completed her senior year in high school, Carla gave birth to a healthy seven pound, three ounce daughter, who she named Carla. She and her parents decided to raise the child and keep her with them.

Meanwhile, the public welfare worker had helped Carla obtain nutritional help from the local health department through the Women's, Infants, and Children's program and also referred her back to the family planning clinic, where she obtained contraceptive help which would assist her in preventing future pregnancies, unless she chose to have additional children.

Five years later Carla had married, and both she and her husband, Wade Turner, were doing well. Little Carla had a two-year old brother, and the family of four seemed to be prospering both socially and economically.

Charlie Moore

Charlie was the oldest of three children born to Hazel and Charles Moore. When the boy was three years old, Hazel told her husband Charles to get out of the house because he was a nuisance. Charles was a disabled veteran who called himself a victim of "nerves" during the Vietnam war. For a time he used alcohol excessively but, after treatment in a Veteran's Administration Hospital, he was able to stop drinking. However, his emotional problems were such that he was unable to hold a steady job. His veteran's disability benefits were sufficient to support his family, but Hazel could no longer tolerate Charles. They were both thirty-four years old when she told him to leave.

Hazel's real reason for wanting to be rid of her husband was her desire to, as she put it, "get more out of life," which meant frequenting taverns and developing romantic liaisons with a series of men. From the time Charles left, Charlie and his siblings—a nine-month-old brother, Billy, and a two-year-old sister, Susan—were subjected to men temporarily visiting and living in the house. One rainy day after Charlie had been playing outdoors, he came into the house with mud on his clothing. Hazel's resident boyfriend at the time told Charlie to take off his clothes and spend the rest of the day nude because, as the boyfriend said, "You can't take care of your clothes, anyway, so you don't deserve to wear them." One night, Hazel and another boyfriend battled physically in a neighborhood tavern. The tavern owner summoned the police who arrested the couple. Hazel protested that she could not go to jail—she had to return home to take care of her children. When the authorities asked if there were infant children at home alone, Hazel acknowledged that there were but said that she had only left for a little while—just long enough to drink one beer.

The police took Hazel and her boyfriend to the police station but immediately sent a police officer to her house to investigate the condition of the children. The police found all three in the house, unsupervised, and, in the opinion of the police and a protective services social worker from the welfare department, in danger of accident or illness because of neglect. The children were immediately taken to a children's shelter. All three were subsequently placed in foster homes.

Although efforts were made to reconcile the mother with her children, Hazel's lifestyle did not change sufficiently to convince the protective services social worker that the children would be satisfactorily cared for in her house. Although she verbalized a desire to have her children back, her behavior did not indicate any strong desire for their return. She did not seek employment, she did not care for her house, she only asked to visit with the children once, and even on that occasion she spent only an hour with them when a whole day was free for them to be together. Two years after the children were removed from her household, Hazel died in an auto accident.

Throughout the time the couple had been separated, Charles had sent her monthly allotments from his Veteran's Administration check to care for herself and their children but he had had no direct contact with her or with the children. When the children were removed from her custody, the welfare department was unable to locate Charles and he volunteered no interest in having the children placed with him.

Meanwhile, the foster parents adored all three children, particularly Charlie. With the mother dead, there seemed no reason for William and Veronica Huddleston not to adopt all three children. The courts had been unwilling to terminate Hazel's rights to care for the children but that was no longer an issue.

So the foster parents applied for the adoption of the children. No one imagined that Charles Moore would protest the adoption, even though he still had a right to the children as their natural father. But if he had been interested, all the parties assumed, he would have let that interest be known long before.

The public welfare social worker who conducted the adoptive study contacted Charles so he could sign the appropriate documents to relinquish his rights to the children. But Charles unexpectedly balked at signing and said that, in fact, he had fallen in love with another woman who had two children of her own. The two of them were living together and between them had sufficient income and a large enough house to care for all five youngsters. The worker asked why Charles Moore had not made his desire for the children known before and he replied that he was afraid of the men who had lived with Hazel. One had threatened to kill him if he came on her property and, therefore, he simply avoided any direct contact with his family until he learned Hazel was dead. His nerves did not allow him, he said, to get into conflict with Hazel or the men she saw. But now he wanted the children and asked that they be brought to him immediately.

When Charlie and his brother and sister were brought to see their father, Charlie immediately began to cry. When he returned to his foster parents after that visit, he told them about the man who had made him walk through the house without his clothing and, somehow, he believed Charles was that man.

The Huddlestons, who desperately wanted to keep Charlie, concluded that the child's natural father had sexually abused him and that he was not a fit parent. They challenged the removal of the children from their home in court and were represented by an attorney who they paid for representing their interests. Mr. Moore also appeared in the court and was represented by a public defender because the state's laws clearly stated that although a child could not be removed from foster parents without cause under most circumstances, removal for return to the child's natural parent or parents was allowable.

The foster family, during the hearing, had raised the sexual abuse charge as a means of convincing the judge to terminate Mr. Moore's rights to the child. But the only evidence was the child's recollection of being forced to walk nude through his house, and Mr. Moore's testimony demonstrated it was unlikely he would have been with Charlie at a time Charlie would have remembered.

Charlie is now living with his natural father and stepmother, along with his natural siblings and his stepmother's children from an earlier marriage.

CHAPTER 7

Providing Group Services in Public Welfare Agencies

Social work methods have traditionally included helping people in groups. The methods of social group work, which is the name usually given to social work's services to groups of clients, arose from a number of the traditions of social work practice, particularly the settlement house movement and youth-serving organizations. Social workers have known for many years how important the group may be in helping people resolve difficulties that they may face and in taking action to improve their lives.

In more recent years, services to people in groups have captured the interest of a variety of other practitioners such as psychiatrists and psychologists, who practice "group therapy;" researchers in the social sciences, who have been intrigued by the influence groups have on individual members as well as by the behavior or dynamics of small groups of people; and by educators who are aware of the impact of the group in teaching and learning.

But social group work predates most modern interest in and activity with groups, including group therapy and other efforts to help people overcome their problems through group methods; it has evolved through the years in ways that make it a useful method in all social work settings, including public welfare. It is social work's way of helping people through groups (Alissi, 1980).

Social group work has the advantage of using program activities of all sorts as a means of helping group members with their problems, whatever those problems may be. If the focus that seems best for the group is talking about problems and discussing ways to overcome them, as is often the case in group therapy, that can be the program effectively used by the worker. On the other hand, groups can deal with a wide range of problems encountered by public welfare clients. Education on nutrition, exposure to new and exciting activities available to most children but not always available to protective services clients, and various forms of play can be quite helpful and they mean a great deal to public welfare clients as part of their group activities.

Some of the originally used social work group methods have potential benefits for public welfare within the agencies which sponsor them. Work with youngsters in youth-serving organizations such as the YM and YWCAs, 4H clubs, Jewish Community Centers, Catholic Youth Organizations, Boy Scouts, Girl Scouts, and Camp Fire, has significant application for work with dependent and neglected children, with youngsters who are in trouble with the law, and with some groups of young adult public welfare clients. The early social group work practice with preschool children, which was often a forerunner of modern day care, has significance for working with day care programs in modern public welfare agencies (Konopka, 1972).

Settlement houses—recreational, educational, and leisure time facilities, usually located in large cities—were instrumental in helping many immigrants to the United States integrate into American society. They were among the first sponsors of group activities for aging people and, with their "self-help" activities for new residents and the poor in the neighborhoods they served, were forerunners of the National Welfare Rights Organization and other client movements. They were called settlement houses because university students, ministers, and others from well-educated backgrounds came into the impoverished sections of large European and American cities to "settle." Part of the concept of the settlement house was for the residents, as the staff members who settled in the area were called, to have influence on their neighborhoods and their residents. Settlement house residents were clearly the first social group workers and were among the first full-time, professional social workers too.

Employment Groups

Group methods may also be useful in providing services to clients who may be seeking or who may be qualified to seek employment. In many cases, the basic problem of the unemployed person is discouragement. Those who have been employed and find that they cannot obtain employment, and must receive assistance because of this, frequently find that talking in groups with others in like circumstances is a significant means for dealing with the problem. Just as in any other kind of group service, learning that there are others who face the same problem and talking with them is often one of the solutions to the problem.

When potentially employable people meet in groups and talk about seeking work, the mutual support and encouragement of others who are attempting the same thing can be an emotional and practical asset. Members of such a group can criticize each other's job-seeking skills, can offer hints on where and how to find jobs, can role play the search for jobs, and can reinforce the notion that each member has talent and a contribution to make to the work force.

Social Group Work Practice in Public Welfare Agencies

The social group work method usually relies on one or more social workers assisting a small group—as few as three or four or as many as fifteen to twenty people—in overcoming a problem or in resolving a need. The social group work method has a number of advantages for use in public welfare, over and above the advantages of working with individuals for the resolution of individual problems (Northen, 1969). Some of these advantages are enumerated below.

1. Working with people through groups tends to reduce the stigma associated with the problem being addressed. For example, when a recipient of public assistance sits in a room with a group of recipients, that individual realizes that economic need is a problem faced by many people and therefore should not be a source of shame.

2. When one is a member of a group, one can receive help not only from the social worker who is serving the group but also from each of the individual members. Sometimes these peers can help one another more than a professional expert can. The professional expert is there to help the individual members but also to help the members help one another. Therefore, assistance with one's problems is available from a number of people on a number of different levels in a number of different ways.

3. Being a member of a group is a familiar experience for most people. It is comforting and common for most individuals to participate with others in learning about something, in discussing the possibility of mutually solving a problem or meeting a need, in participating in worship, and in socializing. The social casework interview and its focus on therapeutic services to help individuals change themselves is a less com-

mon and often more threatening experience than participation in a group.

4. Groups can act as well as talk. Although groups of people may effectively clarify and resolve problems through group discussion, problem identification and resolution, and the development of insight into one's behavior with the help of the social worker and other group members, groups of individuals are also able to come to conclusions about concerns and take actions to resolve them.

A group of public assistance recipients might, for example, explore their feelings about the stigma many citizens place on public welfare recipients, may share their feelings about their very small disposable incomes, but may also visit with a legislator, write to a governor, or call a press conference to protest those conditions.

Similarly, groups of youngsters who meet together can play billiards, shoot basketball, and otherwise engage in activities other than talking about the problems that may concern them. At times, game playing is an excellent situation for discussions of personal problems with peers.

5. Both verbal and nonverbal behavior are dramatically displayed in groups and the members can learn from both. That is, a group member who admits engaging in self-destructive behavior may be told by one member that the behavior is self-defeating. And all the other members may be in agreement, which profoundly carries the message to the individual.

The public welfare social worker who serves a group also needs special skills in working with the group (Klein, 1972). The following are some of the skills required.

1. Determining group composition: The worker must give some thought to the people who will be in the group. How large should it be? Should it include males and females or just one sex? What should be the age range? A social worker carefully planning group experiences will consider all of these factors because each will have an impact on the ways the group progresses and affects its members. The larger the group, for example, the less pressure on each individual member to participate and change because of the group. The broader age span will perhaps create a pattern of leadership that is different than it might be if all the members were the same age. The conversations and activities of a single sex group are likely to be different than those of groups that have both males and females in them.

2. Programming: That is the term social group workers use for the activities in which groups engage. Programming may include discussions of problems, social and recreational activities for the group members, and unplanned but significant events in the group's life that may

have a profound effect on the group and its members. Social workers who work with groups need to know how to use these planned and unplanned activities to the maximum benefit of the members.

3. Observing and analyzing verbal and nonverbal behavior: An effective social group worker is always alert to developments in the group. The physical movements of the members, their facial expressions, the words they use, their postures, and their tones of voice all give the alert observer clues to what is happening to the members and to the total group. That information can be used effectively to help the members of the group.

4. Discussion leadership: At least when a group begins, the social group worker needs to be skillful in helping people talk about the concerns that have brought them together. The social worker should know how to elicit a response from group members—by asking open-ended provocative questions or by introducing topics that will arouse the concern of everyone present—as well as how to settle a group down when controversy has led them into shouting or arguing, rather than talking.

5. Summarizing and ending group activities: Beginning a group of people is important but ending it properly is equally significant for benefitting the members. How they use what they have gained from the group is as critical as how they engage in group activities.

Types of Public Welfare Group Services

Public welfare departments work with clients in groups for many different purposes and in many different ways. The format, size, and content of a group's activities vary from group to group depending upon the purpose, composition, and behavior of the group, itself. Some public welfare groups meet only once, others may meet weekly over a period of years. Some meet for twenty or thirty minutes while others meet for several hours. All of these factors vary with the agency, the group, the social worker, and the members.

GROUP INTERVIEWING FOR SERVICES

Welfare departments often use group methods in explaining and taking applications for the many services they provide. For example, instead of one social worker interviewing one client about public assistance or food stamps, in some agencies a group of clients meets with a worker and discusses, as a group, the program, the benefit levels, the eligibility requirements, and the application. It is possible for a group of ten or twelve applicants to meet in a conference room with a single worker to go over these matters. Through the process of answering questions and discussing the program, many applicants will understand that they are not eligible and will not bother submitting applications. Others will be especially accurate about providing full information to the agency because they have learned the information requirements from other members of their group. Individual, confidential questions can be asked after meetings but, for most issues and for most clients, a group application process for assistance can be implemented.

Similarly, groups of applicants for adoptive children may also meet and learn about agency policies and procedures. They may be reassured, because of the group setting, that favorites are not played and that all applicants for adoptable children are treated in the same way by the agency. They may also learn more about home visits, opportunities to provide foster care, legal issues surrounding adoption, and other matters of concern from one another, as well as from the worker.

Applicants for social services such as day care, homemaker services, and other kinds of help may find it useful to be part of a group when they apply for assistance.

Of course, these activities may conserve the time of the worker as well as making the process of applying more efficient.

GROUP TRAINING

In addition to training its staff, a public welfare agency may also find it necessary and helpful to train many other people who are connected with the agency and its programs (Smith and Farrell, 1979). These may include foster parents who frequently need training on the agency's programs, foster care policies, legal responsibilities, and resources for help. Many also need special instruction in raising children, in dealing with the special problems of developmentally disabled children or children who have been delinquent, in dealing with biological parents, and in working with the schools on behalf of their foster children. Often the learning for foster parents is more profound through participation in a group with other foster parents than it may be in any other way. People who have never before raised children may learn from experienced parents. Potential adoptive parents can learn from those who have adopted (Prochaska and Coyle, 1979). Families that have raised children who are in conflict with the law can teach foster parents who have not shared that experience what to expect. Special lecturers can be brought in on health, nutrition, and child behavior. Legal consultants can help foster parents learn the statutes governing adoption and foster care.

Whereas the applicant group mentioned above may only require a one-hour meeting, altogether, a training group of foster parents may meet over a period of a year or more for two or three hours weekly.

NUTRITION EDUCATION

Many public welfare departments have sponsored groups for food stamp recipients on improved shopping skills and nutrition. These groups often educate their members through shared menus, films, and guest presentations on obtaining the best quality and value for the lowest price when shopping. The preparation of pleasant and balanced meals is the subject of some meetings. These groups often lead into discussions of child-rearing practices, family relations, and other family matters. These may be sources of grave difficulty that members may not have agreed to come to discuss but which they may desperately want to examine and resolve with the help of one another and the social worker.

GROUPS OF CHILDREN AND YOUTH

Some of the youngsters served by welfare departments such as children on probation or neglected youngsters may lack the resources, the inclination, or the experience to participate in group activities for young people in their own neighborhoods (Timm, 1980; Larsen and Mitchell, 1980). Such activities can help boost the morale of young people and can provide them with opportunities to develop better self images and social skills as well as to participate in satisfying and pleasant social and recreational activities with other children. Therefore, many agencies have clubs for young people which meet periodically.

SELF-HELP GROUPS

Some groups of clients in public welfare agencies come together to help one another to resolve problems with which the welfare department is deeply concerned. A national association, Parents Anonymous, is for parents who abuse or neglect their children. They use the kinds of methods developed by Alcoholics Anonymous to meet one another's need for control of neglectful and abusive behavior toward their youngsters. Although groups organized for self-help often meet without the participation of a professional social worker, many do use social workers to help them carry out their activities. There are similar national groups for people with various health and social problems, such as The Lost Chord Group, which serves persons who have had their tracheas removed, Parents Without Partners, an association of men and women who are raising children without spouses because of divorce or death, as well as groups for people suffering from a variety of developmental disabilities, former inmates of mental hospitals and penal institutions, and compulsive gamblers (Lieberman and Borman, 1980; Silverman, 1981).

Physical Exercise as a Group Activity

Some groups of older people have benefited from a program called Preventicare, which was developed by Lawrence Frankel and Betty Byrd Richard. It has been used by welfare departments and other agencies to provide mobility through exercise for older people in nursing homes and community centers for the aging. A description of Preventicare, an exercise program, is found in the book, *Be Alive As Long As You Live* by Frankel and Richard (1980).

Physical exercise through sports and games is also appropriate and often a part of many other group activities for public welfare clients of all ages.

Referral to Other Groups

In addition to groups operated by welfare departments themselves, many clients can be helped by referral to groups sponsored by other agencies or organizations (Mathews and Fawcett, 1980). It is a common practice for workers in protective services to refer parents for group services to mental health and family service agencies. Such agencies may have or may be willing to organize groups of abusive or neglectful parents in cooperation with public welfare agencies.

Groups such as these often find it helpful to meet outside welfare offices—in community buildings, volunteer fire departments, churches, and schools. Meeting in such decentralized locations both removes any negative feelings the clients might have about receiving welfare and also brings the meeting closer to the members' own residences.

Mental health centers and family service agencies may also be quite helpful through the organization of groups for clients who abuse alcohol or drugs (Hawley and Brown, 1981). Settlement houses, YM and YWCAs, Jewish Community Centers, Boy Scouts, Girl Scouts, Camp Fire, and similar youth-serving organizations are often valuable resources for helping children who are in trouble with the law or who come from families where there is abuse or neglect to deal with some of their problems.

Health departments or family planning clinics may have group instruction on family planning, childbirth, or nutrition. Other community agencies may sponsor classes on skills in child rearing, and agricultural extension agencies may provide group opportunities on meal preparation and home economics.

Values of Group Experiences

Many of those who become clients of public welfare agencies lack opportunities for positive group experiences. Poverty and the other socio-economic problems that bring welfare clients into contact with public welfare agencies often reduce the clients' ability to expend additional energy on personal growth and learning or on some of the social and educational activities that can help them forget about their economic and emotional burdens. Public welfare recipients—particularly those who need the cash assistance and food stamps provided by public welfare agencies—may benefit dramatically from participation in groups, either those operated by the agency itself or those to which they are referred by social workers in the agency.

Limitations of Groups

Of course, there are also problems associated with serving people in groups in public welfare departments. If there were not, more group activities would be used and more people would be served exclusively through groups in public agencies.

Not all services of public welfare departments—whether counseling abusing and neglecting parents (McNeil and McBride, 1979; Kruger *et al.*, 1979), taking applications for assistance, or otherwise providing the benefits of welfare programs—can be conveniently offered in group contexts. The reasons for the occasional impossibilities are rather obvious and simple. For example, it is not always possible to gather a whole group together for an activity or an application. An applicant who comes into a welfare office in a rural area on a Monday, for example, has a right to apply for assistance immediately and to be provided it as soon as his or her eligibility is determined. Waiting until the following Thursday when five or six others may have applied is not fair or reasonable.

Some problems require very confidential treatment, particularly when they involve behavior that might lead to arousing the anger of other group members. For example, a father who has committed incest with an infant daughter may be physically attacked by other members of a group of protective services clients if he or the worker reveals the reason for his being a group member.

So groups do not lend themselves to emergencies or to highly confidential or embarrassing subjects. They can, however, be used in most situations and services offered by public welfare agencies.

The following example shows how a public welfare agency can use group methods.

The Nutrition Knowledge Club

The agency's purpose in establishing the club was to improve the nutrition of food stamp recipients. All eight members of the group understood they were to meet every Tuesday afternoon for two months with the food stamp outreach worker to discuss better nutrition and better food purchasing.

All the members were recipients of Aid to Families with Dependent Children as well as food stamps. They had been chosen because they were influential in their neighborhoods and were likely to pass along the information they gained from the club to their neighbors who also received food stamps.

At the first three meetings, the worker introduced them to nutrition experts from the local community college home economics department. They learned about the essential food groups, preparing balanced meals, purchasing food at low cost that would provide their families with adequate numbers of calories, vitamins and minerals, and about the negative affects of alcohol and sugar on the body.

The first meeting ended with a few minutes' discussion, led by the worker, about the ways the members would like to use the following meeting. The worker had served refreshments to the members which included coffee, fruit juices, and raw vegetables which the members were able to eat with a dip-dressing of sour cream and onion soup. For the second meeting one member, Mrs. Atlas, agreed to bring some refreshments that would support the nutrition information brought to them by the home economics nutrition expert at the first meeting and she suggested that each member take responsibility for bringing refreshments to each other meeting. The worker encouraged that idea and said the agency would reimburse each of the members who brought the refreshments if they would bring receipts.

By the end of the third meeting the members asked the worker what the agency really thought of them. Were they viewed as people who didn't know how to care for their families? Did they seem to be so ignorant that they knew nothing about food and its preparation? The worker responded that the agency thought very highly of the members and had invited them because of their influence with their friends. The worker further suggested that the agency knew most people lacked adequate knowledge about nutrition and could therefore benefit from the education provided by the agency on nutrition. But, more important, the worker suggested, how did the women feel about themselves? The agency felt very positively toward this group of clients and thought they could help not only themselves and their families but others in their community too. But did receiving public assistance cause them some demoralization? And did the members want to talk about their feelings toward the agency and toward the problems associated with being dependent on others for financial assistance?

The members—who after three meetings felt comfortable with one another, and who also felt that the group was theirs because each had at least the minimal role of being responsible for the refreshments at one meeting—used the worker's questions to talk among themselves about their feelings toward the agency and toward the public, which they believed "hated" public assistance recipients, even though most people did not know who was or was not a recipient of aid.

CHAPTER 8

Community Organization Methods in Public Welfare

AMONG THE OLDEST APPROACHES to the provision of human services is community organization. Before social welfare evolved the concept of the professionally educated social service provider, whose mission is to identify client need and work with clients in meeting those needs, societies had developed organized efforts for the provision of services to the disadvantaged.

Whether organizational efforts are geared to helping people share resources with one another in order to solve mutual problems, to avoid duplication of services, or to bring about the development of new services, organization of communities and their resources has traditionally been a part of the social services and social work (Ross and Lappin, 1967).

Community organization can be traced to the earliest private and church provision of services to people (Dunham, 1958, 1970). Community organizers for churches and private charities coordinated and rationalized those services by developing programs to meet identified needs and by curtailing services where needs were being met to a higher degree than necessary while other needs were starved for resources. Perhaps the most common concept of community organization is the adjustment of resources to meet needs by creating more resources as new and greater needs are identified, diversion of resources to unmet needs, and elimination of unneeded and duplicated programs. This concept was stated in some early writing about community organization by Robert D. Lane. He wrote about the "field of community organization" in 1939 as part of the Proceedings of the National Conference of Social Work (Turner, 1977).

More recent developments in community organization have gone beyond the balancing of needs and resources to helping communities resolve specific issues or problems.

Even more recently, "social planning" has become, for some scholars and practitioners, the successor to traditional community organization. Social planning—the process of identifying social welfare problems and developing the means for overcoming them through community change, the development and application of new resources, and changes in community patterns and practices—constitutes a modern form of community organization practice.

The Process of Organizing and Planning

Dr. Robert Perlman has synthesized the various ideas of community organization and social planning into a variety of steps that seem common to all such efforts. Writing in the 1977 *Encyclopedia of Social Work*, Perlman outlines the steps as follows:

1. Choosing among values or goals.
2. Analyzing a present state and calculating how to reach a desired future state.
3. Using political agitation and settling issues among groups interested in various goals.

Murray Ross, author with Ben Lappin of a major text on the subject, *Community Organization: Theory, Principles and Practice* (1967), adds several other steps to the process such as developing the will to overcome a problem or need, ranking problems and needs according to the community's own judgment about what is most important, developing the external and internal resources to overcome the problem, and, once the problem is addressed or resolved, redefining that problem or choosing among new concerns which are crucial to the community.

In all its approaches, the community organization method relies upon bringing together the leaders of a community who are concerned about an issue or problem.

There are few matters of greater interest and concern to effective community organizers than identification and involvement of the community's real leaders, rather than those who may simply appear to be leaders. Murray Ross and Charles Hendry wrote many years ago about the processes of identifying and understanding leadership in *New Understandings of Leadership* (1957). They and others point out that those who may seem to be leaders—because they hold high positions, because they are articulate, or because they have attractive appearances—may not be the genuine leaders of organizations.

Those who must be reached by community organizers are the people who have the respect of those they lead and who, in turn, fully understand and appreciate their members. One can only identify leaders by understanding something about the dynamics of the groups of which they are members. Effective leaders are those whose influence is significant in the process of making decisions about matters of concern to the group, who are described by their colleagues as important influences on their lives, and who seem to have deep and detailed understandings of the interests and the needs of the group.

Community organization draws upon fields such as anthropology, sociology, business administration, political science, and public administration to develop its theoretical base (Cox et al., 1979).

Community Organization Practice in Public Welfare

Public welfare departments began seeing the need for community organization methods during the 1960s, when organization and involvement of client groups became a fact of public welfare administration. Groups such as the National Welfare Rights Organization which, for a time, operated throughout the United States, sought to change public welfare programs through community organization methods. They organized low income people to work for changes in public welfare programs. The NWRO, which was founded and led by Dr. George Wiley, a university chemistry professor and long-time civil rights activist who died from accidental drowning in August of 1973, used tactics of confrontation as the primary means of changing department of welfare programs and practices (Kotz, 1977). The tactics were taken from the writings and practices of the late Saul Alinsky, an early community organizer who operated the Industrial Areas Foundation in Chicago and whose best known work was *Reveille for Radicals* (1969).

It is unquestionable that public welfare programs were transformed by the efforts of NWRO which demanded higher benefit levels, readily available information on the rules and regulations governing welfare programs, client representation on welfare advisory groups, and courteous treatment of clients by public welfare employees. Many of the changes demanded by NWRO were translated into policy throughout the United States either by administrative action or through court decisions based upon suits brought by NWRO members or their sympathizers, often in cooperation with publicly funded legal aid groups.

Dr. Wiley and his supporters had discovered a need or discontent among the poorest Americans—recipients of public assistance—and had taken steps to overcome that need, primarily through confrontation, both direct and in the courts, against public welfare departments. NWRO used a number of dramatic tactics for achieving their objectives. They occupied welfare offices and refused to allow directors of those offices to enter. In fact, during the early years of the Richard M. Nixon administration, they took over and occupied the office of the Secretary of Health, Education, and Welfare, Robert Finch. In 1969, NWRO leaders and supporters from other radical causes and groups took over a general session of the National Conference on Social Welfare in New York. The coalition of change-oriented organizations locked several thousand participants in the Conference's opening general session in a New York Hilton Hotel ballroom and demanded cash contributions from the individual members and the National Conference on Social Welfare to pay for the participation of public welfare clients in future meetings of NCSW. Riot-equipped police from the New York City Police Department were required to free the hostage conference-goers.

It is likely that the National Welfare Rights Organization experience was the most dramatic example of the use of community organization methods to change American public welfare.

Social Services Planning

The public welfare field has learned to use community organization methods to achieve its purposes. In some cases, the public welfare department at either the state or local level participates in the social welfare planning efforts for its locality (Ecklein and Lauffer, 1972). The social welfare planning group—whether it is called a council of social agencies, a community welfare council, or goes by another name—attempts to bring together all of the service providers so that duplication is avoided and the maximum use is made from the voluntary contributions and publicly appropriated funds available for services to the community.

Public welfare agencies frequently initiate service planning by participating in community organization. An example might be the development of a plan for serving juveniles who are in trouble with the law. This service is often shared by a corrections department, state police, local law enforcement authorities, public school officials, and the welfare department. By bringing together a representative group from the concerned agencies, the public welfare department can make effective efforts to plan services for youngsters in trouble with the law. By pooling resources, each agency can avoid creating services that already may be provided by existing agencies. For example, if one of the solutions to the problem of delinquency is considered to be the creation of vocational training and employment opportunities in detention centers operated by counties, a better solution might be to arrange for the enrollment of youth in existing vocational and rehabilitation programs operated by the public education program. Or if counties find themselves facing the responsibility for operating secure, safe detention facilities for youngsters who are arrested, they may find it is more feasible for them to contract with the welfare department to operate those facilities than operate them themselves. They might also find it expedient to purchase meals from the school system, rather than creating and operating their own food preparation and distribution facilities.

In many cases, a community's problems must be resolved by the community itself. Frequently, the department of welfare takes the lead in identifying and dealing with community concerns even though community organization is not always a formally identified and staffed process in welfare departments. Sometimes people who are directly involved in the agency's work take leadership in organizing community endeavors on behalf of clients.

On many occasions, solutions to community problems are more important than all of the direct services an agency might be able to provide to clients because setting up a system to identify and deal with problems has the effect of creating a mechanism for problem resolution (Weissbourd and Grimm, 1981).

Resources—Internal and External

Writers about community organization all recognize that resources are needed in order to solve community problems. Many prefer that the community rely most heavily on its own local funds and people—and they often seek to avoid the use of external resources. Others have viewed the community organization process as one of developing proposals and applying for grants from government, foundations, and other sources of assistance in the development of programs (Ross and Lappin, 1967). Effective community organization usually relies on a judicious use of internal and external resources. The good will, concern, and funds available within the community—coupled with the experiences of other communities, grants from organizations that provide assistance, and expert consultants—can all combine to provide a community with solutions to problems. It is important for a community to use its own resources so the people will be involved in and committed to the program being organized. However, it is unwise to forego money and help from sources outside when those are available. Effective community organization tends to use a balance of internal and external resources.

Welfare departments also use community organization efforts to define and set priorities upon community problems. These efforts can include almost any service, but the most common experience of public welfare departments has been in the field of social services planning. By federal law, each state has recently been required to prepare, disseminate, and solicit public comment upon its annual social services plan. Many states use a committee of agency representatives and interested citizens who discuss the social services funds available and determine the priorities for expending them. The plan is negotiated and agreed to by the citizens who develop it, in cooperation with agency staff members who explain and enunciate the agency's required uses for some of the funds. Then the annual plan is printed and disseminated to libraries, social agencies, and interested community groups. Subsequently, public hearings on the plan are organized as a means of obtaining citizen comment everywhere the plan is to be implemented. These public comments are recorded, either by staff members who take notes on the discussions or by using tape recorders. The most frequent objections, suggestions, and other comments are then considered by the welfare department as a basis for modifications of the plan, prior to its being implemented by the state. Of course, widespread information is made available to citizens about the plan and the public hearings.

Many welfare departments, both local and state, apply similar approaches to organizing licensing programs for nursing homes, setting rates for health care, developing budget proposals for governmental programs, and structuring the delivery of their services.

Public Involvement in Public Welfare Operations

The planning efforts described in this chapter are an example of the useful involvement of citizens in the operation and sustenance of the public welfare program (Neuber, 1980). Many state welfare departments—as well as local branches of the state agencies or local, freestanding public welfare programs—create and counsel with citizen advisory groups whose role is to assist the department in setting priorities and in making decisions about the operation of the program. There are several reasons for organizing citizen advisory groups in welfare departments (Trohanis, 1980; Tucker, 1980). Among these are:

1. They can obtain advice which will make the program more acceptable to and therefore successful in the community.

2. They can develop citizen understanding of the public welfare program. Citizen advisory group members can be highly effective carriers of messages about the values and virtues of public welfare programs. Citizen advisors who are favorably impressed by public welfare programs and who want to build support for the program in the larger community can do so without being accused of having special interests as welfare officials and employees may. They can be highly influential with government decision-makers such as legislators.

3. They can provide information to public welfare departments on the actual impact of their programs. Misspending money or operating services that do not reach the clients—or at least the clients who need those services most—may not come to the attention of the welfare department without the participation of the citizen advisors.

It is generally helpful to have representatives of the clients or consumers of the services themselves serve on citizen welfare advisory groups (Carroll, 1980). They can represent the special perspective of those who rely on the programs for help and can, in turn, help the nonclient members develop new perspectives on public welfare programs and services which they might not otherwise obtain.

OPERATING CITIZEN WELFARE ADVISORY GROUPS

These organizations can come about in many ways, sometimes through the voluntary initiative of concerned citizens but more often through the efforts of the public welfare agency itself to organize a group of citizens for involvement in the program. The organization and operation of an advisory council often requires the assignment of a staff member to develop interest in and concern about such an organization, to help select the members, and to serve as the leader of the advisory group as it begins. Of course, the staff member's objective is to turn over the full operation of the council to the members themselves once they feel they are sufficiently knowledgeable and independent to do so. Often the staff member helps the group organize itself and operate by providing members with training and education on welfare programs, on parliamentary procedure, on the development of by-laws, and consultation with others from other welfare advisory groups who have had more extensive experience in their operation.

As soon as it is feasible to do so, the staff member will want to turn over all the decisions about the advisory council to its members so they can select their own leaders, outline their own objectives, and carry out their own projects for reaching the objectives they have set for themselves (Ross and Lappin, 1967).

OPERATION OF VOLUNTEER PROGRAMS

Another element of community organization is public welfare in volunteer work (Haeuser and Schwartz, 1980). Public welfare grew out of voluntary efforts on behalf of the poor. Today's public welfare efforts, though supported by taxes, use the efforts of volunteers to operate the programs.

There are two general classifications of volunteers in public welfare—those who work on the policies of the department as advisors, such as the citizen welfare advisory board members discussed above, and those who work to provide direct services to clients.

The goals of volunteer programs include not only obtaining the advice that policy volunteers provide and the services that direct service volunteers offer but also educating the larger community about public welfare needs and problems and introducing new people and new ideas into public welfare programs.

It is true that volunteers provide perspectives on public welfare and services to public welfare clients that departments would not often be able to provide on their own (Thursz and Vigilante, 1978). A sound volunteer program can include such activities as Foster Grandparents, a federally financed effort to make use of the time, skills, and affection of older people to help with the problems faced by children in public welfare. Foster Grandparents can serve as tutors and also serve as recreational friends for children, taking them fishing, to cultural programs, and teaching them to play games and sports.

Volunteers in public welfare have also served as counselors in domestic violence centers and children's shelters and as visitors in the homes of public assistance recipients to assist them with nutrition, home maintenance, and child care. In some communities volunteers also provide "mother's day out" services, which enable public assistance mothers to participate in recreational or educational programs while volunteers care for their children in the mothers' homes. Volunteers also assist in determining eligibility for clients, in investigating child abuse complaints, in monitoring juvenile courts, and in virtually every other operation of public welfare.

INVOLVING CIVIC GROUPS IN PUBLIC WELFARE

One form of promoting volunteer activities in public welfare through community organization is to involve whole groups or associations in the operations of the programs (O'Connell, 1980). In many communities, groups such as the Jaycees, Business and Professional Women's clubs, Lions, and Kiwanis are recruited to carry out special programs on

behalf of public welfare clients. Civic groups such as these often organize annual parties for foster children, recruitment campaigns for foster
parents, and other specific civic projects on behalf of public assistance
clients. These activities meet the needs of the agency to involve the
public in its programs; the needs of the clients are met by the activity
itself; and the volunteering organization is often able to fulfill its commitments for serving the community through the use of its services by
the welfare department.

The following are some examples of community organization activities sponsored by departments of welfare on behalf of clients:

1. A child support enforcement worker discovers that a majority of
her clients require help because they are not receiving court-ordered
child support payments from the fathers of their children. This causes
several problems—the mothers are stereotyped as irresponsible collec-
tors of welfare; they and their children are demoralized; and they live
less adequately than they would if the court-ordered child support payments were being made. With the worker's help, the mothers form an
association which obtains publicity in newpapers and on radio and television and which visits with the local prosecuting attorney to complain
about the lack of action on their child support. They also visit with the
judges in their community who ordered the payments so the judges are
aware that their orders are not being followed. Shortly thereafter legal
action is taken to require child support payments. Husbands are threatened with prosecution and incarceration for failure to follow court orders. The child support enforcement worker uses her time and efforts,
coupled with the initiative taken by the mothers, to obtain support for
the families instead of—or as a supplement to—public assistance grants.

2. A number of families receiving public assistance who live in an
isolated, rural neighborhood have no public transportation for themselves. The school bus their children use stops only across a dangerous
bridge. A public welfare social worker recognizes that the problem is
one shared by many members of the community and works with them
to form a transportation alliance. The families organize an escort service
across the bridge to the school bus stop, after discovering that the school
buses are too heavy to cross the bridge. Parents take turns halting traffic
and escorting the children back and forth across the bridge for connections with the school bus. They also visit with the county transportation
authority to express their concerns about the lack of public transportation.

3. The same group, identifying other problems with the help of the
public welfare social worker, takes note of an increase in prices at the
local food store coincidental each month with the distribution of public
assistance checks. The association keeps careful records on the prices of

specific grocery items in the store and after documenting their case, a committee is formed to visit the store owner and protest the pricing practices. The owner agrees to keep the prices level throughout the month and to stop raising the prices, except when documented increases in wholesale costs and other expenses make it necessary. In return, the association drops its plan to report the owner to the state attorney general and agrees not to publicize their findings or their meeting with the store owners.

4. The county welfare director notes that throughout the area civic groups, churches, and professional associations provide Christmas gifts and food baskets to low income families. But some families receive more help than they need or want, while others receive nothing. The director calls a meeting of the groups that have provided Christmas assistance and helps them organize a coordinated system for obtaining the names of people who need help, maintaining a master registry of those who receive it, and avoiding duplication of aid. That Christmas the whole community is satisfied that help has been given to those who need it most and that the assistance has been distributed efficiently.

Conclusion

Community organization is one of the means by which departments of public welfare serve their clients. Community organization activities include planning services, seeking and obtaining advice from the public on the operation of programs and program plans, the creation and operation of welfare advisory councils, the organization and operation of volunteer programs, and the sponsorship of programs for public welfare clients by voluntary and civic associations. Together, these activities are as important to the well-being of public welfare clients as are the more direct individual and group service methods common to public welfare agencies.

CHAPTER 9

Public Welfare Work Programs

TENSION and philosophical disputes over the role of work in public welfare are part of the field's history. In the western world, work has always been seen as a preventive or antidote to welfare.

In the early days of American public welfare, public assistance was provided almost exclusively through work programs. Governments might "rent" needy people to farmers who would pay them to work in their fields and assist in raising their crops. They operated work-houses—institutions that provided food, clothing, and lodging, but which required residents to earn their keep by making clothing or other items under contract with private entrepreneurs. These were similar to the debtors' prisons and poorhouses often described in English litera-ture (Friedlander and Apte, 1980).

The assumption was that if people genuinely needed help, they would not object to working under any kinds of circumstances in order to earn a livelihood. Some communities, when public assistance was primarily a local responsibility, supported people by giving them jobs in public work. Some labored on county farms, where the produce was sold and the profits used to support the poor. Others worked on con-structing and maintaining county roads and schools, among other pro-jects deemed useful to the public and appropriate responsibilities for public charges.

Of course, the physically handicapped, the aged, and very young children were treated somewhat differently, and in a manner more in keeping with treatment of the "worthy poor."

The Great Depression of the 1930s changed the relationship between public assistance and poverty and created new approaches to helping those who could not care for themselves (see Chapter 1). In addition to the public assistance and social insurance that were components of the Social Security Act of 1935, the federal government also provided work opportunities for the massive number of unemployed men who were able-bodied and willing to work but unable to find employment because of the nation's severe economic problems. These work opportunities were available through two major programs, the Civilian Conservation Corps and the Works Progress Administration.

The Civilian Conservation Corps took young men into national parks and other rural areas for agricultural development, reforestation, road building, and other improvements to the national parks. The development of the national parks and forests by the CCC was a remarkable episode in American history and did much to make outdoor education and recreation such as camping and hiking available and popular in the United States. But the main purpose of the program was not reforestation or park development but support for families. The CCC provided room and board for young men in areas where they worked, and paid small allowances which could be sent to their families for support. The CCC removed large numbers of men from the cities and towns of America, where they were idle and a potential source of discontent, crime, and violence, and put them to work with opportunities for them to help their families as well.

The Works Progress Administration provided for various public projects in cities and towns throughout the nation. Local parks, municipal auditoriums, and public schools were built, post offices were decorated with murals—people were hired to do the things they knew how to do best and were paid by the federal government to do them in a way that benefited their communities. Artists decorated; writers wrote plays and produced them; actors performed; researchers conducted research; engineers designed facilities; laborers constructed buildings—in short, the people were put to work at modest wages on projects that would improve their communities.

The legacy of these programs continues today in the national parks and in many of the community facilities that were originally constructed by the WPA.

Public assistance, which originally had no work components, was designed as a short-term, temporary program that would disappear when the economy improved and the unemployed returned to work. Social Security insurance was to provide economic security to individuals and families to prevent their becoming publicly dependent. The planners of the Social Security program believed that women with young children would be supported by Social Security in case of the death or disability of their husbands and that aged people would be able to retire with dignity on their Social Security pensions.

As the programs evolved, however, it became clear that desertion, divorce, and children born without breadwinners to support them were problems that Social Security had not anticipated and that had to be handled through the public assistance component of the federal program.

So a major question for operators and planners of public assistance programs became whether or not and to what extent recipients of public assistance should be required to work (Macarov, 1980).

Of course, there are contradictions in this because, as the characteristic studies of public assistance clients mentioned in Chapter 3 demonstrate so clearly, most public assistance recipients work to some extent. They do not work as regularly as they might, their wages are not high, and their employment is often part-time or temporary—but they work.

Over the years, those responsible for public welfare programs have attempted to find ways to insure that public assistance recipients can be employed, encouraged to work, or required to provide public service as a means of repaying the public for the assistance they receive (Ginzberg, 1980).

To accomplish these goals, some communities have from time to time established work programs for participants in their general assistance programs. Examples have included work on highways and other public roads, sanitation and beautification work, and assistance in public schools.

For many years federal regulations did not allow specific work requirements to be associated with the receipt of assistance. More recently, a variety of changes in federal regulations permitted and in some cases required recipients of AFDC to participate in training programs, accept work when it is offered, and to perform public service tasks in payment for their assistance.

Perhaps the most important modern development in work programs is the Work Incentive Program (Garvin et al., 1979), which requires most public assistance recipients—particularly unemployed persons seeking assistance because of their unemployment, and women whose children are of school age—to register for and accept work to which they are referred.

Some of the employment programs for public welfare recipients include federal programs not unlike the CCC and the WPA. One of the most important is the Job Corps, which provides work experience and training in residential situations for young people who are unemployed. Some of the Job Corps Centers are located in rural areas, often at or near the sites of the CCC facilities. The federal Comprehensive Employment and Training Act (CETA) which followed a number of other federal initiatives to employ the unemployed, has been a major force—somewhat like the WPA—in providing work training and federally subsidized jobs for unemployed men and women. These jobs have included work in private industry but have also concentrated on public positions, including some that are similar to WPA project jobs (Hallman, 1980). Professional employment, including social work, services to the aging, law enforcement, and engineering activities, was also offered under CETA, which was reduced early in the administration of President Ronald Reagan.

The Opportunities Industrialization Center, or OIC, also provides vocational training and skills to low income young people in cities throughout the United States. The Reverend Leon Sullivan has been internationally recognized for creating this major service for low income and other disadvantaged men and women.

Vocational training is also available throughout the United States, primarily at vocational and technical centers operated by public school systems in most parts of the nation.

Often, the public welfare social worker refers individuals who need jobs or job skills to these programs as a means of helping people become self-sufficient through employment.

The Work Incentive Program, which is operated jointly by the U.S. Department of Labor, the U.S. Department of Health and Human Services and, in most states, jointly by the public welfare agency and the employment security program, made extensive use of CETA positions for placement of individuals in jobs in addition to training assistance clients for work and placing them in private industry jobs.

Some state departments of public welfare have also developed their own programs to locate and develop jobs for public assistance recipients and to place people in those jobs as alternatives to providing them with public assistance.

Public welfare departments also work closely with employment security agencies in other ways. Many times, people who are unemployed need help and unemployment compensation, which is provided through employment security agencies, is often available to those who are in need because of job lay-offs. In some cases, the major effort of the social worker in public welfare who is working with a client who has recently lost a job is to help that client make use of the services of the employment security agency—both economic assistance available through unemployment compensation and help in finding an alternative job. On occasion, employment security agencies can also help potential public welfare clients enroll and obtain support for training that will lead to employment.

Another agency available to employed or recently employed public welfare clients is worker's compensation. These agencies, which exist in most states, provide assistance, medical care, and other services for persons who have been employed but who lose that employment—or find themselves forced to change or refuse their work—because of injuries related to their jobs. In some situations, the primary role of the public welfare social worker is to help an applicant for assistance make use of worker's compensation programs.

Contradictions in the Work-Welfare Cycle

There are many contradictions to using work as a major alternative to public assistance, and these must be considered by public welfare managers and planners.

Perhaps the most critical is that most public assistance recipients are young children and their caretakers, such as mothers and grandparents, who are often not physically able to work. Those who can work, as has been mentioned, are likely to be employed (Borus, 1979).

Finding employment for a woman who has young children is also complex. The woman may be willing to work but may need training before she is able to be employed satisfactorily and productively. She may also be willing to work but unable to arrange on her own for child care. For most public welfare planners and theorists, this means the woman's children must be cared for at public expense through day care services.

Employment in the private sector or in unsubsidized public jobs that would have existed without CETA, public welfare, or other public efforts has some promise for the placement of public assistance recipients in permanent and publicly unsubsidized work. In fact, part of the Work Incentive or WIN Program provides subsidies and other incentives to employers who hire public welfare recipients.

The creation of public, subsidized jobs for public welfare employees is a wholly different matter, and requires a different set of activities and services. In fact, many budget planners and public welfare theorists believe that creating work for public welfare recipients is more costly than providing them with cash because it costs money to work. For example, employees may need a supervisor to develop and manage their work. Materials will be required in order to produce or develop some service or goods, and there may be other costly supports for work including health insurance, fringe benefits, day care provisions for children, and uniforms and tools. In other words, in the short run, providing a person with created employment is more costly than providing the same person with cash assistance, which basically costs only the amount of money provided to the person or family.

Some believe that no matter what the cost of creating work it is a much better alternative than providing assistance without work. Others dispute this and say that if the goal is to provide temporary assistance to individuals and families, the preferred alternative is to provide that assistance as cheaply and as directly as possible. Still others believe that the major value of public assistance is providing support to families and keeping mothers at home with their children so they can be raised with the security and guidance of a parent.

In 1981 Congress granted states permission to establish Community Work Experience programs. These allowed states to require AFDC recipients to work at the minimum wage in community, nonprofit sector jobs up to the amount of their assistance. In later months, some executive and legislative branch leaders proposed replacing the WIN program with these community work experiences.

A number of programs were attempted and met with varied results. Some were limited to requiring unemployed heads of households to work. Others placed AFDC recipients in state government jobs. Still others focused on job training and counseling as a means for helping clients attain employment and self-sufficiency.

Work Programs and Public Controversy

Work is such a controversial and emotionally charged subject that somehow no matter how it is handled in public welfare, it always leads to controversies. Work that is created under government assisted programs is often simply viewed as paid malingering.

In essence, the dispute is philosophical and economic. In economic terms, cash assistance is less expensive than public employment. In philosophical terms, however, there are differences of opinion and conflicts of values. Is work under all circumstances the best answer to the problem of need and dependency, or is cash assistance without any work requirement equally satisfactory? These are the issues which welfare policy makers frequently need to answer under changing and conflicting circumstances.

Social Workers in Work Programs

The public welfare social worker involved in a work program carries out many responsibilities (Ginsberg, 1975). These include counseling a client about employment after assessing the client's capacity to perform work. The worker may arrange for the client to take vocational tests to determine his or her capacities and interests. These tests may assist the worker in placing the client directly on a job. For clients who cannot be employed without additional preparation the worker may seek out and arrange for participation in basic education or specific skill training. Most communities offer training courses which can provide the unemployed with skills needed to become satisfactorily employed. The selection of an appropriate training course is based upon the client's abilities and gaps in the client's training and education as well as on the labor market. In a community that has a shortage of jobs for manual laborers but a number of vacancies for bookkeepers and accountants, clients may be trained in those fields. A community that has a need for additional health workers may benefit when clients are trained to care for patients in hospitals and nursing homes.

The social worker also must often assist the client in satisfactorily performing work. Sometimes a client needs the guidance of the social worker to help him or her demonstrate adequate work habits, including such basic factors as proper dress, office courtesy, and punctuality.

Social workers in employment programs also work directly with employers. For example, they develop contracts for on-the-job training programs with private employers that enable public assistance recipients to go to work in jobs that may be subsidized with public funds. Other workers advise employers who have jobs available on using welfare recipients in those jobs. The federal government provides tax incentives to employers who use public welfare cash assistance recipients in meeting their labor requirements.

Public welfare social workers also inform the public, through speeches and consultations with corporations and other employers, of the ways in which they may benefit from employing public welfare recipients in their work forces. At times, workers also help supervise the work of clients who are placed in jobs to make sure they are succeeding. Workers may also organize group meetings for clients who are placed in jobs to assist them with any problems they might be having and to help them help one another perform satisfactorily.

Criticism of work program employees who "lean on their shovels" or who otherwise seem to be paid for activity that is less than productive began in the 1930s New Deal programs and continues today. The great expense of work programs is also often a cause of public concern, because work programs almost always cost more than direct assistance. And those who criticize the high cost and perceived wastefulness of work programs are often also the same people who ask about public assistance recipients, "why don't those people go to work?"

Work programs seem to cause controversy for two fundamental reasons. First, work is a common experience for most people. Those who are employed and who understand their own work are often quick to criticize those in other kinds of work who do not seem to be performing as diligently or productively as they might. But most work looks less than productive to those who observe it from the outside. In very few forms of human endeavor are people fully engaged every working hour of every working day in the activity for which they are being paid. In most work, time is needed to think about the task, for breaks, or more commonly, for other people to complete other tasks before one can complete one's own. The typical observer of a highway construction project sees dozens of people standing and waiting for something to happen. This may appear to be a form of time-wasting. In fact, however, the crews have often completed their preparatory work and are waiting for another crew to complete its work before they can continue. Most of those who criticize are unfamiliar with the sequence of activities in construction.

The second major source of controversy about work is the lack of a clear definition of precisely what work is. Is the social work professor who sits and thinks about social work solutions to problems working? Is the messenger who is waiting for a message to deliver working or not? Some have even suggested that women who receive public assistance grants to raise their children are, in fact, performing highly productive work when they stay home and care for those children. Nevertheless, for many people the question often addressed to a mother—"Do you work or do you stay at home?"—seems appropriate.

One doubts that these questions will be speedily or satisfactorily answered. But the lack of clarity about the nature of work is a source of controversy for many people, particularly those who work as professionals in or who receive public welfare services.

The following is an example of a public welfare work client.

Nelson George

Nelson George at age 31 had never held any job for more than two months and, for most of his life, had not been employed. On occasion, he provided casual assistance to furniture movers, highway cleanup crews, and park maintenance projects. For a few weeks he was a dishwasher and for a period of two months, three years ago, he worked as a hospital orderly. He was not usually laid off or fired from the jobs he held. Instead, he tended to notify his employers, after a few days of diligent work, that illness would keep him away for a few days. After a week he simply did not return to work nor did he notify his employers that he had resigned. Instead, he tended to drift out of jobs in approximately the same way he drifted into them.

He had no physical handicaps. In fact, his health was rather good. But he frequently felt that he was ill or too tired to work or in too much pain to continue with a job. Fatigue, aching sensations in his lower back, and nervousness were the symptoms he often described when explaining that he did not feel well enough to carry on with his job.

For most of his life, Nelson had no permanent address. On most evenings he returned to his parent's home, but at times he stayed for several weeks with his married sister and her family. And, from time to time, he stayed with friends he met during the day in the park or the recreation center where he sometimes went to pass the time. He had dropped out of school when he was sixteen, but even before that he had barely mastered the skill of reading. Although his I.Q. was in the normal range, his lack of education and lack of work skills made his behavior equivalent to that of someone who is mildly mentally retarded. Some six months ago, Nelson and his female friend, Lottie Grosscup, began living together in anticipation of the birth of their child.

When the couple discovered that Lottie's income, which they lost when she quit her job, had been all they could rely on, she and Nelson visited the local public welfare office to seek assistance. They lived in a state where cash assistance was provided to families who were expecting children.

Nelson was referred to the Work Incentive unit so that he could find some means for being self-supporting. When the Work Incentive program social worker spoke with Nelson, the worker learned about Nelson's poor work patterns, lack of specific employable skills, and lack of training. He referred Nelson to a variety of training and educational programs as a means of preparing him for self-support. Nelson enrolled in a class that would provide him with basic education through which he could earn a high school equivalency diploma. He was also enrolled in an employment skills training course offered by a local vocational school in which emphasis was placed upon maintaining regular hours at work, staying on the job, working for advancement in employment, as well as such personal skills as communicating with other employees, appropriate dress and hygiene, and the need to notify an employer any time one was likely to be away from work.

A physician checked Nelson and found nothing organically wrong with him that would cause the backaches and other problems he described. The physician attributed the aches and pains to a general lack of a feeling of self-worth and frustration over his inability to perform as effectively as other people employed in the same industries in which he had been a worker. Nelson did not feel good about himself or his performance and did not feel that his work was competitive with that of others around him. Therefore, he tended to withdraw from jobs not out of any unwillingness to work but because he felt he would surely be terminated as an inadequate employee.

Nelson was also enrolled in a course on roofing. Paralleling these practical educational opportunities, Nelson was counseled by the Work Incentive social worker who encouraged him to develop greater self-esteem through self-sufficiency. The worker helped Nelson understand that for the first time in his life, he was living independently, had responsibilities for a mate and a child, and had the ability to support them through his own efforts.

By the time Nelson's daughter was born, he had acquired a full-time job with a local roofing company and was earning well above the minimum wage. Although he occasionally missed work, he always called to report in and to explain why he was gone and when he would return, and he always kept his word.

Conclusion

As this chapter has indicated, one of the major strategies for dealing with the problem of economic dependency is work. Programs to provide work to those who are dependent upon public welfare services include counseling and training to make it possible for recipients of help to become employable; the creation of jobs through on-the-job training contracts and various federal efforts; and work training programs such as the Job Corps which include vocational training, and other similar services. On many occasions, the public welfare social worker is responsible for establishing, operating, and helping clients use work programs as a means for overcoming their dependency.

CHAPTER 10

Practice in Rural Public Welfare

ALTHOUGH social work programs are essentially the same within any state, special adaptations are necessary for the practice of social work in rural public welfare agencies as opposed to metropolitan or urban offices. This chapter discusses ways in which rural offices and activities differ from their urban counterparts.

How the Rural Community May Differ from the Urban

Rural or non-metropolitan areas in the U.S. differ from larger communities in a variety of ways that affect the manner in which public welfare services may be organized and delivered (Ginsberg, 1975).

First, the rural community, which this text defines as a community of fewer than 50,000 people not contiguous to a metropolitan area, is likely to have few social agencies. Health services may also be limited (Hayslip et al., 1980). Therefore, the public welfare department is viewed as the major contributor to the treatment and solution of community social problems. Second, the public welfare program in a rural community is often a major economic factor in that community (Neely, 1979; Farley et al., 1982). It may be a major employer of people with college or university educations. It may rent an office in a community that has few real estate transactions. Its food stamps, cash, and medical assistance to low income citizens of the community are likely to have a profound effect on the community's commerce and employment patterns. Its key professional staff, including the office manager or director, may well be perceived as significant community leaders whose opinions and participation are sought on many public issues. Its deposits of funds in banks have a major impact on the capacity of those banks to loan money and otherwise invest in the community's economy.

The department also frequently serves as the major resource for dealing with such problems as marital discord, parent-child problems, juvenile delinquency, and care for the aging. As such, the public welfare agency is a more important community institution in rural areas than one expects it to be in metropolitan areas. For those reasons, the practice of social work in rural communities is often somewhat different than it is for urban practitioners (Magel and Price, 1979).

There are other differences between rural public welfare offices and their urban and metropolitan counterparts. Turnover of staff in rural offices of public welfare is somewhat less than in urban or metropolitan offices. Many staff members come from the community where the rural office is located, own property in the area, and have spouses or other family members who cannot leave. And for the college educated professional person, there are often few alternatives to public education and public welfare for employment. Similarly, the office manager or director is often a long time resident of the area. Most people who live and work in small communities—whatever their employment—remain in them by choice. Many could relocate in large cities but prefer the slower pace and lower levels of pressure common to small communities. Many prefer the small town patterns of knowing and being known by virtually everyone, of being related to many community members, including colleagues and clients, by blood or marriage (Poole, 1981).

Although compensation and advancement in smaller offices are not always so generous because the caseload is smaller and the responsibilities are less complex, many find that living costs are lower as well, although some economists disagree with the notion that living costs are really lower in rural areas. For people without personal cars, transportation in rural areas is prohibitively expensive. So is quality entertainment because it usually requires a trip to a nearby city. Higher education and training are more expensive too, because they often require living away from home.

Food, utilities, and other essentials cost the same in rural and urban areas. However, for rural people with relatively modest expectations living expenses may well be lower. Rural recreational activities differ in quality from those in cities. Often they revolve around socializing with one's relatives, outdoor sports such as hunting and fishing, and activities sponsored by churches and fraternal organizations.

The rural lack of anonymity also creates a different kind of pattern. In rural areas, taking applications and determining eligibility for various assistance programs may be profoundly different than it is in the urban office, where clients are likely to be strangers to workers. It is not un-common for a worker, after taking an application for assistance from a rural client, to receive unsolicited contradictory information about that client's economic condition, family situation, and social behavior from a colleague, neighbor, or friend (Martinez-Brawley, 1980).

Confidentiality also poses difficulties in the rural office. When a client comes into the office to ask for help in solving a problem, the whole office may soon learn who the client is and what the client needs. This may lead to gossip about the client's family as well as other families.

For example, Trudy Weatherall, age 17, came to the rural public assistance office to seek help in planning for the baby she expected six months from the date of her visit. She was eligible for assistance and was provided with a medical card so she could receive care from the local family practitioner. However, it was clear from her visit and from the interview that her parents had not yet learned about her pregnancy, although they were not financially able to help her, even if they had known. It also became evident that most of the workers in the office could guess who the father of the child was. Although the worker who interviewed Trudy did not discuss the case with anyone but her super-visor, within an hour and a half of Trudy's departure from the office, every employee knew she had been there, knew why, and knew what it meant for many other people in the community.

Workers in rural public welfare offices tend to share the same values as other members of the community and could be related to many other members of the community. At times, their values may conflict with agency policies and professional ethics about the acceptance of clients and the provision of assistance to clients for overcoming problems.

Special Skills Needed for Service in Rural Public Welfare Offices

Workers in rural public welfare offices need a variety of special skills, perhaps more complex than those required of their counterparts in ur-ban and metropolitan areas. Rural workers often find that the problems they encounter are much more complex than they had ever imagined they might be. Many also discover that even though they may have grown up in the rural area where the office is located, they may not have the detailed understanding necessary for effectively serving clients who seek help in the rural area served by the office.

COMMUNITY ANALYSIS

Rural public welfare social workers need to understand their commu-nity. The relationships among people in rural areas, particularly when they have to do with major community matters and financial issues, may affect feelings about what is or should be done in the community (Watts, 1980). Rural public welfare employees particularly need to know what the power and political relations are in the community if they are to do their jobs adequately. Metropolitan workers are often insulated from political and other power matters, but that is less likely to be the case in a small town, where everything is a bit more obvious and public.

Who receives the leases for space, who is hired, where bank deposits are made, who obtains the janitorial contract for keeping the building clean, who provides furnishings for the building—all of these may be highly significant issues in a rural community, and rural employees must know about and prepare to deal with these questions.

OBJECTIVITY, SENSITIVITY, CONFIDENTIALITY

Rural public welfare workers must also pay careful attention to issues such as guaranteeing objectivity, sensitivity, and confidentiality to clients. In a rural community, where everyone knows and is known to everyone else, it is too easy for workers to make judgments about the eligibility and character of a client without listening to all the information and treating the client as if he or she were a stranger. Similarly, in some rural areas, because the worker believes he or she knows something about a client's circumstances, he or she may pre-judge the client as eligible without taking a detailed application and verifying the need and eligibility for assistance.

Clients with serious personal problems also need to have the protections of confidentiality which are so critical to effective social work practice and which are crucial in public welfare. This may mean that workers interview clients on home visits or in neutral sites such as churches or libraries, rather than in public welfare offices. A client who faces problems such as poverty, marital discord, unplanned pregnancy, or the need to decide how to handle a senile parent has a special need to avoid public knowledge of the problem. The rural public welfare social worker needs to be particularly objective about the client and the client's problem, partly because objectivity is always required for competent social work practice in public welfare but also because the worker may be the only person who can be objective about the client and the problem.

LONG HOURS

Rural public welfare social workers also need to be prepared for almost constant duty with the community (Johnson, 1980). Whereas in the metropolitan community one can be on the job during the day and a private citizen in the evening and on holidays and weekends, in the small community one is always on the job and one is always cast in the role of the professional. Therefore, many workers find themselves contacted at home, on the street, in the grocery store, and in church about public welfare clients and issues. For many public welfare social workers in small towns, the only escape from work is found out of town, which is why many public welfare social workers spend their weekends and other free time in other small communities or in cities.

DISCRETION

Public welfare social workers in small communities also need to learn that it is a mistake to gossip about their clients or to speak disparagingly about the agency, their fellow workers, or their supervisors (Handler, 1979). Even when the use of names is avoided, many small community people will immediately know who one is talking about simply from their knowledge of the community. Social gossip about clients who try to abuse programs or about employees who are less than responsible about their work can eventually reach the ears of a public official, such as a state legislator, who may then attempt to cut back services or employment in the agency. It is not at all uncommon for small community legislators to propose such reductions in help on the basis of worker comments. So far as the legislator is concerned, an anecdote about one client or employee reflects the behavior of all clients or employees. Of course professional social workers should never share information about their clients because doing so violates the client's right to confidentiality, but the consequences of doing so can be much more damaging in a rural area.

Unfortunately, minority groups and low income people are often stereotyped so severely in rural communities that they have few opportunities to be relieved of the roles they may have played all of their lives. Rural public welfare social workers must be vigilant in helping minority group members, members of families that have long known poverty, and other disadvantaged people to grow and change in the direction of independence from public assistance.

INITIATIVE

Rural public welfare social workers must also be prepared to take the initiative in dealing with community problems they encounter. Their work is not nearly so specialized or limited as the work of a similar employee in a metropolitan agency (Ginsberg, 1975). The rural worker may find, for example, that no institution in the community provides day care for young mothers who are receiving public assistance so they can complete their educations or become employed. The worker may find it necessary to devote time to organizing a day care program. An urban or metropolitan counterpart may simply arrange for day care through an established center or may call upon some community institution to plan day care services.

DIVERSE SERVICES

Similarly, the rural public welfare social worker may find it necessary to speak to civic groups about social problems and solutions to them, may be called upon to present programs in public schools on topics ranging from public assistance to sex education, and may find it necessary to provide guidance to clients who might otherwise be referred to community mental health centers. Rural communities which may have only limited resources for mental health, rehabilitation, community planning, and other urban social welfare efforts may be called upon to offer any one of these to individual clients or the community. Being able to do so may help far more clients than one would ever hope to assist individually over a period of years. It may also help the community cure problems that would otherwise continue to cause public welfare and other social problems for years in the future (Johnson, 1980).

SELF-DIRECTION

Rural public welfare social workers also need to pay special attention to their own professional and personal development, which may mean making special efforts to attend professional conferences, participate in courses offered by colleges and universities, visit other offices, and otherwise learn about programs in other places. There is a chronic danger in small communities that people will become so attentive to their own local problems and issues that they will miss opportunities to learn about ways in which other communities solve problems. Stimulation and growth within the small community are not often as common as they are in cities, where staff turnover may be greater and where there is more exposure to other social workers and other agencies (Wijnberg and Colca, 1981).

Rural Positives

It should be understood that many rural workers prefer small community practice to urban and metropolitan work because it offers sustained relationships with people, opportunities to make a real difference in the community, and a chance to practice without extensive supervision or direction so that one may be creative in carrying out responsibilities. And rural social workers, like many other people, may enjoy rural living—the relative tranquility, avoidance of traffic and other kinds of congestion, and the opportunity to be more closely associated with natural phenomena.

Conclusion

Public welfare services in rural areas are often different in style and significance than they are in metropolitan areas. Rural workers require exceptional sensitivity to community norms and relationships.

Services to rural clients often have to be delivered in a more personal manner because almost everything is more personal in rural areas. In addition, public welfare departments must often take on responsibility for more services than they are likely to assume in more metropolitan areas. Working with existing institutions is also more critical in rural communities.

In many ways, public welfare services in rural areas are more significant for those areas and their citizens than are the same services in cities and metropolitan communities.

PART III

SUPPORTIVE METHODS IN PUBLIC WELFARE

IN ORDER to make public welfare's direct services to clients possible, public welfare agencies carry on a number of supportive activities. Although not part of the core of social work methods, they constitute activities and services that make it possible for the central, direct activities to take place.

Among the supportive activities described in this text are research, statistical analysis, and evaluation of programs. These services make it possible for the department of welfare to understand what it is doing and how well it is accomplishing its objectives. No program of services as comprehensive and extensive as public welfare can function adequately without careful attention to the dimensions of its services and without evaluating the extent and quality of the service. Many professional social workers play significant roles in the research and evaluation activities of public welfare departments.

Two chapters of this part of the text are devoted to administrative activities in public welfare. Because the programs are so large in clientele, staff, and budgets, adequate administration in public welfare takes on special significance. In addition, many professional social workers, either at the beginnings of their careers in public welfare or after they have completed periods of professional activity, become administrative and management specialists within welfare agencies. Therefore, they need special preparation in the supervisory, fiscal, training, and other managerial activities that are described in these chapters.

In addition to research, evaluation, and administrative management functions, public welfare departments also have significant responsibilities in carrying out enforcement and investigative efforts. Again, because programs of public welfare are so extensive and, in some ways, so controversial, American public welfare has made strong efforts to police its programs carefully. Virtually all public welfare agencies have small investigative units which operate in a fashion similar to law enforcement agencies—they follow up on complaints of client, employee, or vendor fraud, and they take action, when appropriate, against those who abuse public welfare programs.

In addition to investigations, public welfare departments also make major efforts to locate and obtain support payments from parents whose children may be receiving public assistance because of the failure of the parents to support those children. Under federal requirements, all states sponsor programs designed to locate and obtain support payments from parents who are required to provide support for their children.

Because of a variety of court decisions and statutory provisions, all public welfare departments carry out adjudicatory activities which provide clients, vendors, and employees with a right to seek redress, through administrative channels, of grievances that they might have toward an agency. These grievances may be brought by clients who are not satisfied with decisions on their eligibility for help, by employees dissatisfied with their compensation or assignments, and by vendors who wish to appeal suspension from public welfare programs or who have other complaints against programs.

Public welfare departments also carry on policy development activities, and set standards for and license various human service activities. These may include child care agencies, day care centers, adult care homes, nursing homes, and other residential facilities.

Throughout the United States, social work professionals serve as supervisors of all these supportive activities, manage or work with investigative, standard setting, and licensing organizations, and function as hearings officers in cases of adjudication procedures.

This part of the book describes the processes in detail, discusses the roles social workers play in them, and provides examples of these supportive social work methods in the public welfare field.

CHAPTER 11

Administration and Management of Public Welfare Services

ORGANIZATIONS AS LARGE and complex as public welfare departments face major difficulties in insuring that their objectives are sought and that their resources are properly used in working for the attainment of those objectives. Management and administration of public welfare programs are among the major tasks of welfare agencies. Social workers, because their preparation and interests have led them to become career employees, frequently become managers in public welfare.

At times in the history of social work, professionals have resisted becoming administrators or managers of social welfare programs. The motivation for entering the profession has tended to be more toward providing services to clients and their families through the application of social work methods than on organizing and working toward the effective delivery of those services by others. Historically there has been some tension within public welfare agencies over the appropriate use of social workers. Their educations and inclinations have traditionally caused them to be most interested in service delivery but their salary requirements, length of preparation, and agency tenure often cause agencies to hope for a broader use of the talents of social work staff members.

Over the years, social work educators and social work professionals have begun to understand the management requirements of agencies and it is now common for professional social workers to expect to be required to perform managerial as well as direct service tasks. It is also increasingly common for social work education programs to offer and occasionally require courses and field experiences in social work management as well as in direct service methods.

The Nature of Management

Management is never an end in itself. Managing of programs and resources is always directed toward achieving some set of objectives; i.e., the well-being of clients in public welfare, the maximization of profits in private industry, the improvement of the health of patients in medical programs. The skills required for and the principles of management are common to all organizations. Effective management requires many of the same activities in all organized human endeavors. The objectives change but the means used in attempting to reach them remain constant.

Hundreds of texts have been written on the concepts of administration and management. There are also many specialized texts on social welfare management alone. Public welfare management draws upon many of the same theories and practices as does management in other fields. However, there are some specialized social work management texts which deal with the special problems and concerns of public welfare and other social work fields as well as adaptations of management theory and practices to the specialized issues faced in social agencies (Dumpson et al., 1978; Lohmann, 1980; Perlmutter and Slavin, 1980; Prottas, 1979).

LEVELS OF PUBLIC WELFARE MANAGEMENT RESPONSIBILITIES

Social workers play management roles in public welfare programs at every level of the department's work. They range from chief executive officers of state agencies to supervisors of small units in local offices who are responsible for delivering services to clients.

The program areas supervised by social workers include almost every function within public welfare departments. However, because most of the employees are engaged in determining eligibility for economic assistance or in delivering social services, most of the social workers who administer programs are administrators of eligibility determination programs or social services programs (Patti et al., 1979).

Managing Eligibility Determination

The management of programs is similar for all functions of agencies in terms of the methods used for defining objectives, monitoring the work of staff, evaluating results, and planning future activities (Austin, 1981). In content, however, there are some differences between management of eligibility determination and of social services because the content of the work differs.

In eligibility determination supervision, the rules and regulations are generally precise and the task of the unit is to insure that those who are eligible for assistance receive that assistance in the amount prescribed for the clients' circumstances by the rules and regulations of the agency. It is also an objective of these efforts to insure that no one who is ineligible for assistance receives it and that no one who is eligible receives more than the policies of the agency permit.

Good supervision also implies the establishment and conduct of regular training sessions by the supervisor on new policies and procedures, possible improvements in the performance of the unit, and other subjects such as the needs and characteristics of clients. Skill training in interviewing, recording, and investigating client applications may also be a part of the supervisor's training efforts. In some situations, the training is carried on by specialists from the agency's training unit, in which case the supervisor arranges for the training, participates in its design, prepares the workers for the training, and follows up on the training in subsequent supervisory conferences (Witkin and Shapiro, 1980).

Much of supervision is also conducted in groups. Some of the group methods suggested in Chapter 7 can effectively be applied to the supervision of eligibility determination work. Providing supervision to workers in groups has the advantages of allowing the workers to learn from one another and of formalizing the normal exchanges between workers that are part of the operations of most organizations. Encouraging such exchanges of ideas and information helps the supervisor correct any mis-sharing of information while still allowing peers to learn from one another.

Group supervision also tends to minimize any threat that workers might feel directed toward themselves by the supervisor. If they discover through group supervision that their colleagues have questions and that everyone makes mistakes but that not everyone is chastised for those mistakes, they may be more willing to go to the supervisor for help and to avoid errors that they might make without such help.

Supervision of Social Services

Supervising social services requires extensive knowledge of social casework and, on occasion, of social group work methods as they are applied in public welfare and described in some of the earlier chapters of this text. In addition, supervising social services requires a significant understanding of the ways in which children and adults behave under normal as well as stressful situations.

This knowledge is required because the supervisor of social services must often guide the social services worker through the process of working with child and adult social services plans.

In child protective services, the supervisor will generally be consulted about the proper course of action for a worker. Many times the worker will want to know if the child should be immediately removed from the family, lest its life or health be endangered, or whether other intervention, such as direct counseling with the family, or referring the family to a family service or mental health agency, will be sufficient. Or the worker may determine that some supportive service in the home such as a homemaker, day care for the children, or a public assistance grant, will help solve the family's problem to such an extent that the child will not suffer.

A wrong decision in a neglect or abuse case may lead to the child's serious injury or even death. Therefore, the degree of guidance and the quality of supervision provided to the protective services worker is crucial.

In protective services, supervisors, who are able to help workers because of their education, experience, and skill in communicating that experience and special knowledge, often meet weekly with those for whose work they are responsible. In addition, they provide supportive service and information to workers when it is needed, outside the regular supervisory contacts. Frequently this advice is provided by telephone both during and apart from office hours. The importance of protective services supervision is so great that in many public welfare agencies, if a supervisor is going to be away or out of reach, he or she must be backed up by one or more alternative supervisors who can provide instant guidance to the protective services worker in the field.

Experienced protective services workers often make the best supervisors. They can tell with a relatively high degree of certainty when a child is in imminent danger and requires at least temporary removal from the endangering circumstances or when the child is facing only temporary problems which can be cleared up with the brief passage of time or with a modest addition of services to the child's household.

ADULT SERVICES

Social services for adults also require high quality professional supervision, although the problems and alternatives are not always so problematic or dramatic as they are with children, primarily because adults, by and large, are able to speak for themselves and make their own decisions about the degree of danger in which they are living.

The supervision of social services workers who serve adults may require the same kind of judgment about whether or not it is necessary to seek a court order to remove an adult from his or her own living situation as one expects in child protective services. This is particularly true when older, physically or mentally disabled adults come to the attention of the public welfare agency because their living situations endanger their health and safety. One encounters "hermits," mentally ill people who live in unsanitary surroundings, and older people who may die from exposure if they are not properly treated. The distinction between the adult who simply wants to live his or her life as he or she chooses to and the adult who is in genuine danger is one that must often be made with the help of a social services supervisor.

ALLOCATING HELP AND RECORDING SERVICES

The social services supervisor must also help decide on the priorities for helping families or individuals with various kinds of supportive services. Some social services in some states and cities are provided on the basis of absolute financial guidelines, and therefore the need for professional discretion is only minimal. In other cases, however, whether family A or family B is in most need of day care, homemaker services, or some other social assistance is one that staff members must make. The more discretion left to the staff of a public welfare agency, the more responsibility is placed upon the social services supervisor.

In many circumstances, particularly when children are removed or are recommended for removal from their residences through courts, the accuracy of the record on the child and his or her family is critical for the court that must decide whether or not to accept the public welfare staff member's recommendation. Record-keeping varies significantly from agency to agency. In some, records are maintained almost exclusively by computer, whereas in others the only records are typed and stored in traditional filing cabinets. In some agencies there is a combination of records—some typed and filed and others primarily computer-stored.

Crisis Management

In public welfare, crisis management is often the main task of supervisors, local office directors, and state office administrators. That is because the problems addressed by public welfare programs are not always under the control of the manager. Emergency situations, crises arising from disasters, and other phenomena often require the social worker who is an administrator to take rapid action to overcome a problem. The higher one's level of management within the organization, the more likely one is to be required to exercise crisis management.

By definition, the middle and lower levels of management deal with more or less routine matters. Workers are able to predict with some certainty what they may encounter each day. Their time and their labors are subject to direction from higher level managers who respond to a larger environment, to political leaders, and to other persons and institutions over whom they have minimal control themselves. Most of the activities of public welfare agencies are quite routine and are handled by people at the operational level. In fact, one could demonstrate that over 90 percent of the services provided by the typical welfare agency are handled routinely by the workers who directly serve clients.

But policy changes, major innovations, and the most publicized welfare activities are those small number which are exceptions to the normal routine of the welfare program. These kinds of decisions and these situations are the subject matter of most of the work of the highest level managers, who must often deal with crises about which the agency has little information and experience.

For example, an earthquake may necessitate the best available services from sanitation departments, hospitals, funeral homes, and public maintenance services. The public welfare department, may be called upon to coordinate these activities—perhaps in cooperation with the American Red Cross—and may also be responsible for distribution of emergency food, operation of emergency housing and shelters, distribution of clothing, as well as the development of procedures for reuniting families, dealing with the grief experienced by survivors who have lost relatives, and the implementation of a transportation plan to help victims obtain the services they need. Although welfare departments have staff experts on problems of delivering food, clothing, and shelter, and may have specialists in disaster recovery as well, earthquakes are so rare that it is unlikely most offices will have anyone who has previously experienced that specific problem.

Dealing with an earthquake would require cooperative activities with top administrators in other departments, consultation with people who are familiar with the damage caused by earthquakes and the recovery processes used in their aftermath, and some new procedures and directions for the department and its staff. It is that kind of exceptional situation and others which are outside the normal routine of the agency and the normal control of the staff that often call upon the talents and skills of top agency management.

Public welfare's top managers often function at their best in organizing services to overcome crises. Similarly, crises often call upon the best efforts of managers to exercise their responsibilities.

Conclusion

Administering and managing are among the most important social work functions in public welfare departments. This chapter has described some of the general principles of managing public welfare programs, with emphasis on the management of economic and social services. In the following chapter, the means necessary for managing some of the supportive services in public welfare are described.

CHAPTER 12

Management of the Administrative Support Activities

IN ADDITION TO the administration of a public welfare agency's core services of economic and social assistance, there are a variety of additional activities which must be carried on to insure that the core services are adequately and efficiently delivered. This chapter covers some of the methods of managing those activities.

Monitoring

One means used by public welfare departments to evaluate their success in reaching their objectives is monitoring (Epstein and Tripodi, 1979). Monitoring is the name used for on-site inspections of programs that departments operate. Monitoring may take several forms, depending upon the mission, staff, special problems, and special concerns of a public welfare agency.

For example, an agency may want to evaluate its foster care program periodically (McCurdy, 1980). The state office of a public welfare program may achieve its evaluations of foster care by developing a monitoring team which visits each local office periodically, reads case records, interviews foster care workers, visits with foster families, meets with foster children, consults with public school teachers who teach foster children, and uses whatever other means they may devise to evaluate the agency's services to children who are in the custody of the department.

Ordinarily a monitoring effort will follow a predesigned schedule of information to be obtained and questions to be answered. Attempts are made to apply this schedule of information to each activity that is monitored (Hyde and Shafritz, 1979).

In addition to questions about the program, examinations are also made of the fiscal systems and the expenditures of funds on the program. An analysis may be made of records kept on the program and efforts made to evaluate the impact of the program on resolving the problem addressed by the service.

As a result of the monitoring exercises, staff may be removed or reassigned from the project, additional training may be offered so that the program becomes more effective, staff may be promoted or otherwise rewarded for the excellence of their efforts, or programs may be revised in other ways.

For the social worker who is involved, monitoring requires a combination of knowledge of the program that is being studied—skills that are closely related to skills in research methods—and an ability to be objective and factual in one's work. High quality monitoring activities are based upon knowing what to expect, knowing something about the ways in which services have been delivered and are delivered by the agency, and knowing how to determine when a program is within or outside the usually expected performance of an organization dealing with the service being monitored. For example, one may discover that although the foster care program in the county being studied is far from perfect, it appears to be superior to foster care services offered in comparable counties for comparable children because it is more efficiently administered. Or a community mental health agency that provides services to public assistance recipients may appear to be less than efficient in identifying and providing services to low-income clients. However, one may discover that the organization is twice as effective in reaching and providing mental health services to low-income clients than any other mental health center in the state. While that would not mean there are no problems with the contract being monitored, it could mean that the problems are much less severe than one might initially imagine.

SUPERVISION OF PURCHASE OF SERVICES

The monitoring or supervision of services purchased from other public or private agencies such as the mental health center mentioned above is a major responsibility in public welfare departments. The agency wants to assure itself that funds are properly expended and that the welfare department receives the best value possible for its investment.

This may mean that monitors and auditors will read sample cases, report on those cases to their own supervisors, and make recommendations on continued contracts with the agency. Or it may require competent accounting specialists who go through the agency's budget and financial records to insure that expenditures are both proper and properly accounted for.

Without supervision, some agencies which sell their services to welfare departments may use public welfare funds for unauthorized expenditures or may report expenditures incorrectly in ways that are advantageous to the agency but disadvantageous to the welfare department. But even when agencies are completely accurate in their bookkeeping and totally responsible in their expenditures, the public welfare program still needs to collect information that demonstrates that its contracts are valid and prudent expenditures of public funds. Therefore, the administration of purchase of service agreements is a major responsibility of most public welfare departments which increasingly purchase, rather than deliver their own services.

EVALUATION OF LOCAL SERVICES

Some of the same techniques are used by public welfare agencies when they evaluate and supervise regional and local offices. Supervision requires monitoring and studying case records for the purpose of determining the quality of the service provided, auditing the fiscal records to determine that expenditures are appropriate and responsible, and otherwise making on-site visits to offices as a means of keeping staff and management of those offices aware of the fact that others are interested in the quality, honesty, and accuracy of their performance (Maas, 1978).

Staff Development and In-Service Training

Public welfare departments, because their turnover is high and because their services are complicated, always have programs of staff development and in-service training designed to increase the efficiency of the organization through better-trained staff members. This is common in most large organizations, whether they are public or private, nonprofit or profit making. Just as telephone companies provide training to their employees, welfare departments must train theirs.

Frequently, professionally educated social workers in public welfare become trainers or staff developers in employee development and training programs.

An effective training program is essential in all of the various functions performed by public welfare departments for clients. Clerical staff need to be trained in the use of the many forms and procedures required for welfare work. Financial specialists need training in the accounting procedures public welfare agencies use. Social workers, too, need specialized training so that they can be effective employees of welfare departments (Witkin et al., 1980).

The professionally educated social worker has a high degree of conceptual knowledge about social work programs and services, the process of policy development, some of the fundamental issues that face social work, and specialized preparation in use of the social work methods on behalf of clients. However, social workers obviously cannot be specifically prepared for all of the work done in all of the agencies where they might be employed once they graduate (Cohen, 1977).

Therefore, agencies must instruct new social workers and retrain continuing employees when there are changes in actual agency operations. For example, when the law governing juveniles changes, workers with young offenders must be re-trained. When the regulations governing eligibility for public assistance change, workers who have been trained in the previous means of determining eligibility must be retrained (Petty and Bruning, 1980).

In addition to training social workers for dealing with new procedures, programs, and regulations, there is value in constantly re-educating social workers on trends in the field, on developments in other aspects of social work—such as services to the aging, health, and mental health—and on newly completed research and its results.

THE SOCIAL WORKER AS EDUCATOR AND TRAINER

The social worker in public welfare who is assigned to develop and direct training and education programs for staff has a major responsibility that may dramatically affect the quality of service offered to the agency's clients.

An effective training program requires those who are responsible for it to take several steps in its design and development (Munson, 1980).

It is generally useful for those who direct training programs to conduct a survey of training needs. Research skills are often helpful for this task, which may include meeting with supervisors and others with administrative responsibilities within the agency, surveying a sampling of line workers, observing operations of the program to determine where there are needs for more extensive training, and otherwise attempting to spot weaknesses in the agency's operation that might be overcome through more extensive and more effective staff training.

Once the survey is completed, the staff developer or trainer will often find it useful to work with a team of staff members in defining more precisely the agency's training requirements. Although one pattern or set of findings may seem to arise from the analysis of the survey, the advisors on training may have different impressions. For example, the workers in a child protective services unit may identify their greatest need as that of learning how to speak to parents when making home visits. Their supervisors or others who advise on the training program may agree that this is a problem but may persuade the staff developer or trainer that the workers have a greater need for information on community resources and the best means for using them.

Once the content of the training is specified, the trainer may find it useful to obtain guidance from professional educators in social work such as those at nearby colleges or universities. Or the trainer may wish to employ specialists on in-service training and staff development as consultants. Educators may have greater experience in defining learning problems and may have some ideas on how the desired information can best be transmitted to staff members.

The next and perhaps most crucial step in designing an in-service training or staff development program is to define the learning objectives. The trainer will find it helpful to define specific objectives in terms of the learner, rather than the teacher. For example, a program designed to enable child protective services workers to make better and more extensive use of community resources to help families would be likely to list, as some of the learning objectives:

1. To become knowledgeable about more community resources.
2. To become skillful in helping protective services client families make better and more extensive use of community resources so they may more effectively rear their children.

Quite often inexperienced trainers state objectives in terms of what they will do, such as, "To teach about available community resources." Teaching about something is what a trainer does or arranges for someone else to do as a means of meeting the objectives that have been set for the trainee. Objectives should focus on *learning* instead of on *teaching*.

The bulk of the training plan should consist of learning experiences but the learning experiences should be geared to reaching the objectives specified for the trainees.

After the objectives have been defined, those who establish the training program must create activities that will help achieve the objectives. The most effective training design will include a variety of learning experiences and, therefore, a training plan should be much more than an outline of the content to be covered. Instead, it should be a list of experiences and activities that the trainees will obtain in learning the things they will need to reach their objectives.

The learning experiences ought to be incorporated into a training calendar or design that specifies the dates on which training activities will take place, the locations, instructors, and materials needed, as well as information on the trainees who will attend in terms of numbers, backgrounds, and levels of responsibility.

After the learning experiences have been accomplished and applied to the workers, the trainer will want to conduct an evaluation of the work. This may be in the form of a quiz or examination. In some cases, it may be in the form of a questionnaire or evaluation instrument to determine the reactions of the trainees to the training program. The value of a quiz or examination is that it allows the trainer to determine how much and what the trainees have learned from the training program.

Another effective evaluation method is that of observing workers in the field to determine the impact the training program has made on the quality of their services to clients. Of course, the objective of all agency training programs is to improve the quality of the service that is provided. Therefore, the most useful evaluation is one which examines the actual result of the training in terms of client services. However, such an evaluation is not always practical and it is often necessary instead to use some of the other evaluation methods suggested.

Effective training and staff development draw upon a number of resources as a means of pursuing and reaching the objectives of the training program. These include films, video and audio tapes, lectures by experts in the field, and reading by the trainees.

Personnel Administration

Because people are so critical to the operations of public welfare, personnel administration is a major administrative activity and one that can determine the degree of success an agency has in reaching its objectives.

As has been discussed in other chapters, there are certain characteristics of public welfare personnel that create a special personnel administration situation in welfare departments. First, agencies use very large numbers of employees. Some two hundred thousand people work in welfare departments in the United States. These large numbers are needed because so much of welfare work is "labor intensive." Taking and verifying applications for assistance, investigating and dealing with child abuse and neglect, arranging for and monitoring foster care and adoptions, investigating fraud and abuse, and keeping and preparing and maintaining records are all activities that require large numbers of people.

Second, welfare departments characteristically have high rates of turnover. When other jobs in other fields are plentiful, as many as 20 or 30 percent of an agency's staff may be replaced every year.

Third, part of the reason for the rapid turnover is the relatively low wage structure in public welfare. Social workers generally have chosen a low paying profession and the salaries in public programs such as welfare, corrections, and mental hospitals are particularly low.

Fourth, welfare departments employ people from a number of fields, many of whom seize opportunities to leave public welfare and enter other kinds of work for which they have been more specifically trained and which they may find more attractive, including education, business, and some clinical fields such as speech therapy. There have been times in the history of public welfare when the demands for personnel were so great that virtually anyone with enough education or credentials could be hired.

Public welfare employees are very much like soldiers in an army. Large numbers of people come in, require training and close supervision, leave for other kinds of work, and are replaced by others who also need extensive training and supervision. An equally large number of employees are employed for their whole lifetimes in public welfare agencies and over the years become comparable to the career noncommissioned and commissioned officers one finds in an army.

Among the characteristics of organizations such as armies—and public welfare departments—is the need to focus on the job rather than on the individual, and to standardize the work as much as possible so that people are interchangeable.

Public welfare salaries tend to lag behind those of private social welfare agencies largely because public welfare employees are parts of very large cadres of personnel all of whom must be treated equally. A privately funded social agency—or more realistically one that relies upon grants from public welfare agencies and other governmental bodies—can often grant a $2,000 or $3,000 salary increase without great difficulty because all it needs is $2,000 or $3,000 in new money. A public welfare agency, on the other hand, might have thousands of employees even in a small state, and would require hundreds of millions of dollars for major staff salary increases, not to mention the costs of giving equal raises to employees of other state agencies such as the police, transportation department, and school teachers. Thus a decision to grant major salary increases for public welfare is a controversial political decision that often requires new taxes.

Affirmative Action and Equal Employment Opportunity

Public welfare departments have special interests in and obligations to employ people without regard to race, religion, or sex. In the United States, federal and most state laws require that public welfare employees be hired in a nondiscriminatory way (Farley, 1979; Hoyman, 1980). For public welfare it is particularly important that an agency hire and retain large numbers of ethnic minority group members and women because the clients of public welfare are disproportionately represented by minority group members and women. Black, Chicano, Indian, and Puerto Rican clients may be better and more fairly served when there are sufficient numbers of minority group employees in agencies to handle at least some of the cases of minority group members (Hammer, 1979). And minority group members may find it less difficult to communicate with minority clients, particularly when there are language differences. For example, a non-Spanish speaking worker who tries to work with a parent found to be neglectful of his or her children and who speaks only Spanish would have grave difficulty both in assessing the family's circumstances and in working with the family on improvements to those circumstances.

Public welfare departments, not unlike the rest of United States society, have not hired proportionately large numbers of minority group members, and although the majority of employees in public welfare are female, women have not attained status equal with men in the hierarchies of most welfare departments. In many welfare agencies, a top management team of white men presides over a large contingent of females and a smaller contingent of ethnic minority employees.

Affirmative action and equal employment can be achieved in a number of ways in public welfare agencies. These include recruitment of minority applicants for jobs by visiting campuses, agencies, and neighborhoods where such potential candidates are likely to be found. Convincing minority group members to take civil service tests and to become candidates for jobs is often a major step in building a pool of minority group members from which to employ staff.

In some agencies, when two or more candidates for a position have relatively equal backgrounds and only one is a minority group member, the agency requires that the minority group member be appointed. That is the essence of affirmative action—not selecting lower qualified minority group members but requiring that equally qualified minority group members be given preference for positions.

In some public welfare departments, special career advancement programs have been developed specifically for minorities. These programs provide special training and counseling to assist minority group members in moving up the organization's job structure.

In some agencies, where women have clearly been discriminated against in career advancements, similar efforts are made on behalf of female employees (Hoyman, 1980). Still other agencies, faced with the need to employ minority group members but finding it impossible to locate enough candidates who are qualified under the state's merit system, have changed some jobs into positions with lower educational requirements. Thus jobs that might have been reserved for people with college degrees are modified into jobs for people with high school diplomas, and minority group members are hired as case aides or assistants.

Since affirmative action programs began in the 1960s, some have criticized them as "discrimination in reverse." They suggest that such programs, by discriminating in favor of minority group members, tend to discriminate against white males. Of course, there is truth to such ideas. An agency cannot treat minority group members with special concern without also discriminating against some other group. The reasons for affirmative action are, however, quite clear. Minority group members have faced discrimination over long periods of time and, in order to be treated equally, need to be treated with special concern to wipe out the years of discrimination. And public welfare departments, with their large complements of minority group clients, need employees who can understand and deal with ethnic minority cultures, language differences, and the results of discrimination.

Unions and Collective Bargaining

In some states, public welfare employees are members of organized labor unions—sometimes the American Federation of State, County, and Municipal Employees, and at other times members of other local or national labor organizations. These unions seek to improve the compensation and working conditions of public welfare employees through negotiating contracts with public welfare agency management that spell out salaries, fringe benefits, and other personnel considerations over a specified number of years (Alexander and Speizman, 1979; Alexander, 1980; Tambor, 1979).

In some states, government agencies are not permitted to bargain with labor unions. In still others, although collective bargaining is legal, strikes by public employees are not.

There have been strikes by public welfare employees in some states over wages and working conditions. In some cases skeleton crews of public welfare employees have remained on the job to handle emergencies, to insure that applications are taken and processed, and to investigate and deal with child abuse and neglect complaints. Nonunion member supervisory personnel have also fulfilled such functions to insure that clients continue to be served, even during work stoppages.

Promotion, Tenure, and Compensation Policy

Among the most crucial personnel matters handled in public welfare departments is the determination of how much people will earn, what rights they will have to continue employment, and the procedures to be followed for promoting them in rank when that is possible and advisable.

In general, ranges of salary are established by civil service or merit system regulations. A combination of educational qualifications, classifications based upon test scores and the responsibilities one has, and the number of years one has served yield a range of salary levels or steps. Depending upon the availability of funds, individuals may be paid the highest rate possible with their qualifications or at some lower level. Some states provide for periodic wage increases based upon increases in the cost of living while others combine such increases with salary increases based upon meritorious performance by employees. In many states, the upgrading of staff salaries depends upon action by the state's legislature, which rarely has all the money available that it would like for all of its various objectives. Its only means of increasing available funds is to raise taxes, a highly unpopular act which may lead to the defeat of some legislators when they next seek election. Legislators usually act on fiscal matters only once each year, and in some cases, once every two years. These are some of the reasons why compensation for public welfare employees is generally lower than it might be in private agencies or in nongovernmental employment.

The bright side of personnel policies for public welfare employees is that tenure and fringe benefits are available. Public employees usually have the right to remain employees, and although all systems have plans for eliminating jobs and reducing their forces, these occurrences are relatively rare. In public welfare the high turnover rate generally means that those who want to remain employees are able to do so. The ability to keep one's job is much higher in public welfare than it is in business or industry.

For a variety of reasons, public welfare employees also enjoy valuable fringe benefit programs. Retirement, health insurance, paid vacations and sick leave, as well as a number of legal holidays each year, are all advantages which public welfare employees have over many of their counterparts in nongovernmental employment.

Promotions also have substantial benefits for employees both by affording employees more challenging career opportunities and as a means of earning higher salaries. In most public welfare departments, able employees who stay with the agencies are promoted rather rapidly and find themselves assuming responsibility for larger and larger segments of the agency's operation. Relatively young people can become supervisors and top level managers who are responsible for expending millions of dollars on behalf of public welfare clients. The public welfare employee tends to grow on the job much more rapidly than might be true in other work (Yankey and Coulton, 1979).

Public Relations

In the public welfare field, public relations includes informing the public about welfare programs and services, molding public attitudes about welfare so people will feel more positive toward the field, developing supporters of public welfare programs, providing specific information to clients on programs and services and creating and distributing literature on programs (Voros and Alvarez, 1981).

Public relations efforts are carried on through formal and informal contact with representatives of the media, through educational encounters with individuals in the media and in organizations, through the agency's direct relationships with its clients, through the activities of its employees both on and off the job, and through the words and deeds of others such as volunteers, advisory council members, foster parents, and vendors of services. Public relations may be positive or negative depending upon the image of the public welfare agency portrayed to the public by the agency and by others who know and have relationships with the agency. Sound public relations is not deception or simple image-making. The best public relations are maintained by those agencies which perform humanely, efficiently, and effectively. The public relations program is simply a process of conveying the truth to the public about the agency. Good programs and truthful stories about them are, without doubt, the best forms of public relations.

A sound public welfare department is highly conscious of public relations. Those who answer telephones, respond to mail, speak to clients, and carry on all agency responsibilities must hold and communicate positive attitudes about public welfare. This means that the agency's public relations with its own staff is as important as its public relations with the broader community. Keeping the staff well informed, helping the staff understand how they each contribute to the success of the agency in meeting the needs of clients, and sharing information about the agency and its programs fully and openly can create a positive attitude about the agency among its staff members. In many circumstances all of the positive, professional public relations carried on by welfare agencies during the day can be destroyed by the negative comments on the agency's clients and programs by its own staff in the evenings. It is difficult for one who is positive about public welfare clients and programs to counter a comment such as, "Why, your own staff says that most of the clients are lazy cheaters who ought to go to work." Such statements are frequently a reflection of poor information about clients and poor staff morale. But employees have high credibility with their friends and with the general public. Because they do, the whole image of the agency can be spoiled by an ill-informed, perhaps unfair, comment.

PUBLICATIONS

A sound public relations program includes publications and other communications to staff and the general public. Many agencies prepare news stories on welfare services for use in local television and radio broadcasts. Some also prepare public service announcements to be used as unpaid commercials for public welfare.

In addition, agencies prepare brochures on their programs which they distribute in their offices and in other places where clients, potential clients, or the general public might see them. Most agencies also have mechanisms for sending press releases to weekly and daily newspapers in order to provide information to the public or to get across specific information on services, changes in services, and other essential data. Information of that sort is essential and is often legally required by state or federal laws. The federal government requires official legal notice to be given to all clients of any major changes in services to which they are entitled, particularly any reductions in the size or scope of grants. And state or local laws often require public notice to be given regarding formal meetings, hearings, or other events at which decisions on public matters are likely to be made or considered.

Written materials alone are not particularly effective, however. When one hopes to communicate about something as complex as public welfare, a combination of media is often required. For example, a full explanation of the food stamp program may require a combination of newspaper, radio, and television accounts supplemented by brochures for those who want more details on the subject. Simply announcing a program in the media or producing and distributing a brochure are insufficient. A combination of the two, coupled with personal explanations to those who want and need the program, are often the combined answers for those who need information.

Conclusion

This chapter has covered some of the supportive services necessary to make public welfare departments work administratively.

Effective services require careful monitoring, supervision, training, fiscal supervision, personnel administration, and public relations. Maintaining high quality in the services provided by the agency—whether those services are economic or social—is the goal of these supportive services.

CHAPTER 13

Adjudication, Investigation, and Enforcement

PUBLIC WELFARE DEPARTMENTS include a number of activities that are relatively far removed from the organization and delivery of economic assistance and social services. These activities, which include adjudication of disputes, investigation and prosecution of fraud and abuse, and enforcement of laws governing public welfare clients, are significant elements in the process of keeping public welfare departments operating. They make it possible for the funds available for public welfare to be appropriately spent, they help insure fair and equal access to public welfare services for all people without discrimination on the basis of religion, race, or political affiliation, and they help insure that those who have obligations under public welfare meet those obligations.

The Fair Hearing Process in Public Welfare

Under various laws and court decisions, states must provide those who apply for assistance with hearings if they request them (*Goldberg* v. *Kelly*, 397 U.S., 254–1970). These hearings, which are like court hearings or trials, put the department in the position of defending its decision before an independent examiner who may be a social worker, an attorney, or someone educated in another field who has been trained to conduct hearings on welfare matters. Many of the hearings officers are experienced social workers who have received special training in the conduct of hearings and on public welfare regulations and laws. The hearings officer has to be an impartial official who has not been directly involved in the determination of the action in question.

There are several reasons why a client may request a hearing. The basic one is the denial of a service or access to a service. A client may claim that he or she was denied the right to apply for or denied cash assistance, food stamps, or legal rights, or was discriminated against because of personal characteristics such as race, color, national origin, age, sex, handicap, religion, or political affiliation. Clients may also appeal when there has been a reduction in the assistance provided to them, when the services being provided are closed to them, or when there is a delay in providing services to them.

Clients who are denied assistance must be advised of their right to a hearing and must also be advised of any legal services available to them to help them. And the agency or its employees are not allowed to make any suggestions that the client abstain from making an appeal or to intimidate clients into believing that such an appeal would cause them to lose their assistance.

Clients are also entitled to timely notification and there are regulations specifying how much advance notice must be given before any kind of assistance or service is terminated or reduced. All of these matters are spelled out specifically both in federal regulations and in state policy and procedural manuals. These manuals and regulations have the effect of the law and are based upon state and federal statutes, court decisions, and procedures developed by the public welfare agency in conformity with the law.

The client who chooses to appeal appears before the hearings officer, often with a lawyer but sometimes without any representation, to appeal the agency's decision. The hearings officer makes a decision based upon the laws and policies that have been established.

Appropriate information is made available to the hearings officer. This may include results of medical examinations when a client has been denied cash assistance because he or she is physically and mentally able to work but chooses not to do so, testimony from witnesses, and the client's own comments about the appeal and the hearing of the appeal.

In some states, group hearings are held when several people have a similar objection to a decision. These may include cases where a large group of clients had their assistance denied, reduced, or terminated, all for the same reasons and all at the same time.

In most cases, if a client wants to appeal a decision and asks for a hearing, the agency must provide the hearing promptly and the client's case is not closed nor is the assistance denied while the hearing is being scheduled. Therefore, the public welfare department may work hard to have its hearings conducted as promptly as possible so that those who seem to be ineligible for assistance and who are appealing decisions receive assistance for the shortest possible period of time.

Clients who are dissatisfied with the decisions of welfare hearings officers may appeal their cases to state or federal courts, which may hear the case or refuse to hear it because the court believes the hearing and the decision were proper or because it believes that it lacks jurisdiction in the case.

Nonclient Hearings

Clients are only one group for whose benefit public welfare departments hold hearings. In addition, departments hold hearings on other matters that are in contention for employees and vendors.

The most typical kind of nonclient hearing is that which is held when an employee appeals a dismissal, demotion, or transfer. These hearings can either be internal, within the welfare department, or may be held by the merit system agency which handles employee qualifications, appointments, and concerns. In some cases, employees are able to appeal administration decisions within the agency and, if they are not satisfied with the results, may then appeal to the merit system for resolution of the problem. These matters are discussed in some additional detail in the section of this text on "Personnel Administration" (Chapter 12).

Vendors of services who are suspended from participating in programs such as Medicaid are also entitled to hearings on those actions. Although each welfare department has a different system for hearing appeals, all must afford the suspended vendor an opportunity to state his or her case before some kind of administrative hearing, which is usually handled by an agency hearings officer or by a high official of the welfare department. Hearings are provided because no person may be denied the right to sell services to a public agency without "due process," or the right to a fair hearing.

These hearings are defined as "civil," rather than criminal. Generally, departments of welfare can hear appeals that do not involve potential criminal activity whereas only the courts can handle criminal matters.

Investigations of Fraud and Abuse

Because the amounts of money expended on public welfare are so large, even the misspending of small amounts in welfare programs may add up to large totals. And public confidence in public welfare, which is often low, may be bolstered by vigorous investigations of potential fraud or program abuse. Therefore, welfare departments employ or contract for the services of fraud investigators.

HEALTH SERVICES

More public welfare money is spent on health services than on anything else and the largest amount of money improperly taken is probably taken by health care vendors. Of course, most vendors of health services, such as physicians, pharmacists, hospitals, and nursing homes, do not abuse the welfare system. In fact, vendors of health services as a group are uncommonly reputable and honest. But the amounts spent are so large that even small amounts of fraud committed by a few vendors add up to millions.

Fraud and abuse by medical vendors are complicated by the nature of their professions. Traditionally, those who provide medical services work under little or no supervision. Their professional training, dedication to a code of ethics, and certification or licensing by the government give them the right to practice their professions as they think best. Although the law places limits on what they may do, the legal limitations are broad and general. Evaluations are ordinarily made only by their peers. Public policy governing medical practice dictates that only professionals should make professional decisions—that supervision of the work of professionals may lead to government abuse and may reduce the quality of care available to people who are ill.

Vendors of services also may appeal decisions on the rates they are paid or on other matters affecting their ability to earn income from their work with welfare agencies. These, too, are held administratively within the welfare department. When those who appeal are dissatisfied with administrative decisions by welfare departments, they are able to appeal to the courts, as clients are.

Fraud and abuse by health care vendors must often be dealt with by welfare departments themselves. Local and state law enforcement agencies are often too small and burdened with other responsibilities to carry on the specialized investigations needed to spot and eliminate medical abuses. In addition, those who abuse health care programs often have the resources to avoid prosecution—they may have sufficient funds for excellent legal defenses and connections with local officials who are responsible for prosecutions. Many welfare departments find that the only sanctions applied against abusive health care vendors are suspensions from participating in the welfare reimbursement program.

The following are some examples of abuses that need to be investigated in public welfare agencies.

1. An agency worker is discovered to be the beneficiary of a large life insurance policy held by an aging client. The department's policies say that no employee may take money or other items of value from a recipient of services. When confronted with the charge that she will benefit monetarily from the death of the client, the worker says the client made the decision freely and that she has no intention of telling the client to change the policy.

2. A welfare office maintains a local bank account with assets of some $3,000 to help clients who have emergency needs for food, clothing, or rent. An audit of the account arouses some suspicion in the auditor who decides personally to visit with three families which have received cash help during the past year. The auditor discovers that none of the three families can be found nor is there any record that they have ever lived in the community where the office is located.

3. A social worker is needed immediately at school because his son is ill and his wife is out of town. The supervisor calls the home of the client the worker has reported he will visit and discovers that not only is the worker not in the home, but he had no appointment to visit the client on this day.

4. Citizens in a small community report that the residents of a nursing home in that community are regularly "punished" by denial of food, by being forced to stay in their rooms, and are regularly denied visits to doctors. Furthermore, they insist that the facility is usually filthy but that it is cleaned up whenever health department inspectors make their periodic, announced visits. The public welfare department pays for the care of most of the patients in the home and, therefore, initiates an investigation into the quality of care provided.

CLIENTS

Welfare fraud or abuse by recipients of assistance is usually carried out by few people, for relatively short periods of time, and for small amounts of money or other assistance. Although the extent of client fraud and abuse is often misrepresented in the minds of the public, it is still a serious problem and one that requires investigation and action (Eaton, 1980).

The most common form of abusing or committing fraud against public welfare programs is the failure to report income. People who are not as much in need as they claim to be may receive cash assistance, food stamps, medical care, and social services to which they would not be entitled at all or at a level higher than they would be entitled to receive if they honestly reported their income and assets. And there is a small but significant number of clearly fraudulent applications by people who are not in need at all and who use welfare fraud as a means of livelihood.

Most cases of client fraud or abuse should be prevented rather than stopped after the fact. They should be detected by careful screening during the application process or at subsequent reviews of the family's situation. Careful interviewing, verification of information—particularly suspicious information—and more frequent checking of cases likely to be prone to errors can often prevent client abuse or fraud. Prevention is preferable to investigation and prosecution because it is less expensive and more likely to yield satisfactory final results. It also can serve as an effective deterrent to abuse of public welfare programs when the word is spread that it is difficult to qualify for welfare assistance.

But the myth of widespread, extensive welfare fraud seems to be perpetuated by occasional publicity that is given to clients who are able to fraudulently collect hundreds of thousands of dollars from welfare departments. These cases receive national publicity that convinces many people that large scale abuse of assistance programs is common. In fact, the reason these cases are so well-publicized is that they are unusual. These accomplished criminals may collect erroneous assistance payments by establishing multiple identities documented by forged birth certificates and driver's licenses. Fortunately, few cases of welfare fraud are so dramatic or accomplished. The more typical client welfare abuse is by an ordinarily eligible assistance recipient who steadily fails to report a monthly child support check her ex-husband sends her and thereby receives assistance to which she is not entitled.

Although there are clients who improperly obtain public welfare assistance, the amounts are usually small and the length of time the benefits are received is relatively brief. Clients could not ordinarily receive more than $5,000 improperly in any year. Therefore, client fraud investigations and prosecutions are most important when they enhance public confidence in welfare programs and when they deter others from committing fraud or abuse. Each individual case is not very costly.

Clients may, on occasion, also be abusers of medical programs. Examples include clients who over-use physician services, visiting one physician or another almost every day for illnesses that are more imagined than real. In other cases, clients use their medical coverage to obtain, often through deception, prescriptions for narcotic drugs.

Investigative Personnel

Although many public welfare agencies employ professional investigators trained in police work, most find it desirable to employ a balanced investigative team of professional social workers along with those who have police training. The social worker's knowledge of programs, skill in interviewing, and skill in recording—all of which are essential in investigative work—can make a social worker with some extra training in law enforcement and investigative methods a rather effective investigator. A social worker's skill in communication, both oral and written, can be a major factor in effectively supervising or carrying out investigations.

Public Welfare Quality Control

Quality control is a method, first developed in manufacturing, to ensure that the product of an organization's work conforms to pre-established specifications. A typical example is the manufacture of parts for airplanes. An inspector takes a sample of such parts from the assembly line and examines them in detail for conformity to design and specifications. Any evidence that the parts are out of compliance with the standards may lead to some corrective action, which depends upon the source of the difficulty. A supervisor may be reassigned, retrained, or terminated. Manufacturing personnel may be retrained or disciplined. The design of the part or the manufacturing process itself may be re-engineered. In other words, quality control identifies problems that are subsequently corrected so the company's product is satisfactorily produced.

Quality control does not replace the normal supervision and inspection that is a part of any organization's program. Instead, it is a further check on the supervisory and inspection system which can prevent the organization from appearing to do well while making dramatic errors in the actual production of its goods or services (Budde, 1979; Bendick, 1980).

Quality control methods are used in public welfare in much the same way they are used in industry. A sample of cases is identified and rigorously re-evaluated by specially trained and supervised quality control workers to determine the extent to which that sample conforms to agency policies and practices.

Quality control methods assume there is always some error in the cases examined, because no human endeavor is ever perfect. However, the objective is to hold the error rate to a minimum low tolerance. If the error rate exceeds that low tolerance, administrators of the program know that corrective action must be taken. Either the policies must be changed, the procedures need re-evaluation, or the workers who carry out the policy require retraining or replacement.

Although quality control methods in public welfare are most commonly associated with assistance in the form of cash, food stamps, or medical services, quality control methods can also be used as a means of monitoring the administration of social services, particularly those that are of monetary benefit such as day care.

Quality control is not primarily a means for identifying and reducing fraud or abuse in public welfare programs, but it can reveal illegal or improper activities by clients, vendors, or employees, which can, in turn, trigger investigations.

Child Support Enforcement

The primary reason for welfare dependency in the United States, as this text pointed out earlier, is that parents of children do not pay for their care, even when they can afford to do so and are ordered to do so by the courts. Approximately two thirds of all the families receiving public assistance in the United States receive it because of this failure of fathers, primarily, to provide support to their children (Krause, 1981; Chambers, 1979; Cassetty, 1978).

For that reason, public welfare departments operate child support enforcement programs as part of their obligations under the Social Security Act. Failing to do so leads to reductions in the money the federal government provides the state for public assistance programs.

Many social workers in public welfare are engaged in these child support enforcement activities, which are specified in the Social Security Act. The Act requires that paternity be established and support sought and secured for children who receive public assistance and who have been voluntarily abandoned by their morally and legally responsible parents or "putative," biological, fathers.

The activities of child support enforcement units in public welfare departments include the establishment through court procedures of paternity for children who are born out of wedlock; locating the absent legal parent or putative father; contacting the absent parent to determine the financial ability to provide support; seeking to secure and enforce a court ordered support obligation against the absent parent; and collecting and distributing child support payments received both voluntarily and by court order (Schossler, 1979; Cullen, 1980).

To aid in the location of absent parents, the United States government has established a parent locater service, which makes it possible to find parents in other states through a computer matching of their Social Security numbers with their employment records. In addition, each state is authorized to pay incentives to local prosecuting attorneys and other officials so they will assist in locating absent parents and in establishing their responsibility as well as in securing payments from them for the support of the children.

In many cases, state departments of public welfare collect child support payments from absent parents and distribute these payments to the client family, after deducting the amount that the department pays the family in public assistance.

Of course, the ultimate objective of this child support enforcement effort is to help families become self-supporting by causing those who are legally responsible for children to exercise their responsibility for them.

The natural parent who receives public assistance must, in turn, cooperate with public welfare agencies to provide information about the deserting spouse and to take legal action against that spouse for support. Failure to do so, except when the recipient is in danger of being harmed by the absent parent, may reduce the family's grant and remove the uncooperative parent from the assistance rolls.

The same system established for locating absent parents of children dependent on public assistance is available to the general public for a small fee. That is, any person who is entitled to child support payments and is not receiving them may, for a fee, obtain help from the public welfare agency in locating and enforcing the absent parent's obligations to the child. This child support enforcement activity is one of the more significant recent developments in public assistance programs and has the potential for reducing public responsibility for dependent children.

Conclusion

The adjudication of disputes, investigation of fraud, and the enforcement of statutes and regulations are all part of public welfare social worker responsibilities. Although they are not often included in the traditional preparation of social workers for serving clients and administering programs, they are methods increasingly used in public welfare in order to improve the delivery of public welfare services with smaller staffs. They are required to implement judicial decisions which require welfare departments to provide fair hearings for clients and concrete evidence for actions taken when providing or denying public welfare benefits.

CHAPTER 14

Research, Statistics, and Evaluation

ONE OF THE MOST commonly used activities in public welfare is the scientific study of public welfare problems, programs, and performance. In social work, these functions fall under the social work research method which includes systematically studying, defining, and evaluating problems, clients, and agencies.

It is part of the public welfare department's daily operation to collect information on the clients they serve. In order to know what they should do on behalf of those clients, the agency needs to know something about them and the difficulties that brought them to the welfare program. In order for public welfare departments to do their jobs effectively it is also necessary to collect and evaluate information on the activities of the departments themselves. In addition, departments must monitor the services they provide and must use scientific methods to gather and evaluate the information on those services. Departments must also evaluate their own operations and they do so by collecting information on programs and their impact on clients.

Data Collection

The fundamental research activity in public welfare is the collection of statistics on clients, services, and on the department itself. Virtually everything done by every public welfare department is converted into statistical form and maintained as information on the service. Public welfare agencies print periodic statistical reports on their caseloads, expenditures, and the services they provide (Abert, 1979).

This information comes from the work economic and social services social workers do when they record facts on the clients they see and the services they provide. This information on clients and services is tabulated for department statistical reports. The need to gather data is a primary reason for the extensive record-keeping required of social workers in public welfare.

These systems provide a means for collecting information, reporting it to some central point such as a state research office, and reporting it to the total agency, federal agencies, and to the public through the medium of a statistical bulletin or statistical reports (Attkisson et al., 1978).

A typical public welfare agency statistical report will inform its readers of the number of clients served during the month in each program category. Comparative information on clients served in the same categories during the previous month and, perhaps, during the same month in a previous year, may also be provided. The number of dollars expended in each program, the number of people served in each family, and the breakdown of the numbers of cases and the dollars expended by city, county, or neighborhood may also be included.

This information serves a variety of purposes for the public welfare department. It provides facts to the agency's top management on trends in the department's services. If there has been a dramatic increase in the service provided, the agency needs to know about that. If there has been a large decrease in services provided, it may reveal that the agency is providing a service that is no longer needed. Or the information may reveal that the agency is spending more money than it can without incurring a deficit, which means the agency may have to reduce its services, cut its caseload, or obtain supplemental funds in order to continue providing services to its clients (McCurdy, 1980).

Agency management may also learn from these statistical reports that some counties are experiencing great growths in their caseloads while others are remaining level and while still others are experiencing decreases. The management will want to know if there are some special social or economic problems being encountered in those counties with great increases and they may want to reallocate some of the agency's resources from the counties with fewer problems to the counties with great problems. Or the management may believe that those who are working in a specific county are not providing adequate services to those who come for help and they may send an investigative team to evaluate the situation.

In addition to serving as a management tool, the information system also provides legislative bodies with information for use in planning. These bodies need factual information in order to decide on budgets and other legislation for public welfare programs. A state or local government's budget agency or financial management office will also be interested in these data. Other agencies of government also use this kind of information. Boards of education use it to find out about the needs of school children. Learning that more children are receiving public assistance may cause the school to increase its budget for free textbooks, hot lunches, and other special services for low income children. Employment service offices may make special efforts to find work in a designated area for public assistance recipients when they discover there is an increase in the unemployed parents' category of public assistance recipients. Health departments may also find it necessary to increase their services based upon statistical information provided by the welfare department (Fink and Kosecoff, 1980; Maas, 1978).

Statistical information of this sort is also useful for dissemination to the public through the media. Newspapers, radio, and television stations often use welfare statistical reports as the basis for news stories on trends in welfare. Some specific information on research of interest to the media is provided later in this chapter.

The gathering of statistical information is a responsibility of many social workers in public welfare. It often requires the ability to design information systems and to collect and tabulate the statistical data for dissemination purposes. Workers in public welfare who conduct data collection and statistical analysis often need to be familiar with automatic data processing and computer systems. But all employees, including those who are principally involved in providing direct services to clients, provide statistical information for the agency to collect, evaluate, and disseminate.

RESEARCH AND EVALUATION ON PUBLIC WELFARE
CLIENTS, PROGRAMS, AND WORKERS

Genuine research usually extends beyond the simple collection and dissemination of facts about the welfare program. Research projects define a problem or a need for information, collect data as a means of answering the question, evaluate the data, and report findings which result from the research process. (Weiss, 1977; Wright, 1979).

Some examples of statements of research problems may be:

1. Why is the number of employed people who seek public assistance increasing?
2. Why are there more adolescent female applicants for public assistance than ever before?
3. Why do the needs for protective services for abused and neglected children increase in early June and decline in October each year?

If a researcher seeks information that has not been calculated before, the questions might be:

1. What are the characteristics of families in which child abuse and neglect are found?
2. What are the characteristics of the families most likely to have case errors? Are some families more predictably inclined to commit fraud against the welfare agency than others?
3. What might be the effect of charging families receiving medical assistance for the first one dollar of each prescription, as opposed to providing prescription drugs without any cost at all?

In some situations, data may be collected through examination and analysis of case records. Research workers may, for example, simply look up information on computer screens or in file folders about a case to determine some of the characteristics of the clients such as their age, number of people in the household, previous work experience, or other material that is stored in the computer or in the case record file.

When more detailed information on the feelings or reactions of clients is needed, researchers may talk to clients by telephone or in face to face interviews and record their responses on the forms that have been designed for the data collection process (Hyde and Shafritz, 1979).

Researchers may use computer methods to select the sample to be studied or they may choose cases at random from the case files. In sampling, the major effect is to insure that every case to be studied has an equal chance of being represented in the research with every other case. The researcher wants to be sure that there is no bias toward older people or younger people or people who live in better sections of town. That is true except when the researcher wants a *stratified* sample, which provides the researcher with specific information on a specific portion of the population under study—younger women with young children, for example. In that case, the researcher will try to study only those kinds of cases.

In some instances, a small survey will suffice to provide the information the agency needs about the clients. In such surveys, workers develop written questionnaires which they mail to clients for their responses.

Evaluation of Data

After the data are collected, the information is tabulated and analyzed with various statistical measures. Conclusions are then drawn from the data analysis which will answer a question or which will reveal that the question cannot be answered without additional data or additional research (Tripodi and Epstein, 1980).

The following are certain matters in research that are critical for the public welfare researcher.

1. One of the most crucial decisions the researcher must make is about the sample to be studied. How many cases will be analyzed, how will they be chosen, and how can there be certainty that they are representative of the total *universe* being studied? A good sample of a very few cases—perhaps 200 or 300—can be effective in providing facts about tens of thousands of clients. But the sample must effectively represent the total group being studied.
2. How can the information best be collected to answer the research question? If one is asking questions of public welfare recipients, the clients may misinterpret the questionnaire or the interview and believe that the answers they give will positively or negatively affect their continued receipt of financial assistance or social services from the agency. How can researchers minimize bias or misinformation in the data that are collected?
3. What kinds of statistical measures will help the welfare department better understand the facts it is studying? Should clients be compared with nonclients or should their characteristics be compared with former clients of the agency? Perhaps it is worth the time and effort to compare them with both. Is one factor clearly dependent on another? That is, is unemployment the major reason for an increase in the number of cases served or has there been a change in the administrative philosophy of the office that experienced the caseload increase?

Researchers know about or have access to others who know about various forms of statistical analysis that will help them answer some of these questions (Rothman, 1980).

PROBLEMS WITH RESEARCH USE

At times, public welfare departments make the mistake of believing their research findings or the findings of others are conclusive. However, situations differ from community to community, from client group to client group, and from welfare department to welfare department so that something that has proven workable in one situation will not always work in another.

COMPUTERS AND PUBLIC WELFARE RESEARCH

Computer systems and automatic data processing have made some research possible that may not have been possible before. Although computers are not fundamentally capable of doing anything that human beings with pencils and paper cannot do, they can, in fact, make some kinds of research possible that would otherwise be completely impracticable. For example, computers can amass and deal with vast quantities of information which would be quite cumbersome for people and which would require more human effort than might be worth expending on the project. In addition, the computer can handle a variety of calculations simultaneously and can also hold several pieces of information in its own memory and, in effect, think about those various pieces of information at the same time—a feat that is nearly impossible for human beings (Schoech, 1979).

For example, a computer system might in a matter of seconds tabulate the total number of people in a county receiving assistance, compare those numbers to the numbers served in the previous month, analyze the change in relation to unemployment statistics for the county during that period of time, and project changes in the caseload.

Examples of Public Welfare Research

Some studies are regularly conducted on public welfare. For example, every two years the U.S. Department of Health and Human Services publishes a study on the characteristics of Aid to Families with Dependent Children recipients.

CONTRACTED RESEARCH

Welfare deparments do not always conduct their own research with their own staff. In many cases they pay colleges, universities, or private research firms to study a problem or concern and report to them on the findings. This contract research has the advantage of buying only the time and skills necessary to carry out the specific research that the welfare departments wants to do.

COST ALLOCATION STUDIES

In addition to studying clients and social problems, most public welfare agencies try to find ways to determine precisely what activities they perform. This kind of information is important not only for management purposes such as assigning personnel but also for determining the costs of the service and the formula for allocating those costs among the various levels of government which pay for them. In all public welfare departments, the costs are shared by the state and federal governments.

DEMONSTRATIONS

Another research approach frequently used by departments of welfare is the demonstration. The agency pays the cost of trying new ways of providing services to people, more effectively managing their programs, or more efficiently providing cash assistance. Some agencies of the United States government and some private foundations provide special funds for demonstrations. The idea is to try something new to see if it works. The new endeavor is usually tried on a small scale in a state, county, or city. The results of the demonstration are evaluated and reported widely so other states and localities may try the new approach if it has proven successful, or avoid it if it has not.

Demonstrations have included giving cash assistance to families in the form of a guaranteed income, rather than in the form of an Aid to Families with Dependent Children grant; using cash instead of food stamps for people who qualify for nutritional assistance; developing new ways for delivering social services in local offices through coordination between the social service workers and other parts of the welfare department; using intensive social casework services to help overcome the poverty of AFDC families and requiring work on public projects in payment for food stamps.

Research for Public Education

Since the 1960s, when public welfare clients grew in number because of economic and governmental policy changes, the term "welfare" has become inflammatory. Merely mentioning it ignites the passions of some citizens. For a variety of reasons discussed in earlier chapters, there is a strongly held belief that millions of people receive assistance from public welfare because they are too lazy to work and "choose" to become public charges and live on the tax payments of the rest of the population (Ginsberg, 1982).

Some critics simply confuse public welfare services with other federal, state, and private programs such as worker's compensation; Social Security payments to the retired, widowed, handicapped, and dependent children; Supplemental Security Income; Veterans' Administration benefits; and private pensions. These programs, which are designed to reach the same ends as public welfare, enjoy better reputations than public welfare. However, many of those perceived as receiving help improperly are clients of those agencies, not public welfare.

The myth of the welfare cheat or loafer is strongly held. Even aspiring recipients of public assistance often prefix their requests with, "Now, we all know there are many people receiving welfare who don't deserve it. But believe me, I am not one of them. I need and am entitled to public aid." Belief in the welfare cheat is so strong that those who need help assume they are exceptions rather than typical families with financial need—a common human experience often beyond the family's control. They do not understand the public welfare system as one that primarily tries to help people surmount those short-term difficulties.

These attitudes toward welfare services have negative consequences for low income people in the United States. The myth of the welfare cheater makes welfare budgets prime candidates for budget reductions. Legislative supporters of welfare services risk loss of support by those who oppose it. Alleged welfare abuses are popular subjects for discussions in the media and wherever nonrecipients gather. Because of this, those who operate public welfare programs have a responsibility to educate the public about public welfare, both to ensure continued support for welfare services and to minimize the demoralization of those who need public welfare's help.

RESEARCH AS A TOOL IN PUBLIC EDUCATION

The following are two research projects which were initiated by the author while serving as commissioner of a state public welfare department in West Virginia. The projects were designed primarily to educate the public on welfare issues.

School Clothing Allowance. The first study was on the impact of changing the distribution of school clothing allowances for children in public assistance families from an annual voucher to a check. This aroused widespread public concern that the money would be used for purposes other than purchasing clothing for low income school age children.

Although there had been relatively little disagreement with the state's helping families with school age children purchase clothing for those children at the beginning of each school year, a change in the format for distributing that assistance aroused protest in 1977 which was also the first year of a new governor's administration. Under the previous governor, the department of welfare issued vouchers to be spent in retail stores for children's clothing. The state waived the sales tax on these purchases and many merchants gave discounts to those who used vouchers. However, in 1976, federal authorities insisted that the use of vouchers violated federal regulations.

So the assistance was provided in the form of checks, accompanied by a letter stating the purpose of the check. Extensive information was provided to the public on the purpose of the program. However, many nonclient families and individuals complained that the funds would be used, at worst, for alcoholic beverages or, perhaps a bit better, for adult clothing

The uproar led to the development of a study of the actual use of the school clothing checks by client families.

The department research staff, in consultation with university research specialists, coordinated a mail and telephone survey of 1,286 clients, teachers, clothing merchants, and randomly selected members of the general public. Each group was asked different questions to determine, as closely as possible, how the money was used and how people, other than clients, perceived the program.

Among the school administrators and teachers who were surveyed, three-fourths were aware of the program and a similar number were aware of students who were eligible for the clothing assistance. Of those who knew children who were eligible, 58.5 percent said that the children's personal appearances indicated they had benefited from the program, while 14.1 percent said their personal appearances did not indicate any benefit. The rest didn't know. Seventy-five percent of the administrators and teachers said that the state should use a restricted voucher, even if it meant using only state funds for the program. Parenthetically, it is interesting that in subsequent years, when legislative action threatened the survival of the school clothing allowance, pressure from school personnel was a major factor in convincing the governor and the legislature to continue the program.

Of the clothing merchants, 88 percent were familiar with the program and had processed the vouchers in the past—not surprising in a program that served over 16,000 families with children at the time the study was done, in a state of some 1.8 million citizens. When the merchants were asked if a change to a check had affected their dollar volume of school clothing sales, 59.1 percent said it had. However, the balance of the respondents (300 merchants participated in the study) said that the change either had no effect or that they could not determine whether or not it had had an effect. When the merchants were asked about the "frugality" of families in purchasing school clothing, 52.3 percent said the families were less frugal when using checks than they had been with vouchers. The rest thought the families were equally frugal or else they did not know. When asked if there was ample evidence that the allowance was being spent for school clothing, 47.4 percent thought there was not ample evidence but the rest said they either didn't know or that there was good evidence of such expenditures. Those who thought there was such evidence—17.8 percent—were a clear minority. And 75 percent of the merchants said that the allowance ought to be given in the form of a restricted voucher, even if no federal funds could be used for matching purposes.

Of the 300 members of the general public who were polled by telephone, a minority, 44.3 percent knew that there had been a clothing allowance and the rest did not; 80.7 percent of the respondents looked favorably upon the state helping with such a program. But, when the difference between a voucher and a check was explained to them, 66.3 percent of the respondents believed that a restrictive voucher was more desirable than an unrestricted check, even if federal funds were lost.

As for the recipients who were the subject of this program, 642 clients received questionnaires and 417 of those were returned to the research staff within a few weeks of the school clothing allowance checks being mailed. By that time, 97.8 percent of the clients, which included low income and foster parents, had spent the total amount and nearly half had used their money in more than one store. This flexibility represented an advantage of the check over the voucher, which had usually required the recipients' spending the entire check in one store, whether or not the store had precisely what they wanted. And the clients reported purchasing ordinary clothing— undergarments, shirts, blouses, jeans, coats, boots, shoes, and sweaters. When asked if they had found it necessary to spend some or all of their clothing allowance for items other than school clothing, 9.6 percent said they had, but in almost every case the expenditures reported were for other school items such as notebooks and pencils or clothing for other children jealous of their older siblings. A handful of others used part of the money for other basics, such as food, rent, utilities, and medical expenses.

When asked if they preferred a check or a voucher, 62.6 percent of the clients preferred a check, 6.7 percent the voucher, but 30.7 percent had no preference or did not respond to the question.

The study, which received widespread coverage in the media and which was used extensively with legislators in subsequent years when the same issue arose, confirmed the marked difference of opinion between clothing vendors and clients. It showed that using a check or a voucher made little difference in terms of reported expenditures for school clothing by client families. And it also demonstrated that the public attributes little importance to whether the state or federal government is the source of funds, although that is a major consideration for government officials.

Of course, this survey research cannot be described as totally valid. A valid study of the issues would have required an invisible observer or some sort of documented evidence of the expenditures. But this survey comes as close as one may within reasonable expenditures of funds.

The research may have changed some public attitudes about clients and about this program of school clothing assistance. But perhaps more important, it communicated to those who were concerned that the department of welfare cared enough to follow up on the issue and that the department cared enough to question the clients about their use of public funds. It is unlikely that many attitudes were changed about the virtues of checks over vouchers. However, after four years of granting checks instead of vouchers, few remembered that there had ever been another method of distributing these monies.

The Turnover of Cases Receiving Public Assistance. A second study dealt with the length of time families actually used public assistance from the welfare department. One of the tenaciously held stereotypes of public assistance recipients is that assistance is received for many generations over many decades. This notion is even occasionally reinforced by social scientists attempting to document the existence of a "culture of poverty." As the story goes, a welfare-assisted woman raises a daughter who, as soon as she is able to do so, produces a child of her own and promptly becomes a welfare recipient. And that child, too, becomes a recipient of help.

There are such families in the caseload of every public welfare department, and nonrecipient families either know such families or think they do. But statistics on welfare-assisted families indicate that most families use welfare as a temporary expedient and that few families receive assistance for even a year, much less a generation.

The short term nature of public assistance was documented in 1978 when another study was initiated to analyze the turnover rate of the families being served. Department researchers established that 28 percent of the families receiving assistance received it for no more than two months. Those figures applied to families whose cases had been closed between March 8, 1977, and March 6, 1979. Of the cases active on March 6, 1979, a time of relatively poor economic conditions, the mean length of time for receiving assistance was 28.2 months and the median was twelve months. Of the active caseload, some 20 percent received assistance for two months or less and 10 percent for more than six years.

This information was used to demonstrate the nature of the caseload and some of the ways in which it was reduced, such as locating employment as an alternative to continuing to receive AFDC. Other factors which affect the length of time a family receives assistance—such as a child reaching adulthood, which also terminates the assistance—were also described. Marriage, the reconciliation of the family, and relocation to other communities were also explained as other reasons for ending assistance.

The belief that many families receive welfare assistance for all their lives and for generations into the future is widely held. This research showed, however, that most families who receive assistance do so for relatively short periods of time. It did not refute the idea that some families become public assistance recipients when times are very bad but become self-sufficient when economic conditions improve. Families with few economic resources are the most likely to come into and leave the public assistance rolls through several generations.

The research on families and the length of time they have received assistance was useful in explaining more precisely the cycle through which people enter and leave the public assistance rolls.

Error Rate Studies

Another form of research is the determination of the number of errors made in the granting of public assistance, food stamps, and medical services to clients. A sample of cases is selected, often at random but sometimes through the use of a stratified sample of those cases most likely to be in error. Then a special, independent quality control unit reexamines the cases to determine if the client was genuinely eligible and whether or not the client received too much or too little assistance. Out of this analysis and examination, an error rate is determined for the agency. Federal regulations often demand that the agency commit a minimum of errors or face some reduction in the matching levels it receives from federal funds. (See Chapter 13.)

Protection of Clients and Confidentiality

The professional ethics of social workers and the requirements of state and federal laws require that provisions be made to protect public welfare clients from having personal information revealed about them in the process of conducting research. This protection is achieved in a number of ways. When research requires collection and possible dissemination of personal information that may be embarrassing to clients, clients must be given an opportunity to refuse to participate in the research. If there is potential harm to clients, they must be warned, must certify they understand the potential harm, and agree to participate in the research.

Conclusion

Social workers in public welfare often are employed as specialists in research on various elements of the department's operations and on problems with which the department deals. Skill in the scientific study of social, financial, and administrative issues are among the abilities a professional social worker in public welfare should master. This chapter has reviewed some of these issues and the activities associated with these functions.

PART IV

SOCIAL WORK IN THE LARGER SYSTEM OF PUBLIC WELFARE

THE FIRST THREE PARTS of this text have described in some detail the breadth of the public welfare field and social work's role within it.

However, understanding and learning to work in public welfare require knowledge of the larger context in which public welfare exists because that larger context has a major affect on the public welfare field.

This part of the text describes the ways in which public welfare and the social workers who work in this field of practice relate to and work with some of those larger systems.

The relationship between social work and related professions is examined in detail. In addition, the relationships between public welfare—which is an executive agency of state government—and the legislative and judicial branches of government are also described. The relationships between public welfare and other human service executive branch agencies such as the departments of health, mental health, corrections, and rehabilitation, are examined.

The relationships of public welfare with various professional associations and international organizations are discussed. These organizations affect many of the functions of social workers in public welfare. Child welfare services, assistance to migrants and refugees, and efforts to influence national and world policy are all part of the concern of social workers in public welfare agencies. Many public welfare employees are directly or indirectly involved in the provision of services which are directly influenced by these national and world efforts.

This last section of the text is designed to help the reader develop a comprehensive and detailed understanding of the ways in which public welfare programs function as part of the larger international network of human services programs.

Qualified professionals seek to understand themselves and their work in the largest context so they can understand not only what they do, but also why they do it. It is the purpose of this final part to provide such a background.

CHAPTER 15

Public Welfare Social Workers and Professional Associations

MOST PUBLIC WELFARE social workers find it advantageous to participate in professional associations. This chapter describes some of the major professional associations in which public welfare social workers are involved and also discusses some of the ways in which professional association participation may be of benefit in helping them carry out public welfare objectives and assisting in the career development of social workers employed in public welfare.

The National Association of Social Workers

The National Association of Social Workers is by far the largest of all the organizations for social workers with some 90,000 members, although NASW does not connect as directly with or have as much influence over the public welfare field as do some other professional social welfare organizations.

However, because public welfare is so significant for all professional social workers, the Association lobbies heavily in Washington with both the Congress and the executive agencies in order to influence the policies and programs of social welfare funded and operated under the auspices of the United States government. The Association also depends upon its chapters, which are statewide organizations throughout the United States, to influence state procedures and legislation.

SOCIAL WORK LICENSING

Among the top priorities of NASW over the years has been the licensing of social workers and, by doing so, protecting the use of the term "social worker" from use by people who are not educated in the field. Licensing has several objectives including the protection of the public from people who purport to be professional social workers but who are not; enhancing the status of professional social workers; and protecting jobs normally filled by professional social workers from being filled by others.

The Association has also worked to develop social welfare legislation to improve the benefits available to disadvantaged people. In addition, the Association has taken broad public positions condemning discrimination against minority group members, women, and homosexuals.

ADJUDICATION OF DISPUTES

One of NASW's valuable services for social workers in public welfare is its adjudication of conflicts between workers and their employers. When a worker believes he or she has been improperly treated by an employer over matters such as salary, working conditions, layoffs, or assignments, the Association, through a local, state chapter, and national mechanism, can hear those disputes and make recommendations about them. Of course the Association expects social workers to try to resolve their conflicts with employers by talking to those employers and using agency grievance procedures before they appeal to the adjudication procedures of NASW.

Because it is a private organization, the Association has no authority to enforce its opinions in such disputes. Instead, it uses moral persuasion to redress grievances. When employers refuse to compensate or otherwise satisfy workers who appear to have been treated improperly, the Association can place "sanctions" on the employer, which may discourage other social workers from accepting employment in the agency.

American Public Welfare Association

The largest organization exclusively devoted to public welfare is the American Public Welfare Association, an unusual organization which combines individual and agency members. Whereas only individuals may join NASW, whole organizations, including state and local public welfare departments, can and do join APWA. In fact, most of the financial support for APWA comes from the annual dues paid by state and local welfare departments.

As is common in most national organizations, APWA lobbies for improved public welfare in the United States Congress. It also provides training services for welfare employees, publishes journals and other materials for distribution, and conducts research. Its annual public welfare directory is used throughout the United States.

Perhaps APWA is most important, however, because it also sponsors a series of affiliated groups which are part of the public welfare field. Under the APWA umbrella are the National Council of State Public Welfare Administrators and the National Council of Local Public Welfare Administrators. It also has an association of Medicaid directors and an association of public welfare attorneys. Because the top executives of public welfare agencies throughout the United States are very active and influential members of the American Public Welfare Association board of directors and leaders of its specialized organizations, it is probably the most influential of all the national organizations in terms of American public welfare.

Child Welfare League of America

The Child Welfare League of America is a national organization for those interested in and concerned about social services for children. It provides consultation, training, and publications for those who are employed in or who participate in other ways in certain programs. Although it has no national individual memberships, the organization solicits and accepts contributions from individuals and also sells its publications and its services to them (Shyne, 1979).

Most states have some relationship with CWLA because it is heavily concerned with programs such as adoption, foster care, and group service programs for children. However, the most active members are those who are on the boards and otherwise are supporters of child care organizations and youth service agencies.

The Child Welfare League of America also attempts to influence federal and state policies through its Washington office on matters affecting children and youths. It has separate organizations of public child welfare agencies which provide opportunities for the exchange of information and for public policy development efforts.

Family Service Association of America

The Family Service Association of America is a national group of agencies which pulls together the public and the private family service agencies around the United States, advocates for their objectives, and attempts to enhance their activities.

The family service associations in most of the United States are privately funded and operated groups, which provide services to families and children designed to overcome family difficulties ranging from alcohol abuse to parent-child conflicts. Some pubic welfare departments are affiliated with FSAA.

Council on Social Work Education

The Council on Social Work Education is primarily concerned with the education of social workers but, because so many social workers are involved in public welfare, CSWE has to pay special attention, too, to the relationships between educational institutions and public welfare programs.

CSWE is the accrediting body for undergraduate and graduate social work education throughout the United States and Canada. It frequently evaluates the validity and relevance of social work education curricula with regard to any given program's degree of emphasis on the public social services.

National Conference on Social Welfare

The National Conference on Social Welfare is one of the oldest of the national social welfare agencies. It originally came into existence primarily to organize and conduct an annual forum on social welfare issues. For much of its history, NCSW was the only social welfare forum and it provided a neutral sponsorship for its own programs as well as for the national meetings of a variety of other public, private, and religious organizations concerned with social welfare.

White House Conference on Children and Youth

Each decade since 1909 the Presidents of the United States have sponsored White House Conferences on Children and Youth. These conferences have always been important influences on public welfare.

In fact, they predate the federal public welfare system. The Social

Security Act and its various components resulted, in part, from recommendations made at White House Conferences in the first third of the twentieth century.

These conferences bring together providers of services to children and youth, some children and youth themselves, parents, public officials, and others from throughout the United States to identify and describe the current status of children and youth in the United States, to define the needs for new legislation and new services, and to generally chart a plan for the following ten years of children and youth work. In 1981 the United States government chose not to sponsor a White House Conference and chose, instead, to support a series of state conferences.

White House Conference on Aging

Following upon the program for children and youth, the Presidents of the United States began a series of White House Conferences on Aging in 1961, which were highly significant in achieving legislation and programs for older adults in the United States. The Older Americans Act, which is the basis for many of the social, cultural, and nutritional services provided to older people, follows closely upon several recommendations from the White House Conferences on Aging (Vinyard, 1979). The most recent White House Conference on Aging was held in Washington in 1981.

Family Conferences

In 1980, President Jimmy Carter initiated the White House Conference on Families, an idea that seemed to originate with his Vice President, Walter F. Mondale, when Mondale was a U.S. Senator from Minnesota. The idea of the White House Conference on Families was that programs of service to children, youth, and the aging often omitted the fundamental unit in American society—the family. Therefore, it was necessary to look at the impact of social and economic programs on families themselves.

Conferences on families were held in almost all of the states prior to the White House Conference, which was, instead of a single conference, three regional meetings in Baltimore, Los Angeles, and Minneapolis. Some of the state and regional conferences led to controversy over issues that were heavily debated in 1980 and which were important influences in the presidential campaign that year, when President Carter was defeated for re-election by his Republican opponent, Ronald Reagan. Among those issues were abortion, homosexuality, prayer in the public

schools, and family planning. A coalition of groups, particularly funda-
mentalist religious groups, used the activities of the White House Conference to press for constitutional amendments banning abortion, re-
storing prayer in the schools, limiting family planning, and curtailing
the influence of child welfare programs on American families. These
groups ran counter to the positions held by a majority of social workers
who, as a group, tend to support the right of women to have abortions if
they so choose; the complete separation of church and state, which
means a ban on prayer in public schools; open and free access to family
planning information and services for everyone; and the protection of
children and adults from abuse, exploitation, and neglect.

Despite the controversy, the chairman of the conferences, a former
Congressman from Arkansas, Jim Guy Tucker, was able to help the
delegates focus on issues that were of concern to and shared by the total
range of participants in the White House Conference on Families such as
tax policies which penalized families as opposed to individuals, the need
for employment policies which were pro-family life rather than opposed
to it, the need for day care and other services to enhance family living,
and perhaps most important, the general recognition of the need for
government to consider families in every aspect of its decision-making—
something which had not always been the case in the past.

Because public welfare largely deals with families, these efforts were
of significance to all those involved in the field.

State Social Welfare Associations

Almost all states have social welfare conferences or associations
which hold annual meetings for the purposes of providing training,
sharing information among professionals, and otherwise improving social welfare in the states. These organizations usually draw upon participation from public welfare departments, mental health programs,
health departments, vocational rehabilitation, religious organizations,
voluntary social welfare agencies, and other individuals and groups
concerned about human services within the state. In most states, the
majority of the participants are employees of public welfare departments.

Over the years, many of the state associations have become modified
from organizations led by volunteers who were often board members of
local private agencies into associations of social welfare employees with
professionals holding the key leadership positions. By the 1980s, many
state social welfare associations had been led by presidents who were
public welfare employees, a phenomenon that would have been unusual in earlier decades.

Interstate Compact on the Placement of Children

One of the important voluntary associations which serves public welfare is the Interstate Compact on the Placement of Children, which involves many states. This Compact, or agreement, provides means for the states to share information on individual child welfare cases. The purpose of the compact is to protect against children becoming lost in the process of being provided foster care and residential care across state lines. It also facilitates the return of runaway children to their homes.

Many public welfare workers who deal with children make use of this Compact's services.

Social Action

Social action through professional associations is one of the more common ways in which public welfare social workers and professional associations work together. A case example follows.

Protective services workers from the public welfare department became concerned about the Mountain Gospel Mission, which suddenly housed twenty-two children under ten years of age. The children were placed with the church by their parents, who could not cope with them. But neither the parents nor the Mission, which defined itself as a church, would cooperate with the public welfare department in investigating the children's situations, insuring that their health and nutritional needs were met, or in helping them find foster or adoptive homes instead of the institutional care provided by the Mission.

Tales of mistreatment were rumored in the community. Children were seen in the nearby community with welts on their arms and some teachers complained that children came to school from the Mission with lice in their hair. One child was treated for a broken arm at a local emergency room. According to the minister who brought her to the hospital, she fell from a tree, but the child whispered to a nurse that her arm had been broken when the minister's wife had twisted it as a disciplinary measure. The Mission supported itself with contributions. Each Sunday, the twenty-two children were loaded on a rickety blue bus and taken to congregations nearby where the children sang and the Sunday collection was given, in part, to the Mission.

When child protective services workers from the local public welfare office attempted to inspect the Mission, they were turned away by the minister who directed it and who said they had no right to interfere with "God's work." When the welfare department sought an injunction against the Mission's continuing to operate an unlicensed child care facility, the department was challenged in court on the grounds that the Mission was not a group care facility for children but, instead, a church that happened to have children in residence. Legal counsel for the state's attorney did not want to challenge the church, which had many supporters in the community, because it was an election year.

Marian Jordan, a protective services worker with the welfare department who had taken the lead in handling this case, was deeply concerned about the inaction and decided to enlist the aid of her professional colleagues. She brought the matter up at the next meeting of the National Association of Social Workers chapter, which decided to pursue a media campaign about the Mission through the auspices of a local newspaper reporter who specialized in social welfare stories. They also organized a committee to investigate the Mission and decided to organize and offer the services of several other local, mental health, and child welfare agencies to protect and treat the children. In addition, they agreed to find alternative housing for all twenty-two children, in the event that the children could be taken from the Mission.

The NASW investigation proved some of the worst suspicions about the Mission. The children lived in unhealthy and unpleasant surroundings. Many did not go to school but, instead, worked endless hours cleaning the Mission. Some of the children interviewed by the agencies had serious health problems, including chronic bronchitis, untreated and infected sores on their legs and arms, and malnutrition, from which a third of the children suffered. The results of the NASW investigation, which was completed in cooperation with the school some of the children attended and under the auspices of the local health department, were publicized in the newspaper series. Within one month, all the children were placed in licensed children's homes, foster families, or returned to their parents. The minister of the Mission left the state.

Conclusion

Professional associations have always been a part of the practice of social work, including the practice of social work in public welfare. Professional associations have exercised significant influence over public welfare programs and continue to play a major role in influencing welfare policy. Social workers who are employed in public welfare may find professional associations quite helpful in pursuing public welfare objectives, in providing training opportunities for public welfare staff and their colleagues in other agencies, and in helping them advance their careers both through the contacts they make in professional organizations and through the skills they learn by participating in associations.

CHAPTER 16

Dealing with Government Agencies

PUBLIC WELFARE is a part of government, a fact that is occasionally misunderstood or ignored by employees of welfare departments. As a part of government, public welfare is both limited in the scope of its activities and enhanced in its authority to affect individuals and communities. Some of the ways in which social workers in public welfare relate to other parts of government are the subject of this chapter.

The Nature of Democratic Governments

Although there may be some exceptions, social work functions best in societies that are democratically governed. While the forms of democratic governments differ dramatically from nation to nation, there are some commonalities and shared characteristics which pervade all democracies. The most important is the sovereignty or ultimate power of the people. In essence, democracy means that the people (the Greek term for people is *demos*) have the final word on what will and will not happen in their nation. That is different, of course, from a monarchy, in which the ultimate power resides in a king, queen, or other sovereign; a theocracy, in which religion or the religious authority of priests governs; an oligarchy, in which a small number of important people ultimately hold power; or a dictatorship, in which a single individual controls the government. In a democracy, all decisions ultimately rest with the people who have the power to change the individuals who govern, modify the laws or constitution under which the nation is controlled, and, in essence, determine through elected legislative and executive branch officials the kind of nation they will have.

The public welfare social worker in a democracy has a sobering and noble charge—carrying out the will of the people in the operation of programs for the disadvantaged. The public welfare social worker cannot modify the programs for which he or she is responsible in violation of the will of the people without violating the law. In their daily activities social workers in public welfare may tend to forget that they are agents of their democratic governments, which ought to be a source of satisfaction and pride.

Democratic governments also typically maintain a separation of power and authority between their three main branches: the executive, the legislative, and the judicial. In simple terms, the legislative branch makes the laws, the executive branch carries them out, and the judicial branch settles disputes between citizens and interprets the meaning of statutes and decides when people have violated the laws. Of course, the separation is not so neat or clear. For example, many of the laws passed by legislative bodies are proposed by the executive branch. Many decisions about what laws mean are made by executive branch bodies and, if they are not challenged in the courts, they have the effect of law. But that classical separation of functions roughly exists in democratic nations and provides balances of power and checks against usurpation of authority which prevent democracies from becoming other forms of government.

Public welfare agencies are part of the executive branch of government, just as all service agencies tend to be. Precisely how the agency fits into the executive branch differs from state to state. In some, the department is under the direction of the chief executive, or governor, and is governed by an appointee who reports directly to the governor. In other states, the state welfare department is run by a board of directors or commissioners who are appointed for long terms by governors. The department's chief executive is responsible to the welfare board, which hires the chief executive, sets agency policies, and negotiates the agency's budget with the legislature.

In still other states, the state department of public welfare makes general policy and supervises programs in the state but the actual delivery of services occurs on the county or city level, under the control of a mayor or a group of county commissioners, or an appointed county public welfare board. The governmental organizational patterns may differ, but public welfare is always an executive branch activity.

Public welfare departments and their employees must connect with other agencies of government in order to carry out their responsibilities to the citizens. The following section describes organizations with which public welfare must establish relationships and some of the ways in which such tasks are accomplished.

RELATIONS WITH LEGISLATIVE BODIES

In most states, the legislature has a high degree of influence over the welfare department and its programs. It is the legislature that determines the level and content of most welfare budgets, passes legislation affecting the authority and responsibility of the agency, and in some states determines the levels of cash assistance grants, the scope of the medical care program, the size of the agency's staff, and the salaries paid to public welfare employees.

Many of these decisions are based upon recommendations by the governor, the department itself, or a combination of proposals by the governor and the department. Some proposals, particularly those dealing with finances, are based upon recommendations made by the state budget agency, which is discussed later in this chapter (Dear and Patti, 1981).

It behooves workers at the middle and upper levels of public welfare agency administration to know a good deal about the operations of their state legislature. State legislative bodies, although they differ in size and activity from state to state, have some common characteristics. The following are some of those characteristics which can make a difference to public welfare departments.

1. The elected legislative leadership has immense authority over all legislative decisions. They appoint committee heads, often preside over the committees which determine what bills will and will not be acted upon, apply the often complex procedural rules to legislative decisions—which often are more important than the sentiments of the members to the final actions on bills—and, in some cases, are the official representatives of the governor in the legislature.

2. Most legislative decisions are made by committees. The total body merely confirms or rejects committee actions.

3. Most legislatures hold the bulk of their decisions for the final days or hours of the legislative session. In many states, more bills are passed on the last day of the session than during the entire session that preceded that day. Carefully monitoring those final "logjam" sessions is a major task for many state welfare departments.

4. Members of legislatures want to represent their constituents, which often means intervening on their behalf with welfare agencies. Therefore, most welfare agencies receive a constant stream of legislative inquiries on behalf of would-be clients and employees. Representing the concern of one's constituents is perceived as a major factor in whether or not a legislator is re-elected.

These characteristics imply a special set of responses to legislators by welfare agencies. Obviously, welfare departments must work to earn good relationships with and the confidence of the legislative leadership such as the senate president, speaker of the house, and the committee heads they appoint, particularly those who deal with finances and subject matter areas affecting welfare programs. But even the rank and file or minority party members of the legislature require cultivation by the department staff, especially in response to their inquiries on behalf of clients or applicants for employment. This need is often misunderstood by public welfare social workers who assume that inquiries are, in fact, efforts to apply improper political pressure on the agency so that ineligible applicants will receive assistance or unqualified people will be employed. Under most circumstances, however, these are not usually the intentions of the legislator or the effect of their inquiries. Instead, they are primarily interested in demonstrating to their constituents that they are well represented by someone who will be certain that the rules are being fairly applied. And the legislator, too, will want to be assured that the constituent was fairly considered for aid or employment. Only rarely does a legislator want the rules broken or even bent on behalf of a constituent. Those who do often lose that next election because they fail to understand their proper roles in government. In almost all cases a rapid, documented, reasonable response that the legislator can share with the constituent will satisfy the inquiry.

For example, Senator Parsons of the State Legislature called the county public welfare office and asked someone to find a job for his constituent, Martha Winston. The Senator said it was important that something be done to help her because she was unable to find a job anywhere. Mr. Sears, the County Director, called Ms. Winston and asked her to come visit with him. He interviewed her and told her about employment with public welfare. He provided her with the forms necessary to apply for a position under civil service, which she did. Before her name came up on the register, however, she had found a position as a clerical assistant with a local construction firm. Mr. Sears reported back to Senator Parsons what he had done and what had happened to Ms. Winston. The Senator was pleased and thanked Mr. Sears for his help.

For a time in the 1960s social work and other professions proposed the importation to the United States of the *ombudsman* role, a Scandinavian government position. The ombudsman is one who represents ordinary citizens with the bureaucracy, independently intervening on their behalf to insure their fair treatment and the appropriate application of the law to their cases. Some governmental units adopted the position and a few towns and large organizations still have ombudsmen. But in most cases, the use of ombudsmen failed, not because the idea is unsound, but because each United States citizen already had one or more advocates in the persons of state legislators or members of Congress. A legislative inquiry is nothing more than an example of an elected representative playing the role of ombudsman.

Social workers in public welfare are often called upon to testify before legislative committees on their work when those committees are studying legislation affecting public welfare departments (Kleinkauf, 1981). Appearing before legislative committees is often one of the most important activities a social worker can carry out, particularly in terms of the activity's impact on clients. Effective testimony might lead to an increase in public assistance grants for low income families, better arrangements for the adoption of children, or an increase in staff for achieving other public welfare objectives. Testifying before committees requires careful preparation on the part of the social worker who appears. All of the information requested by the committee should be collected and presented to the members in written form, with enough copies for everyone including the committee staff. In addition, related information, even if not specifically requested, ought to be collected and brought to the meeting in case it is needed. Some who testify rehearse their appearances by role-playing with their colleagues, who act as if they are legislators and who interrogate the staff member. In some situations, it is appropriate and desirable to bring some expert colleagues along for the appearance. Good judgment is critical, however. Bringing six staff experts to a committee of five people may prove overwhelming and counterproductive. The committee's first question might be who is watching the operations of the department when everyone employed in it seems to be at the committee meeting. In most cases, the committee will ask for a brief introductory statement, which will be followed by questions and comments by committee members. Experienced witnesses suggest four rules for appearances before legislative committees:

1. Be well prepared and know your subject.
2. Do not evade questions you cannot answer. If you do not know the answer, say that you don't but that you will send it to the committee immediately after the information is gathered.
3. Avoid sarcasm and hostility, even when the questioner seems ignorant or hostile. Treating one committee member unkindly is viewed as an attack on all the members.
4. Do not be defensive. Explain your program and the reasons your agency does what it does. If there is disagreement, acknowledge it but do not attempt to dispel it at the committee hearing.

Most appearances before legislative groups are pleasant experiences for witnesses. Social workers who are attentive to human motivation ought to be able to understand why and how legislators operate in their

professional capacities and can often help them discharge their responsibilities more effectively. If one remembers that the legislator—like the
social worker—wants to do well in a job that is related to, although
different from the public welfare employee's, there should be few conflicts. And one should always remember that the legislature is the body
most closely connected with and most representative of the public. As
such, it is the most democratic of the branches of a democratic government.

A Case Example

Programs of public welfare change in unplanned ways and the
routes by which innovations are developed vary from state to state and
circumstance to circumstance. Quite frequently there seems to be little
or no relationship between an action and the way that action came
about. The following case example of an action on behalf of child caring
institutions by the executive and legislative branches is a case in point.

During the first legislative session of the new governor's administration, the vice
chairman of the State House of Representatives Finance Committee had been both
influential and helpful. Representative Calvin Quinn had defended the governor's
proposals with his colleagues and had been the major force in passage of the Governor's budget. Toward the end of the legislative session, Representative Quinn called
upon an assistant to the Governor and said that he had a request of his own. He
served on the Board of a Roman Catholic Church-funded home for children, which
was populated almost exclusively by wards of the welfare department. But the
welfare department paid only $400 per month per child, which was dramatically less
than the cost of providing the care. The Church needed more money from the state or
it would have to cease providing child care services. No longer was the church able
to absorb a deficit and it was nearly impossible to raise funds from private contribu-
tors and from church collections for a service that the state ostensibly provided.
What would it take, Representative Quinn asked, to obtain enough money for his
church's child care facility to be fully paid for the care it provided? The governor's
assistant, in consultation with the human services director, developed some information for Representative Quinn and told him that, first, it would be impossible for the
department to treat one child care facility any better or any worse than all the others.
Therefore, there was a need for sufficient money to pay the actual cost of care in all
of the state's fifty-seven institutions. Second, that cost would be approximately $2.2
million per year in additional appropriations to the welfare program. Representative
Quinn said that sounded both reasonable and possible. He used his influence in the
Finance Committee to transfer $2.2 million from a special highway program to the
child care line time of the welfare budget.

As the example above demonstrates, decisions are often made on the basis of special concerns of a single individual or group of individuals. The budget priorities established by the welfare agency, the governor's own original program for the state, and many other interests and plans were superseded by the special debt the governor owed the representative and by the concern brought forcefully to his attention by an organization with which he was closely affiliated.

JUDICIAL RELATIONS

Social workers at every level of public welfare work frequently with the judicial branch—the court system. Whether the worker's role is locating and requiring payment from deserting parents whose children receive assistance; making recommendations on the termination of parental rights when children are abused or neglected; conducting adoption studies; providing probation and parole services for youngsters in conflict with the law; or investigating fraud and abuse by clients or vendors; contacts with the courts are frequent (Neely, 1981).

Public welfare social workers need to know the roles of the various officers of the courts—judges, prosecuting attorneys, public defenders, bailiffs, and clerks. They must also understand the functions of all the courts in a court system. These vary from state to state but usually include some form of small claims, justice of the peace, or magistrate court; courts of original jurisdiction, which hear cases and render verdicts; and appellate courts, to which verdicts of courts of original jurisdiction may be appealed for modification or reversal.

Subpoenas are often issued to public welfare social workers which require them to turn records over to a court, appear at a hearing, or otherwise comply with judicial demands. Workers are often intimidated by such commands to appear or comply, in part because there are penalties, including imprisonment, for failure to carry out the specific demands. But precisely how one should respond is not typically known to people with no legal training. Therefore, the public welfare social worker's proper response to a court document is to refer it to the department's legal staff which will know how and to whom the response should be made. Workers in local offices usually reach legal counsel through their supervisors, rather than directly. Social workers who are frequently involved in judicial matters often discover that the judicial proceedings are handled on all sides by attorneys. Only rarely do the social workers come into the process directly and personally.

Public welfare employees also come into contact with the state court systems in some of the administrative activities in which they are involved. Courts are often required to promulgate rules and regulations for probation and parole, juvenile detention standards, and child welfare proceedings. For these purposes public welfare staff often serve as consultants to court systems.

RELATIONS WITH REGULATORY BODIES

Some political scientists describe a fourth branch of government which is neither executive, legislative, or judicial but which is, instead, all of these. These are the independent regulatory bodies, which are established by law and governed by long-term appointees. At the federal level, these bodies include the Federal Communications Commission, the Interstate Commerce Commission, and many others. These organizations make rules, as legislatures do, enforce them, as the executive branch does, and decide appeals of their rules by those affected by them, as courts do.

In state government, public welfare social workers relate to a number of independent agencies. Some welfare departments are, in some ways, independent regulatory agencies themselves. The most common of the regulatory bodies which affect public welfare are the agencies which regulate public utilities, civil service commissions, and independent bodies which investigate and arbitrate human rights complaints.

Contacts with utility regulatory bodies often center upon the rules for terminating utility services to low income people. In colder climates terminating electric or natural gas service may lead to illness or death for low income people who cannot pay their bills. Public welfare emergency assistance programs often enable those facing cut-offs to pay their bills and have their service restored. Many regulatory agencies now require that service be continued during the coldest months or during times when temperatures fall below freezing. In addition, departments of welfare have collaborated in recent years on energy assistance programs sponsored by the federal and state governments.

In some states and localities, there are regulatory bodies which license nursing homes and nursing home operators; set the licensing standards and enforce those standards for pharmacists, physicians, and other health practitioners; and may carry out other activities that relate directly or indirectly to public welfare. In some states, hospital rates are set by regulatory bodies.

Public welfare employee relations with regulatory bodies include commenting on proposed rules and regulations, testifying at hearings, and consulting with staff on cases that are shared by welfare departments and regulatory bodies. And employees often use civil service and human rights agencies for help in resolving their own problems as employees.

The members of regulatory bodies are usually appointed by governors for long terms so they are immune from political influence.

RELATIONSHIPS WITHIN THE EXECUTIVE BRANCH

Perhaps the most vital relationships of the public welfare agency are those that it establishes within the executive branch, of which it is a part. The department's credibility with comparable agencies in other human services fields (or with other units in the umbrella agency, when public welfare is part of that kind of structure) will have a dramatic effect on the fortunes of welfare clients and programs.

Most critical of all are the relationships the agency establishes and maintains with the state's governor or umbrella agency head. The confidence that the agency's top supervisor feels in the ability of public welfare to achieve its objectives, manage its resources, and deal sensitively with the public, will have an impact on everything from the agency budget to the allocation of office space for the agency's headquarters.

In addition to positive relations with the top executives of the state government, public welfare agencies also must work to establish positive contacts with the governmental leadership on the town, city, and county levels, as well. Frequent and courteous contacts between local agency heads and these local elected officials are crucial to the smooth operations of welfare offices, whether the programs are operated from the state or local levels. Invitations for local officials to meet with and speak to meetings of local staff, following up on inquiries by local officials, and collaboration on cases and local community projects are all important in the operations of local welfare units. There are times, particularly in rural communities, when the public welfare program is the only social welfare agency in town. As such, it is often required to fill the gap left by the lack of a social welfare planning council, a community mental health center, or a rehabilitation agency. Local officials will often expect public welfare employees to address or treat all the social services problems the community's citizens encounter. It is generally advisable for the agency to attempt to fill those needs. This may at times mean securing the services of other agencies for the community and its citizens through collaboration and referral.

Centralized Client Services Units

Some state public welfare programs enhance their collaborative activities with other branches and agencies of government by operating centralized client services units in their state offices. These units, often augmented by toll-free incoming telephone lines, deal with client inquiries, investigate and respond to questions from chief executives and legislators, and communicate directly with local offices to determine the status of cases about which inquiries have been initiated. They also draft responses to clients on behalf of the agency and respond to telephone calls from clients and others. These centralized units, which are frequently staffed and managed by social workers, function in some ways as quality control workers do. That is, they assure themselves that the case is being properly handled, in line with established agency policies and procedures. They also work to insure that there is a rapid and clear response to the inquiry. Units of this sort are often effective in maintaining credibility with other agencies of state government and with clients.

Public Welfare and the Federal Government

More than half of all the funding for public welfare comes from the United States government, rather than from state and local sources. The programs are defined by the United States Congress and administered by agencies of the executive branch of the federal government. For those reasons, contacts between the public welfare programs and officials of the federal government are frequent and intense.

Contacts between state agencies and members of the United States Congress—both representatives and senators—are similar to those between the agencies and state legislators. Members of Congress receive inquiries from constituents which require responses from local or state welfare offices. Congresspersons who have a high frequency of constituent inquiries often have staff members who specialize in casework with the public welfare agency and other units of the state and federal governments, such as the Social Security Administration and the Veterans' Administration. Contacts between those staff members and public welfare staff members are frequent.

Welfare departments also maintain contact with congressional offices on federal policies and legislation. It is not unusual for welfare agencies to be asked to react to pending federal legislation. At other times, welfare officials propose legislation to their congressional delegations or alert them to pending federal legislation that could affect public welfare operations in the state. It is not unusual for local and state welfare officials to be invited to testify before committees of the United States Congress. When they are called upon, the same suggestions apply to federal inquiries as were offered earlier in this chapter for appearances before state legislative committees.

Most of the state or local agency's relationships with the federal government, however, are with their counterparts in the executive branch. Federal agencies such as the Department of Health and Human Services and the Department of Agriculture, which supervises the food stamp program, have direct control of and supervisory authority over public welfare programs.

The Department of Health and Human Services maintains close contacts through its central and regional offices with state program specialists in public assistance, emergency assistance, social services, child support enforcement, quality control, medical services payments, fraud and abuse investigations, and cost allocations. In other words, the Department is involved directly with the state and local operations of public welfare for any programs in which it has financial participation. Because it participates in financing almost all of the services of public welfare, it is involved in every aspect of the program. When HHS is not involved, Agriculture is and, therefore, it has direct connections with the staffs of public welfare agencies in the states.

Conclusion

By its nature, public welfare is part of government. Because of the range of services it performs for such a large and diverse population, it crosses paths with many other agencies and branches of government. Effectively carrying out its obligations requires careful work with other agencies in the executive branch, with the legislative branch of government, with the judiciary, and with regulatory bodies.

High quality professional social work in public welfare requires both knowledge of, and skill in, dealing with government in the broadest definition of the term.

CHAPTER 17

Social Work's Relations with Other Professions in Public Welfare

SOCIAL WORK, although it is the predominant profession in public welfare, is only one of many professions and occupations needed to deliver the services offered by modern public welfare departments. Welfare agencies and the social workers who staff them rely upon those other professions and occupations in working to achieve the objectives of public welfare. This chapter discusses the roles played by employees other than social workers in the development and delivery of services and suggests ways in which social work in public welfare may be improved.

Social Workers with Preparation in Other Fields

Chapter 2 discusses the phenomenon of many—often most—of the people who carry the title "social worker" in public welfare who have studied in baccalaureate or graduate programs for degrees other than the Bachelor or Master of Social Work. Many of the long-tenured, key employees of public welfare agencies have degrees in fields as varied as business administration, physical education, and literature, as well as the more closely related fields of sociology, psychology, education, and counseling. Despite the growth of baccalaureate programs in social work, new public welfare workers are hired every day who have never formally studied social work. That contradiction results from a number of factors—many young people do not make career choices until after they have completed their undergraduate work; civil service systems do not always discriminate in favor of professionally prepared social workers because some tests are biased towards people who have knowledge of mathematics and government rather than social work; some political influence continues to be applied for the hiring of those who have supported key elected officials, often to the disadvantage of those who have devoted their efforts to learning social work; even though social work education opportunities have increased, they have not increased rapidly enough to prepare enough people who are willing and able to fill all the job openings in public welfare, wherever they are available.

Therefore, public welfare departments attempt to orient their employees to social work values and methods through programs of in-service training, using their prior preparation as a base upon which to build social work skills. Methods such as sending employees to seminars and short courses, encouraging participation in continuing education credit courses, in-service seminars on social work subjects, and supervision of non-social workers by social workers are examples of the ways in which agencies attempt to build a social work orientation into the performances of increasing numbers of employees. Training efforts are discussed in Chapter 12.

As Chapter 2 suggests, the profession of social work now makes increased opportunities available for those not formally educated in the field to become a part of it. Employees of social agencies may now become members of the National Association of Social Workers. An expanded number of social work journals and meetings—on subjects as varied as social work in rural areas and evangelical social work—are now available to those who want professional orientation and stimulation, and more social work education programs are offering educational opportunities to those who want them.

Although the public welfare field includes employees with a wide range of educational backgrounds, the fundamental orientation has traditionally been toward social work and that orientation is readily translated to the backgrounds of all agency staff members.

Social Workers and Health Professionals

With the increasing emphasis in public welfare on providing health services to low income people—medical services are typically the largest single item in most welfare budgets—health professionals have come to play increasingly important roles in public welfare.

Public welfare agencies employ physicians, nurses, pharmacists, dentists, mental health specialists, and other health care providers who provide a number of services which are essential to the missions of public welfare agencies. Few are direct providers of services to clients. Instead they administer services and assist the agency in the operation of its programs (Bracht, 1978; Brown, 1978; Feder and Holahan, 1979).

Social workers in public welfare often find it necessary to collaborate closely with health care providers in carrying out agency programs. In most of the functions performed by health providers, social workers may play supportive roles. There should be little conflict between the two groups because each has a contribution to make in enhancing the health of clients. Health specialists know how to diagnose, evaluate medically, and communicate with other professionals in their fields. Social workers, on the other hand, are experts in mobilizing resources to pay for health care, are competent in understanding and dealing with the social and emotional components of illness, and can assist clients in adjusting to the results of health problems.

Attorneys

Because so much of the practice of social work in public welfare is based upon legal mandates such as statutes and court orders, attorneys have come to play a significant role in all public welfare agencies. With the advent in the 1960s of public interest law groups, increasingly large numbers of clients or potential clients have filed individual and class action suits against public welfare agencies, demanding that they do something they are not doing or cease doing something that they are.

In some agencies, full-time attorneys are employed. In others, legal services are provided by a centralized group such as an attorney general's office. In others, legal assistance is obtained on the basis of need through retainers and contracts with privately practicing lawyers.

Legal issues pervade every element of the agency's program including public assistance, child welfare services, medical services, investigations, personnel administration, and child support enforcement. Therefore legal counsel is essential. On the other hand, some agencies make the error of allowing the legal staff to make decisions that are more properly the prerogative of the agency administration. Legal advice should never supplant well-informed professional judgements about public welfare services. In essence, an attorney's skills are best used to inform the agency administration of the consequences that might arise from decisions and, if those decisions could lead to litigation, what the courts might do in response to them. Prudent administrators listen to their lawyers and do not take actions that they are told would never be permitted by the courts, if tested, or that are described as clearly illegal.

Good legal advice is worth having and using. But it is only part of the information administrators should use in making decisions for their agencies.

Public welfare workers also help clients use the services of attorneys, often to contest the agency's own actions or to assist clients in appealing adverse decisions (Bernstein, 1980).

Law Enforcement

Public welfare investigative activities, designed to reduce or eliminate fraud and abuse, are described in an earlier section of this text. But the scope of relationships between social workers and law enforcement officials is broader than investigative work. The assistance of state and local police forces, prosecuting attorneys, and others is needed in locating and bringing to justice parents who do not pay for the support of their children; in child abuse and neglect cases, when the assistance of police may be needed in order to make an investigation; in dealing with hostile, perhaps dangerous clients who blame the agency for decisions that affect them adversely; in providing security for offices; and in collaborating in juvenile corrections programs, when those are within the purview of the agency (Parkinson, 1980).

Although social workers and law enforcement officers seem to some as if they were antithetical to one another, their paths cross frequently in many situations. Just as social workers in public welfare often need the assistance of law enforcement specialists for some of the functions suggested above, the police officer often needs the assistance of the social worker in handling a domestic violence case, in placing a child who is suddenly homeless because a crime has been committed by or against the parents, and in dealing with juvenile delinquents. It is often useful for these two groups of professionals to meet and agree on the ways in which they will work together before crises occur. Taking some time to learn about each other's orientations, professional training, and responsibilities can also avert conflict when cooperation is needed. Although they serve people in rather different ways, both public welfare social workers and law enforcement officers are public servants who can help each other serve the public best.

Accountants and Business and Public Administrators

The growth of public welfare in scope and complexity has required increasing numbers of staff to be skilled in the management of organizations, rather than experts in the design and delivery of human services themselves. Therefore, many public welfare agencies have augmented their administrative staff with people educated as accountants and administrators, both business administrators and public administrators.

Social workers in public welfare view these specialists as enablers of the social work process—as people who enhance the capacity of the agency to deliver its primary services of economic and social assistance.

Educators

Educators constitute another profession within the public welfare field. Teachers, early childhood educators, and adult educators all play roles in helping public welfare departments carry out their missions.

Adult educators are often involved in developing and conducting new programs for public welfare staff. Early childhood educators often assist in setting standards for and supervising day care and early child development programs. In addition, teachers may assist with youth services programs.

Besides these specific roles of educators in public welfare agencies, there are large numbers of persons who are professionally prepared as educators who subsequently take employment in public welfare departments in roles that are essentially those of social workers.

Computer Scientists and Systems Analysts

It is unlikely that welfare departments could have become the complex and massive organizations they are had the technology of automatic data processing not been developed in the second half of the twentieth century. The record keeping, check writing, and accounting necessary for managing organizations that serve millions of clients, pay millions of medical bills each month, audit billions of invoices every year, and gather as well as report information on their activities, would require massive populations of clerks were it not for the computers and the computer specialists who use them (Lohmann and Wolvovsky, 1979).

Faced with a task such as fairly, rapidly, and honestly distributing several billion dollars to the several million United States citizens who needed assistance in paying their utility bills—as public welfare departments were in the early 1980s—most departments would have required a year of effort and a staff of several hundred were it not for computers. With computer programs, however, the task was relatively simple and was accomplished in only a month or two, in most cases, with the assistance of a few temporary employees.

Virtually all public welfare departments now rely extensively on computer programs and systems analysts and designers to assist in accomplishing most of their tasks—managing funds, maintaining personnel records, collecting data on clients and client services, paying invoices, monitoring for fraud and abuse, and writing checks. Because of the pervasive use of computers in public welfare, virtually every social worker interacts in some way with the computer system and the computer science staff in the course of carrying out his or her responsibilities.

Improving Social Work's Performance in Public Welfare

Despite the centrality of social work in public welfare, it is only one of several professions in the field. Modern welfare departments cannot rely on professional social workers alone to carry on their functions and reach their objectives. The problems addressed, the services offered, and the magnitude of the organizations are all too great for any one profession to monopolize the staffing and management of public welfare. Public welfare departments need professional social workers, but professional social workers need other professionals in public welfare as well.

In many ways, however, social work professionals could enhance their usefulness to public welfare departments. Modifications of social work performance could be improved by some changes in the education of social workers, by changes in the public welfare objectives of the profession, and by some changes in the attitudes of social workers toward their relationships with other professionals in public welfare.

Social workers who enter public welfare positions would benefit from more education specifically directed toward assisting them in filling such positions. Field instruction placements in public welfare agencies are the most reliable means for assuring some awareness of the realities of public welfare social work practice for potential employees. However, some enhancement of classroom courses may also assist in orienting students for more effective work in public welfare agencies.

For example, it often appears that the major detriment to effective social work practice in public welfare is the blocking of social work-oriented decision making by professionals in other fields whose specialized knowledge goes unchallenged, often because the social workers are ignorant of the realities of those other disciplines. Time and again social workers who have the authority to make decisions about public welfare programs defer to others such as accountants because they are afraid to overrule the judgments made by those fiscal experts. On too many occasions, social workers in key administrative positions develop proposals for activities and subsequently consult with staff comptrollers or finance directors to determine whether or not the activities are financially feasible. If the fiscal specialist says "no," the project is dropped. Obviously programs cannot be operated if there are insufficient funds. And there is little reason to doubt that the fiscal specialist has told the truth. However, such means of making decisions have the effect of placing the fiscal officer in the key administrative role, rather than the social worker whose job may be to render the ultimate decisions. For reasons of this sort, many agencies which are ostensibly directed by professional social workers are really run by accountants.

The ascendancy of accountants can be halted through proper education of social workers. For example, if social workers preparing for leadership positions in public welfare were to take even one course in accounting principles, most could learn how to read a financial statement and how to ask fiscal experts the correct questions necessary for making decisions. That is, the question, "Can the agency afford this activity?" is not the one to ask. It will elicit a "yes" or a "no" when the desired response is a statement of options, consequences, and choices. A more useful question to a fiscal officer would be, "If we raise the levels of cash assistance grants for families without wage earners by ten percent, how many additional dollars would we need? Where might we obtain those additional dollars through program reductions in other areas, program modifications, and supplemental appropriations? How many people would be affected by each of these choices? What are the restrictions on transferring money among these programs?" A social worker skillful in analyzing financial reports could assist in identifying the options.

With regard to the social work profession's agenda for public welfare, some clarifications and modifications might be in order. Traditionally the profession, represented by the National Association of Social Workers, has pressed for liberalization of benefits to clients, better treatment of social workers in public welfare, and other issues discussed in Chapter 2. The profession may be better able to help the large number of its members who are public welfare employees by expanding its role in attempting to change civil service requirements so more professional social workers, as opposed to people who are not specifically educated in the field, may be employed. The profession may also want to further develop its ability to influence the political forces which ultimately determine the fate of public welfare programs, a subject that is more thoroughly discussed in Chapter 16.

Social workers in public welfare may also enhance their effectiveness by participating in the larger social welfare community of which they are a part. Participation in other social welfare organizations such as local community welfare planning councils or councils of agency executives can help build natural coalitions supportive of public welfare in the larger social welfare community. Involvement in community activities can also extend the influence of public welfare to other related social work programs such as mental health, health services, and youth-serving programs, all of which directly affect the destinies of many public welfare clients. Assuming leadership roles in community affairs is an expectation for key social workers in public welfare agencies.

Conclusion

Public welfare employs professionals from a number of disciplines in addition to social workers. These include health care professionals, accountants, attorneys, educators, administrators, computer scientists, and others. Effective social work practice in public welfare agencies requires an understanding of these correlated and supportive professions. Social workers must develop skill in using the contributions of other professions by studying about their work, consulting with them on mutual concerns, and by helping them understand the roles and contributions of social workers. Social workers in administrative positions need skill in using the talents of their co-professionals without allowing non-social workers to make social work decisions for the agency.

CHAPTER 18

International Public Welfare

PUBLIC WELFARE PROGRAMS are an international phenomenon. The programs differ from nation to nation and culture to culture but all have the major purpose of helping people avoid need or deal with poverty and other forms of disadvantage through the provision of economic and social services. The variations in welfare programs arise from differences among nations in historical patterns of helping, religious traditions and affiliations, economic organizations, economic strengths, tax structures, and political systems, among others.

In general, the more industrial and advanced economically the nation, the broader the range of its social welfare programs. Many European nations address virtually every social or economic problem that an individual or family might face with some program or service. In the United States, however, some individuals are not eligible for any public welfare programs. Unemployed women who are too young to receive Social Security or too old to receive it to support their surviving children may be without any public help at all. In many states, families with wage earners, even when those wage earners are unemployed, are unable to receive public help through the Aid to Families with Dependent Children program.

The public welfare system in the United States is far from universal. Some of its features are substantially different than those one finds in the rest of the world. Many programs which are considered part of the public welfare system in other nations are not part of the public welfare program described in this text because, typically, they are located in distinct agencies of state and local government. These programs include workers' compensation, health insurance, and unemployment compensation.

In addition to government-sponsored programs of public welfare, in some countries industry is the major provider of social and economic assistance. In others, foundations and religious organizations are the sources of the basic public welfare programs. Some nations, including the United States, offer public help to disadvantaged individuals in other nations through volunteer organizations such as the Peace Corps.

Universality of Services

The kinds of public welfare services offered in North America and in Europe are generally offered, in one form or another, in every nation of the world. The distinction between nations is not what they provide but the extent to which they are able to provide it. Whereas most working parents may be able to obtain free or low cost day care services for their children in some of the Scandinavian and other Western European nations, only a fraction of the children who might need day care may be served in a developing African nation such as Tanzania. Although residential facilities for children exist everywhere in the world, the extent of these services varies significantly from the more developed and wealthier nations to the poorer countries of the world. In much of Latin America and Africa, youngsters roam the streets in small and large groups and, in some cases, may have no permanent homes. Many of the developmentally disabled, mentally ill, and abused and neglected children and adults in the developing nations must survive on their own, without any special governmental help. Social workers everywhere find that they must help the children they can reach as best they can within the resources—both people and money—available to them. Around the world, public welfare services function on a continuum. There are varying degrees of coverage and levels of assistance from region to region and from nation to nation.

In addition, national objectives are reflected in public welfare programs. Some nations give special help to public employees. Others provide less assistance to farmers than to nonfarmers. Still others make extra grants for married couples, for large families, and for caring for the elderly and disabled in one's home.

The Range of Services Throughout the World

The U.S. Social Security Administration reported in 1979 in *Social Security Programs Throughout the World* on public aid programs in 134 nations. They found that the most common form of assistance is worker's compensation, which is available in all of the nations surveyed. The least common form of assistance is unemployment compensation. In the United States both unemployment compensation and worker compensation are usually provided by agencies separated from those which provide public welfare, with some exceptions (see Appendix 2). Of course, these programs serve only the employed workers in formal, industrial workplaces. In much of the world underemployment is common. Even among the employed, sporadic self-employment is so common that very few of the total population are included in these forms of public help. Many people only engage in subsistence farming and occasional or part-time work, which ordinarily do not make them eligible for services.

Family Allowance Programs

The United States is unusual in providing Aid to Families with Dependent Children. In most other nations that provide cash assistance to families, the family allowance is the primary mechanism used. There are several principles under which such programs operate, although they vary from nation to nation. Usually, the family allowance is provided to all residents of the nation, rather than just to the needy. Wealthier families actually return the assistance in their tax payments, but disadvantaged citizens keep the money and use it to care for their children.

Special additions and allowances also differ from nation to nation. In some countries, grants for education, special grants for birth services, and assistance in providing maternal and child health services are provided. In a few cases, special grants are made to allow for the care of adult dependents, such as aged parents, and families. In some nations, family allowances are provided for special services in urban areas, but not in the rural communities.

The sixty-seven nations that provide family allowances are scattered throughout the world but are most heavily concentrated in Europe and the industrialized nations of the rest of the world. They are a phenomenon of economic strength, unknown in the nations with the lowest per capita incomes and weakest economies.

For example, Poland provides a family allowance for most families with children under sixteen years of age and makes special provisions, also, for older children who are students as well as for disabled family members. Canada provides a family allowance for all families with one or more children, which is indexed to inflation and which increases as the cost of living increases. Some of the provincial governments in Canada supplement the federal allowance, particularly for larger families.

Australia, New Zealand, and most Eastern and Western European nations have family allowance programs. However, such programs are virtually nonexistent in Latin America, Africa, and the Middle East, with the exception of Israel.

In Asia, family allowances vary from rather extensive programs in Japan to none at all in South Korea and Thailand. In Mexico, special funds are made available for child day care services in Mexico City, but in rural Mexico there are no such forms of assistance provided. Few of the Carribean nations have family allowance programs. In some countries, family aid is made possible through the tax system, which provides special tax incentives to families with children.

Some examples of family allowances in various nations include:

Algeria. Family allowances are paid for children under seventeen to families in which the wage-earner is employed in a field other than agriculture or to families which are living on social insurance benefits. The allowance takes the form of a 25 percent bonus for each child of the earnings or insurance benefits.

Argentina. Specific amounts are provided to families with children under fifteen (twenty-one for children who are students), for disabled family members, and for families with pensioners. The amount of the allowance varies from family to family based upon the ages of the children and the nature and status of the family's employment and earnings.

Bolivia. Families with employees in industry, commerce, mining, and government are eligible for allowances. Agricultural workers, domestic servants, the self-employed, and occasional workers are excluded. Allowances include cash grants for each child, housing allowances, money for milk for infants, and special burial allowances.

Bulgaria. Cash allowances are provided for each child to employees of industry, members of collective farms, and social insurance beneficiaries. The allowance only applies to children under sixteen. Special birth grants are provided for each additional child.

Canada. All residents with one or more children are entitled to allowances of some $20 per month per child. The amount is increased in line with the consumer price index. The allowances are supplemented by some provinces.

Chad. Those who are employed in Chad and who have one or more children receive a monthly family allowance for every child under fifteen but up to twenty-one if the child is a student or is disabled. Birth grants are available when children are born, and a prenatal allowance is made available during the time of pregnancy.

People's Republic of China. Subsidies are provided to low income families in this nation. Communes have income maintenance systems for peasants.

Czechoslovakia. Family allowances at fixed amounts per month are made available to families for each child. An additional supplement is provided for handicapped children. The allowances are received for children under fifteen and for children up to twenty-six when the child is a student or is disabled. An income test is required if there are fewer than three children in the family. The allowances are available to all people employed in the nation. A separate system is maintained for those who are employed on agricultural cooperatives.

Denmark. A regular allowance is provided for each child with a special bonus provided to single parent families, orphans, and children of old-age pensioners. The allowances are made available to all resident citizens, aliens who are working in Denmark, and recipients of pensions. The allowances cover children under sixteen.

Finland. Allowances are provided to all residents with one or more children under sixteen and to aliens who have at least two years of residence. Birth grants are provided. The amount varies with the number of children in the family and the ages of the children.

France. Families with two or more children receive family allowances. Children must be under sixteen, but allowances are provided for older children when they are looking for their first jobs or studying, and for disabled children. There is a special supplement for low income families and special allowance systems for agricultural, railroad, and public utility employees.

Democratic Republic of Germany. Residents with one or more children are provided monthly allowances for children under sixteen and birth grants. Those who are self-employed receive allowances when they have four or more children, unless their incomes are low. There is a special system for miners.

Israel. Residents with one or more children under eighteen are provided cash allowances each month. Families with three or more children are given extra allowances in recognition of larger family size. A special allowance is also provided to families in which any member has served or is serving in the armed forces. Welfare recipients and immigrants are provided with extra allowances, too.

Italy. Those who are employed, social insurance beneficiaries, and some self-employed persons with children under eighteen receive family allowances. In addition, families with children who are students under twenty-six years of age are provided allowances. Families with disabled people of any age also receive allowances.

Japan. Residents with three or more children under age eighteen, including at least one child who has not completed compulsory education, receive family allowances for the third and each other child over three. Public employees participate in a special program.

Netherlands. All residents with three or more children sixteen or under receive allowances. When children are students, allowances can be received up to age twenty-seven and up to age eighteen if the child is disabled. Children who are students or who are disabled receive double the amount of other children. Public employees participate in a special system.

Norway. Allowances are paid for all resident children under sixteen each month. Sole supporters receive benefits for one child more than is actually in the family.

Poland. Employees, collective farmers, members of cooperatives, home workers, attorneys, and social insurance beneficiaries receive allowances for children under age sixteen, for any student under twenty-five, and for disabled children of any age. Wives who are unemployed receive special allowances in addition to the regular child allowance.

Portugal. Those who are employed in industry, commerce, liberal professions, as domestic servants, and as fishermen receive family allowances each month for any child under fifteen, for students up to twenty-four, and for disabled children of any age. A special allowance is provided for the birth of a child, for the care of an infant up to eight months of age, and at the time of marriage.

South Africa. Resident employees of low income who have three or more children receive monthly allowances for children up to sixteen and up to eighteen for children who are students. The system excludes Asian, Colored, and Black employees. The father must be currently employed in order to qualify for the family allowance system.

Sweden. All residents with one or more children receive quarterly allowances for each child under sixteen and for each student under nineteen years of age.

Union of Soviet Socialist Republics. All residents with four or more children receive family allowances for those who are between the ages of one and five. If the mother is unmarried, the allowances continue for children up to twelve years of age. Birth grants are given to families that have three or more children and to unmarried mothers who have one child or more. There is a special program of assistance to low income families with one or more children.

United Kingdom. Residents with one or more children receive weekly allowances. An additional amount is provided as a supplement for the first child of a single parent. The program covers children under sixteen and under nineteen when those children are students.

Zaire. Employed persons and social insurance beneficiaries with one or more children in Shaba province receive family allowances for children under sixteen, for students up to twenty-five, and for children of any age if they are disabled. An allowance is also payable for a nonworking wife who is caring for children. There is a special system for public employees throughout the nation.

Industrial Social Work

In parts of the world, public welfare is provided not be government but by industries which serve workers and their families. Assistance is based upon employment. The nations simply require industries to offer assistance to employees and their families as a condition of doing business. Examples include Colombia, which requires family allowances for children under eighteen years of age to be paid by employers with ten or more permanent employees. South Africa and Togo have similar arrangements. In some countries, special programs are provided for the families of public employees. In addition to cash assistance, services may include low cost or free housing, cultural activities such as music and art classes, and primary education as well as help with family emotional problems, mental illness, and alcoholism.

These programs for employed people, of course, benefit the working poor rather than the lowest socio-economic class peasants, family farmers, and others whose employment is sporadic and informal.

Church and Foundation Assistance

In many parts of the world the Roman Catholic Church, through Catholic Charities, provides much of the assistance to the low income population. It works hand in hand with governments to distribute food, clothing, and other forms of assistance to the disadvantaged population of the nation. At times, assistance from other nations is distributed through Catholic Charities or similar organizations.

Missionary services sponsored by religious denominations such as the Church of Jesus Christ of the Latter Day Saints (Mormons), Episcopal or Anglican, Methodist, Seventh Day Adventist, American Baptist, Southern Baptist, Presbyterian, the American Friends Service Committee (Quakers), and many smaller groups provide assistance to fill the gaps in aiding disadvantaged populations where government programs are not sufficient to the task.

In some religious missions, of course, there is a heavy focus on religious training and indoctrination while in others, fundamental social and economic assistance are the primary foci of the services. The Salvation Army and the Church Army, which is an affiliate of the Anglican Church, provide job training and assistance with clothing, housing, and food in much of the developing world.

Foundations such as the Rockefeller Foundation, the Ford Foundation, and the Konrad Adenauer Foundation of Germany also play major roles in developing housing and other forms of social welfare in third world nations. These programs supplement or provide incentives to government to expand their own social welfare programs. The economic development activities organized by some foundations are designed to build the economic strength of the nation and, thereby, improve the general welfare of the citizens.

Inter-Governmental Programs

Services for the low income populations of many nations are sponsored by more advantaged countries. The United States has had an extensive overseas assistance program for most of the twentieth century. The United States assisted in the redevelopment of Europe after World War I and again after World War II. It also has ongoing programs such as the Agency for International Development and the Peace Corps, which are designed to develop and promote services for people through economic and technical assistance. Agricultural development, educational programs, and health services are included in programs sponsored by the United States. Schools have been constructed and economic development activities undertaken by the United States through programs such as the Alliance for Progress in Latin America.

The pattern of more advantaged nations assisting the less advantaged is common throughout the world. The Scandinavian countries, for example, have been active in developing and operating health services for African and Asian nations. Israel has provided training programs and social welfare services in large parts of Africa. Canada has provided social service technical assistance throughout the world.

Conclusion

Public welfare is international and governments in every nation provide assistance to their citizens.

There is no nation without some form of public welfare, though each nation's public welfare system has its own organization and structure. The level of the services provided varies widely, based upon each country's resources, history, and culture. In some, the basic services are provided only indirectly by government, and industries are required to provide social and economic services to their employees. In some nations, foundations and religious organizations are significant providers of services to the disadvantaged population instead of or in addition to the services provided directly by governments. And in still other cases, nations provide economic and social assistance to other nations as a way of aiding the disadvantaged populations of the world.

Epilogue

As THIS BOOK is being published, some of the most sweeping changes in American public welfare since the 1930s are being made.

The presidency of Ronald Reagan, who ran as the Republican candidate in 1980 on a platform of making major changes in American government, has led to some sweeping proposals for change in all human services programs, including public welfare. Many of the proposals for change have been more dramatic than the changes themselves. At the time this book was completed, it was not certain precisely how significantly public welfare would be transformed.

Among President Reagan's actions and proposals are several modifications in the roles of the state and federal governments.

Block Grants

The President and his staff as well as Congress have created "block grants" for some functions that had previously been operated with state and federal funds. For example, social services, low income energy assistance, and some health care programs have changed from matching programs, requiring the appropriation of state funds to match federal funds, to block grants. The federal government, under the block grant approach, simply gives each state a certain amount of money to use as it sees fit for programs under which these funds are appropriated. Little detailed planning or accounting is required. Instead, states are allowed to spend the money as they choose, within some broad definitions, and only routine financial accounting is required to document that the money has been spent properly. The block grants, the format of which satisfied many state and local governments, also included reductions in federal appropriations, which led to reductions in some services in most parts of the United States when they were originally implemented. The federal government theory was that the savings in accounting, planning, reporting, and monitoring of activities would almost equal the losses in money available for services. The federal government hoped that the services could be maintained at the level of the past while the administrative costs would be reduced.

In the process of implementing some of these block grants, the numbers of both federal and state employees have been reduced so that fewer people were working in public welfare after the block grants became law than before they were passed.

President Reagan and some of his staff proposed that other programs become block grants. Congress required that programs for the aging, some children's programs, and some programs for developmentally disabled youth and adults be maintained as categorical programs with specific requirements for services, reporting, and careful monitoring, maintained in the law.

"Turn Back of Programs"

One of the key ideas of the federal administration of Ronald Reagan was to "turn back" the operation of some programs to the states. Among these programs were public welfare services that had always been federal programs. The proposal included giving the states the authority to raise certain kinds of tax revenues in order to fund these programs, for everything from the construction of roads to the operation of fundamental health services.

States and localities were divided on these issues. Many believed that human services ought to be nationally standardized so that no person would be disadvantaged in relation to any other citizen of the United States. Precisely which programs, if any, would be turned back to the states was still at issue when this book was completed. It was clear, however, that the issue of responsibility for human services programs—whether it be federal, state, or local—would remain an issue for many years to come in the United States.

The Swap

One of the key notions of the Ronald Reagan administration was that some programs originally sponsored by the federal government could be more efficiently operated by the states and, similarly, that some programs more typically state and federally administered as a partnership could be more efficiently administered as totally national programs. Out of this belief came plans for a "swap" between the state and federal governments. As originally proposed in the President's 1982 State of the Union Message, the trade would involve asking the states to take over the full operation of the Aid to Families with Dependent Children and food stamp programs while the federal government would take over the full operation of the Medicaid program. Combining Medicaid with Medicare seemed, in the minds of some, to be a means for achieving greater efficiency in these programs. The governors of most states were initially opposed to these federal proposals. In all but a handful of states (generally those with very generous Medicaid programs), the cost to the states of the swap would be much greater than when the state and federal governments jointly operated Medicaid and AFDC, and the federal government funded most of the food stamp program. Later planning, however, hinted that the federal government might be willing to provide emergency federal support for AFDC in states where severe economic disasters were occuring.

For most states, it seemed that programs of cash assistance and food stamps, as well as medical assistance, ought to be national services simply because states could neither control nor effectively limit their own poverty, illness, or other social and economic problems. These were, in the minds of most state officials, national problems that required national solutions. Some state officials felt that the federal government was attempting to pass on to the states its deficits and its needs for additional revenues.

Clearly, however, the issue of the relative responsibilities of various levels of governments for AFDC, food stamps, and Medicaid would be a topic of discussion for years. Therefore, public welfare is likely to remain a source of controversy and shifting responsibilities for the remainder of the decade.

APPENDIX 1

Public Welfare State Agencies

Alabama Department of
  Pensions and Security
64 N. Union Street
Montgomery, Alabama 36130

Alaska Department of
  Health and Social Services
Pouch H-01
Juneau, Alaska 99811

Arizona Department
  of Economic Security
1717 W. Jefferson Street
P.O. Box 6123
Phoenix, Arizona 85005

Arkansas Department
  of Human Services
Donaghey Building, Suite 1428
Little Rock, Arkansas 72201

California Health and Welfare
  Agency
915 Capitol Mall, Room 200
Sacramento, California 95814

Colorado Department
  of Social Services
1575 Sherman Street
Denver, Colorado 80203

Connecticut Department
  of Income Maintenance
110 Bartholomew Avenue
Hartford, Connecticut 06115

Delaware Department of
  Health and Social Services
Delaware State Hospital
Administration Building
New Castle, Delaware 19720

District of Columbia Department
  of Human Services
801 N. Capitol Street, N.E.
  Room 701
Washington, D.C. 20002

Florida Department of Health
  and Rehabilitative Services
1321 Winewood Boulevard
Tallahassee, Florida 32301

Georgia Department
of Human Resources
State Office Building
47 Trinity Avenue, S.W.
Atlanta, Georgia 30334

Hawaii Department of
Social Services and Housing
P.O. Box 339
Honolulu, Hawaii 96809

Idaho Department of
Health and Welfare
450 W. State Street
State House Mall
Boise, Idaho 83720

Illinois Department of Public Aid
316 S. Second Street
Springfield, Illinois 62762

Indiana Department of Public
Welfare
701 State Office Building
Indianapolis, Indiana 46204

Iowa Department of Social
Services
Hoover Building
Des Moines, Iowa 50319

Kansas Department of Social
and Rehabilitation Services
State Office Building
915 Harrison Street
Topeka, Kansas 66612

Kentucky Department
for Human Resources
275 E. Main Street
Frankfort, Kentucky 40621

Louisiana Department of Health
and Human Resources

P.O. Box 3776
Baton Rouge, Louisiana 70821

Maine Department of Human
Services
State House
Augusta, Maine 04333

Maryland Department
of Human Resources
1100 N. Eutaw Street
Baltimore, Maryland 21201

Massachusetts Executive
Office of Human Services
State House, Room 167
Boston, Massachusetts 02133

Michigan Department
of Social Services
300 S. Capitol Avenue
P.O. Box 30037
Lansing, Michigan 48909

Minnesota Department
of Public Welfare
Centennial Office Building
4th Floor
St. Paul, Minnesota 55155

Mississippi Department
of Public Welfare
P.O. Box 352
Jackson, Mississippi 39205

Missouri Department
of Social Services
Broadway State Office Building
P.O. Box 88
Jefferson City, Missouri 65103

Montana Department of Social
and Rehabilitation Services
P.O. Box 4210
Helena, Montana 59604

Nebraska Department
of Public Welfare
301 Centennial Mall, S., 5th Floor
P.O. Box 95026
Lincoln, Nebraska 68509

Nevada Department
of Human Resources
Capitol Complex
505 E. King Street
Carson City, Nevada 89710

New Hampshire Department
of Health and Welfare
Hazen Drive
Concord, New Hampshire 03301

New Jersey Department
of Human Services
One Capital Place
222 S. Warren Street
Trenton, New Jersey 08625

New Mexico Human Services
Department
P.O. Box 2348
Sante Fe, New Mexico 87503

New York State Department
of Social Services
40 N. Pearl Street
Albany, New York 12243

North Carolina Department
of Human Resources
325 N. Salisbury Street
Raleigh, North Carolina 27611

Social Service Board of North
Dakota
State Capitol
Bismarck, North Dakota 58505

Ohio Department of Public
Welfare

State Office Tower
32nd Floor
30 E. Broad Street
Columbus, Ohio 43215

Oklahoma Department of
Human Services
P.O. Box 25352
Oklahoma City, Oklahoma 73125

Oregon Department of
Human Resources
Public Service Building
Salem, Oregon 97310

Pennsylvania Department
of Public Welfare
P.O. Box 2675
Harrisburg, Pennsylvania 17120

Puerto Rico Department
of Social Services
P.O. Box 11398, Fernández
Juncos Station
Santurce, Puerto Rico 00910

Rhode Island Department of
Social and Rehabilitative
Services
Aime J. Forand Building
600 New London Avenue
Cranston, Rhode Island 02920

South Carolina Department
of Social Services
P.O. Box 1520
Columbia, South Carolina 29202

South Dakota Department
of Social Services
Richard F. Kneip Building
Pierre, South Dakota 57501

Tennessee Department
of Human Services

111 Seventh Avenue, N.
Nashville, Tennessee 37203

Texas Department
  of Human Resources
P.O. Box 2960
Austin, Texas 78769

Utah Department of Social
  Services
150 W. North Temple Street
P.O. Box 2500
Salt Lake City, Utah 84110

Vermont Agency of Human
  Services
103 S. Main Street
Waterbury, Vermont 05676

Virginia Department of Social
  Services
8007 Discovery Drive
Richmond, Virginia 23288

Virgin Islands Department
  of Social Welfare

P.O. Box 550
Charlotte Amalie, St. Thomas
  00801

Washington Department of
  Social and Health Services
State Office Building
Mail Stop OB-44T
Olympia, Washington 98504

West Virginia Department of
  Welfare
State Office Building
1900 Washington Street, E.
Charleston, West Virginia 25305

Wisconsin Department of
  Health and Social Services
State Office Building
1 W. Wilson Street
Madison, Wisconsin 53702

Wyoming Department
  of Health and Social Services
Hathaway Building
Cheyenne, Wyoming 82002

Services Provided by State Agencies

TOTALS	53	28	33	52	51	27	26	32	31
State	Public Assist.	Gen. Assist. County	Gen. Assist. State	Services Child.	Services Adult	MR	MH	Blind	Aged
Alabama	●	●	●	●	●				
Alaska	●		●	●	●	●	●	●	●
Arizona	●		●	●	●	●		●	●
Arkansas	●		●	●	●	●	●	●	●
California	●			●	●			●	●
Colorado	●			●	●				●
Connecticut	●		●						
Delaware	●		●	●	●	●	●	●	●
Dist. of Columbia	●		●	●	●	●	●		
Florida	●		●	●		●	●		●
Georgia	●	●		●	●	●	●	●	●
Hawaii	●		●	●	●			●	
Idaho	●		●	●	●	●	●		
Illinois	●	●	●	●	●				
Indiana	●			●	●				
Iowa	●			●	●	●	●		
Kansas	●		●	●	●	●	●	●	●
Kentucky	●		●	●	●	●	●	●	●
Louisiana	●		●	●	●	●	●	●	●
Maine	●		●	●	●			●	●
Maryland	●	●		●	●				
Massachusetts	●		●	●	●	●	●	●	
Michigan	●	●		●	●			●	●
Minnesota	●	●		●	●	●	●		●
Mississippi	●	●	●	●	●			●	
Missouri	●	●	●	●	●			●	●
Montana	●	●	●	●	●			●	●
Nebraska	●	●	●	●	●				
Nevada	●	●		●	●	●	●	●	●
New Hampshire	●	●		●	●	●	●		
New Jersey	●	●	●	●	●	●	●	●	
New Mexico	●	●	●	●	●				●
New York	●	●		●	●			●	
North Carolina	●	●		●	●	●	●	●	●
North Dakota	●	●		●	●			●	●
Ohio	●	●		●	●				
Oklahoma	●		●	●	●	●	●	●	●
Oregon	●	●	●	●	●	●	●		●
Pennsylvania	●	●	●	●	●	●	●	●	●
Puerto Rico	●		●	●	●			●	●
Rhode Island	●	●		●	●			●	
South Carolina	●	●	●	●	●				
South Dakota	●	●		●	●	●	●		●
Tennessee	●	●		●	●			●	
Texas	●	●		●	●				
Utah	●	●		●	●	●	●		●
Vermont	●		●	●	●	●	●	●	●
Virginia	●		●	●	●				
Virgin Islands	●		●	●	●			●	●
Washington	●	●	●	●	●	●	●		●
West Virginia	●		●	●	●			●	
Wisconsin	●		●	●	●	●	●	●	●
Wyoming	●	●		●	●	●	●		●

Chart provided courtesy of Iowa Department of Social Services

198

Voc. Rehab.	Drug/Alcohol Abuse	State Vet. Services	Medicaid	Health	Crippled Children	Youth Serv.	Adult Corr.	Employment Services	TOTALS
23	23	13	47	19	24	27	10	6	
			•						6
	•		•	•	•	•	•		14
•		•						•	10
•	•		•		•	•			13
			•					•	7
•		•	•						7
			•						3
	•		•	•	•				12
•	•	•	•	•	•	•			14
•	•		•	•	•	•			12
•	•				•	•			12
•			•			•	•		9
	•	•	•	•	•	•			12
			•						6
			•		•				5
		•	•			•	•		9
•	•		•			•			12
	•	•	•	•	•	•		•	15
	•		•	•	•	•			13
•	•		•	•	•	•			12
		•	•					•	6
•	•	•	•	•	•	•	•		15
	•		•			•			9
	•		•						10
			•						7
		•	•	•	•	•	•		13
•		•	•						10
			•		•				7
•	•		•	•	•	•			14
	•		•	•	•				10
			•			•			10
		•	•					•	9
			•						6
•	•		•	•	•	•			14
•			•		•	•			10
			•						5
•			•		•	•			12
•	•		•	•	•	•	•	•	16
			•			•			11
•									7
•		•	•						8
			•						6
•			•						9
			•						6
			•						5
	•	•	•	•	•	•	•		14
•	•		•	•	•	•	•		15
									4
•						•			8
•			•	•	•	•	•		15
			•		•				7
•	•		•	•	•	•	•		14
	•		•	•	•				11

Bibliography

ABBOTT, EDITH. *Public Assistance: American Principles and Policies.* Chicago: University of Chicago Press, 1940.

ABERT, JAMES G. *Program Evaluation at HEW: Research Versus Reality. Part 3: Welfare.* New York: Marcel Dekker, Inc., 1979.

ADDAMS, JANE. *Twenty Years at Hull-House.* New York: Macmillan Company, 1910.

AKABAS, SHEILA H.; KURZMAN, PAUL A.; AND KOLBEN, NANCY S. *Labor and Industrial Settings: Sites for Social Work Practice.* New York: Council on Social Work Education, 1979.

ALEXANDER, CHAUNCEY A., AND ALEXANDER, SALLY J. *China View: A Report of the First NASW Study Tour to the People's Republic of China.* New York: National Association of Social Work, 1979.

ALEXANDER, LESLIE B. "Professionalization and Unionization: Compatible After All." *Social Work* 25 (November 1980); 476–482.

———. "Social Workers in Unions: A Survey." *Social Work* 25 (May 1980): 216–223.

———, AND SPEIZMAN, MILTON D. "The Union Movement in Voluntary Social Work." In National Conference on Social Welfare, *The Social Welfare Forum, 1979,* pp. 179–187. New York: Columbia University Press, 1980.

ALINSKY, SAUL D. *Reveille for Radicals.* New York: Vintage Books, 1969.

ALISSI, ALBERT S. *Perspectives on Social Group Work Practice.* New York: The Free Press, 1980.

AMERICAN HUMANE ASSOCIATION. *Child Protective Services Entering the 1980's: A Nationwide Survey.* Englewood, Colorado: American Humane Association, 1979.

AMIDEI, NANCY. "Food Stamps: The Irony of Success." *Public Welfare* 39 (Spring 1981): 15–21.

ANDERSON, DAVID C. *Children of Special Value: Interracial Adoption in America.* New York: St. Martin's Press, 1971.

ANDERSON, JOSEPH D. "Structured Experiences in Growth Groups in Social Work." *Social Casework* 61 (May 1980): 277–287.

———. *Social Work Methods and Processes.* Belmont: Wadsworth Publishing Company, 1981.

ANDERSON, MARTIN. *Welfare: The Political Economy of Welfare Reform in the United States.* Stanford, California: Hoover Institution Press, 1978.

ANONYMOUS. "Infant Adoption: Two Family Experiences with Intercounty Adoption." *Children Today* 9 (November–December 1980): 2–5.

"APWA's R&D: Working Toward Improvement of Human Service Programs." *Public Welfare* 39 (Summer 1981): 38–41.

ARKAVA, M. L., AND BRENNEN, E. C. *Competency-Based Education for Social Work: Evaluation and Curriculum Issues.* New York: Council on Social Work Education, 1976.

ARNAUDO, DAVID, TATARA, TOSHIO, AND ARMORE, SUSAN V. *Income Maintenance Research by State and Federal Agencies 1978.* Washington, D.C.: U.S. Department of Health and Human Services, 1979.

ATTKISSON, C. CLIFFORD; HARGREAVES, WILLIAM A.; HOROWITZ, MARDI J.; AND SORENSON, JAMES E. *Evaluation of Human Service Programs.* New York: Academic Press, 1978.

AUSTIN, DAVID M. "I & R: The New Glue for the Social Services." *Public Welfare* 38 (Fall 1980): 38–43.

AUSTIN, MICHAEL J. *Supervisory Management for the Human Services.* Englewood Cliffs, New Jersey: Prentice-Hall, 1981.

BAER, BETTY L., AND FEDERICO, RONALD C. *Educating the Baccalaureate Social Worker: A Curriculum Development Resource Guide,* Vol. 2. Cambridge, Massachusetts: Ballinger Publishing Company, 1979.

———. *Educating the Baccalaureate Social Worker: Report of the Undergraduate Social Work Curriculum Development Project,* Vol. 1. Cambridge, Massachusetts: Ballinger Publishing Company, 1978.

BASS, DAVID, AND RICE, JANET. "Agency Responses to the Abused Wife." *Social Casework* 60 (June 1979): 338–342.

BELSKY, JAY. "Future Directions for Day Care Research: An Ecological Analysis." *Child Care Quarterly* 9 (Summer 1980): 82–99.

BENDER, THOMAS. *Community and Social Change in America.* New Brunswick, New Jersey: Rutgers University Press, 1978.

BENDICK, MARC, JR. "Failure to Enroll in Public Assistance Programs." *Social Work* 25 (July 1980): 268–274.

———. "Quality Control in a Federal-State Public Assistance Program." *Administration in Social Work* 4 (Spring 1980): 7–20.

BENTON, BILL B., JR. "Separation Revisited." *Public Welfare* 38 (Spring 1980): 15–21.

BERNSTEIN, BARTON E. "Lawyer and Social Worker as an Interdisciplinary Team." *Social Casework* 61 (September 1980): 416–422.

BERRY, JULIET. *Social Work with Children.* Boston: Routledge and Kegan Paul, 1972.

BERTSCHE, ANNE VANDEBERG, AND HOREJSI, CHARLES R., "Coordination of Client Services." *Social Work* 25 (March 1980): 94–98.

BIESTEK, FELIX P., AND GEHRIG, CLYDE C. *Client Self-Determination in Social Work: A Fifty-Year History.* Chicago: Loyola University Press, 1978.

BLOKSBERG, LEONARD M., AND LOWY, LOUIS. "Toward Integrative Learning and Teaching in Social Work: An Analytic Framework." *Journal of Education for Social Work* 13 (Spring 1977): 3–10.

BLOMQUIST, DAVID C. "Social Work in Business and Industry." *Social Casework* 60 (October 1979): 457–462.

BORUS, MICHAEL E. *Measuring the Impact of Employment-Related Social Programs.* Kalamazoo, Michigan: W. E. Upjohn Institute, 1979.

BRACHT, NEIL F. *Social Work in Health Care: A Guide to Professional Practice.* New York: The Haworth Press, 1978.

BRADEN, JOSEPHINE. "Adopting the Abused Child: Love Is Not Enough." *Social Casework* 62 (June 1981): 362–367.

BRANTLEY, DALE, AND WEST, SIBYL. "The Rural Developmentally Disabled, An Underserved Population." *Human Services in the Rural Environment* 5 (March/April 1980): 17–24.

BRIAR, SCOTT. "Needed: A Simple Definition of Social Work." *Social Work* 26 (January 1981): 83–84.

BRIELAND, DONALD. "Bioethical Issues in Family Planning." *Social Work* 24 (November 1979): 478–484.

———; COSTIN, LELA B.; AND ATHERTON, CHARLES R. *Contemporary Social Work: An Introduction to Social Work and Social Welfare,* 2nd ed. New York: McGraw-Hill, 1980.

———, AND LEMMON, JOHN. *Social Work and the Law.* St. Paul, Minnesota: West Publishing Company, 1977.

BROWN, JOHN HAROLD UPTON. *The Health Care Dilemma.* New York: Human Sciences Press, 1978.

BUCKHOLDT, DAVID R., AND GUBRIUM, JABER F. *Caretakers: Treating Emotionally Disturbed Children.* Beverly Hills, California: Sage Publications, 1979.

BUDDE, JAMES F. *Measuring Performance in Human Service Systems: Planning, Organization, and Control.* New York: American Management Association, 1979.

BURGESS, LINDA CANNON. *The Art of Adoption: The "Hows" and "Whys" by an Adoption Worker Responsible for Over 900 Adoptions.* Washington, D.C.: Acropolis Books, 1976.

BURKE, EDMUND M. *A Participatory Approach to Urban Planning.* New York: Human Sciences Press, 1979.

CAIN, LILLIAN. "Social Worker's Role in Teenage Abortions." *Social Work* 24 (January 1979): 52–56.

CANTONI, LUCILE. "Clinical Issues in Domestic Violence." *Social Casework* 62 (January 1981): 3–12.

CARBINO, ROSEMARIE. *Foster Parenting: An Updated Review of the Literature.* New York: Child Welfare League, 1980.

CARROLL, MARY. "Collaboration with Social Work Clients: A Review of the Literature." *Child Welfare* 59 (July/August 1980): 407–418.

CASEY, TIMOTHY J., AND FREEDMAN, HENRY A. "Paying the Rent for AFDC Clients: The Case Against Direct Vendor Payments." *Public Welfare* 37 (Winter 1979): 37–40.

CASSETTY, JUDITH. *Child Support and Public Policy.* Lexington, Massachusetts: D. C. Heath, 1978.

CASSETTY, JUDITH H. "Child Support Enforcement: Program Conflicts and Human Considerations." *Public Welfare* 37 (Fall 1979): 33–39.

CAULFIELD, BARBARA A. *Child Abuse and the Law: A Legal Primer for Social Workers.* Chicago: National Committee for Prevention of Child Abuse, 1979.

————. *The Legal Aspects of Protective Services for Abused and Neglected Children: A Manual.* Washington, D.C.: U.S. Department of Health, Education, and Welfare, 1978.

CAUTLEY, PATRICIA WOODWARD. *New Foster Parents: The First Experience.* New York: Human Sciences Press, 1980.

CHAMBERS, DAVID L. *Making Fathers Pay: The Enforcement of Child Support.* Chicago: University of Chicago Press, 1979.

CHAMBERLAIN, NAOMI H., AND KELLY, JACQUELINE. "Georgia's Approach to Preventing Teenage Pregnancy." *Public Welfare* 38 (Summer 1980): 43–49.

CHAPMAN, JANE ROBERTS, AND GATES, MARGARET. *The Victimization of Women.* Beverly Hills, California: Sage Publications, 1978.

CHARNLEY, JEAN. *The Art of Child Placement.* Minneapolis: University of Minnesota Press, 1955.

CHESLER, JOAN SCHLOESSINGER, AND DAVIS, SUSAN A. "Problem Pregnancy and Abortion Counseling with Teenagers." *Social Casework* 61 (March 1980): 173–179.

CHILMAN, CATHERINE S. "Teenage Pregnancy: A Research Review." *Social Work* 24 (November 1979): 492–498.

CHRISSINGER, MARLENE SONJU. "Factors Affecting Employment of Welfare Mothers." *Social Work* 25 (January 1980): 52–56.

CLARK, FRANK W., ARKAVA, MORTON L., AND ASSOCIATES. *The Pursuit of Competence in Social Work.* San Francisco, California: Jossey-Bass, 1979.

COHEN, JEROME. "Selected Constraints in the Relationship Between Social Work Education and Practice." *Journal of Education for Social Work* 13 (Winter 1977): 3–7.

COHEN, WILBUR J., AND BALL, ROBERT M. "Public Welfare Amendments of 1962 and Proposals for Health Insurance for the Aged." *Social Security Bulletin* 25 (October 1962): 3–16.

COMBS, JOSEPH T. "An Information System that Measures Foster Casework Effectiveness." *Children Today* 8 (May–June 1979): 15–17, 36.

COMPTON, BEULAH R. *Introduction to Social Welfare and Social Work: Structure, Function, and Process.* Homewood, Illinois: Dorsey Press, 1980.

————, AND BURTON R. GALAWAY. *Social Work Processes,* rev. ed. Homewood, Illinois: Dorsey Press, 1980.

CONKLIN, CAROL. "Rural Community Care-Givers." *Social Work* 25 (November 1980): 495–496.

COOK, ALICIA S. "A Model for Working With the Elderly in Institutions." *Social Casework* 62 (September 1981): 420–425.

COOLSEN, PETER. "Community Involvement in the Prevention of Child Abuse and Neglect." *Children Today* 9 (September–October 1980): 5–8.

COOPER, CARY L. "Humanizing the Work Place in Europe: An Overview of Six Countries." *Personnel Journal* 59 (June 1980): 488–491.

COSTIN, LELA B. *Child Welfare: Policies and Practices,* 2nd ed. New York: McGraw-Hill, 1979.

————. "School Social Work as Specialized Practice." *Social Work* 26 (January 1981): 36–43.

COWAN, SYLVIA CAVALIER. "The Rural Poor and Mental Health." *Human Services in the Rural Environment* 1 (November/December 1979): 10–18.

COWARD, RAYMOND T. "Planning Community Services for the Rural Elderly: Implications from Research." *The Gerontologist* 19 (June 1979): 275–282.

COX, FRED M.; ERLICH, JOHN L.; ROTHMAN, JACK; AND TROPMAN, JOHN E. *Strategies of Community Organization*, 3rd ed. Itasca, Illinois: F. E. Peacock, 1979.

————. *Tactics and Techniques of Community Practice*. Itasca: F. E. Peacock, 1977.

COYNE, ANN, AND FLYNN, LAURIE. "The Importance of Other Parents in Adoption." *Children Today* 9 (November–December 1980): 7–9.

CROUCH, ROBERT C. "Social Work Defined." *Social Work* 24 (January 1979): 46–48.

CULLEN, FRANCIS T. "Child Support Collection: A Stick and Carrot Approach." *Social Work* 25 (September 1980): 397–402.

CURNOCK, KATHLEEN, AND HARDIKER, PAULINE. *Towards Practice Theory: Skills and Methods in Social Assessments*. Boston: Routledge and Kegan Paul, 1979.

DATAN, NANCY, AND GINSBERG, LEON H. *Life-Span Developmental Psychology: Normative Life Crises*. New York: Academic Press, 1975.

DAVENPORT, JUDITH A., AND DAVENPORT, JOSEPH, III. *Boom Towns and Human Services*. Laramie, Wyoming: University of Wyoming Publications, 1979.

DAVIDSON, STEPHEN M. "The Status of Aid to the Medically Needy." *Social Service Review* 53 (March 1979): 92–105.

DAVIDSON, TERRY. *Conjugal Crime: Understanding and Changing the Wifebeating Pattern*. New York: Hawthorne Books, 1978.

DAVIS, ALLEN F., AND MCCREE, MARY LYNN. *Eighty Years at Hull House*. Chicago: Quadrangle Books, 1969.

DEAR, RONALD B. AND RINO J. PATTI. "Legislative Advocacy: Seven Effective Tactics." *Social Work* 26 (July 1981): 289–296.

DeCOURCY, PETER, AND DeCOURCY, JUDITH. *A Silent Tragedy: Child Abuse in the Community*. New York: Alfred Publishing Company, 1973.

DELGADO, MELVIN. "Hispanic Staff in Non-Hispanic Settings: Issues and Recommendations." *Administration in Social Work* 3 (Winter 1979): 465–475.

DERTHICK, MARTHA. *Uncontrollable Spending for Social Services Grants*. Washington, D.C.: The Brookings Institution, 1975.

DOBELSTEIN ANDREW W. *Politics, Economics, and Public Welfare*. Englewood Cliffs, New Jersey: Prentice-Hall, 1980.

DODGE, MARY K. "Swedish Programs for Children: A Comprehensive Approach to Family Needs." *Child Care Quarterly* 8 (Winter 1979): 254–265.

DOLGOFF, RALPH L. "Clinicians as Social Policymakers." *Social Casework* 62 (May 1981): 284–292.

————, AND FELDSTEIN, DONALD. *Understanding Social Welfare*. New York: Harper and Row, 1980.

DOSCHER, VIRGINIA R. "Fifty Years of Looking Ahead: A Sketch of the Past/The Shape of the Future." *Public Welfare* 38 (Winter 1980): 16–17.

————. "The First Decade." *Public Welfare* 38 (Winter 1980): 18–31.

————. "Now The Next Fifty." *Public Welfare* 38 (Winter 1980): 52–57.

————. "War and Postwar." *Public Welfare* 38 (Winter 1980): 32–51.

DRUCKER, PETER F. *Managing in Turbulent Times.* New York: Harper and Row, 1980.

DUMPSON, JAMES R.; MULLEN, EDWARD J.; AND FIRST, RICHARD J. *Toward Education for Effective Social Welfare Administrative Practice.* New York: Council on Social Work Education, 1978.

DUNHAM, ARTHUR. *Community Welfare Organization: Principles and Practice.* New York: Thomas Y. Crowell, 1958.

_____. *The New Community Organization.* New York: Thomas Y. Crowell, 1970.

DYWASUK, COLETTE TAUBE. *Adoption—Is It For You?* New York: Harper and Row, 1973.

EATON, JOSEPH W. "Errors and Mistakes in Social Practice." *Administration in Social Work* 4 (Spring 1980): 43–54.

EBELING, NANCY B., AND HILL, DEBORAH A. *Child Abuse: Intervention and Treatment.* Acton, Massachusetts: Publishing Sciences Group, 1975.

ECKLEIN, JOAN LEVIN, AND LAUFFER, ARMAND. *Community Organizers and Social Planners.* New York: John Wiley and Sons, and Council on Social Work Education, 1972.

EDELSTEIN, SUSAN. "When Foster Children Leave: Helping Foster Parents to Grieve." *Child Welfare* 60 (July/August 1981): 467–474.

EFFRON, ANNE KURTZMAN. "Children and Divorce: Help from an Elementary School." *Social Casework* 61 (May 1980): 305–312.

EPSTEIN, IRWIN, AND TRIPODI, TONY. *Research Techniques for Program Planning, Monitoring, and Evaluation.* New York: Columbia University Press, 1979.

EPSTEIN, LAURA. *Helping People: The Task-Centered Approach.* St. Louis, Missouri: C. V. Mosby Company, 1980.

_____. "Teaching Research-Based Practice: Rationale and Method." *Journal of Education for Social Work* 17 (Spring 1981): 51–55.

ESKA, BRUNHILDE. "The Social Security System of the Federal Republic of Germany." *Social Service Review* 54 (March 1980): 108–123.

ETZIONI, AMITAI. *Modern Organizations.* Englewood Cliffs, New Jersey: Prentice-Hall, 1964.

EWALT, PATRICIA L., AND HONEYFIELD, ROBERT M. "Needs of Persons in Long-Term Care." *Social Work* 26 (May 1981): 223–232.

FANSHEL, DAVID. *Far From the Reservation: The Transracial Adoption of American Indian Children.* Metuchen, New Jersey: The Scarecrow Press, 1972.

_____. *Future of Social Work Research.* New York: National Association of Social Workers, 1980.

FARLEY, JENNIE. *Affimative Action and the Woman Worker: Guidelines for Personnel Management.* New York: American Management Association, 1979.

FARLEY, WILLIAM O.; GRIFFITHS, KENNETH A.; SKIDMORE, REX A.; AND THACKERAY, MILTON, G. *Rural Social Work Practice.* New York: The Free Press, 1982.

FAURI DAVID P. "Providing Human Resources for the Rural Elderly." *Human Services in the Rural Environment* 5 (November/December 1980): 17–20.

FEDER, JUDITH, AND HOLAHAN, JOHN. *Financing Health Care for the Elderly: Medicare, Medicaid and Private Health Insurance.* Washington, D.C.: The Urban Institute, 1979.

FEDERICO, RONALD C. *The Social Welfare Institution: An Introduction.* Lexington, Massachusetts: D. C. Heath, 1980.

FELKER, EVELYN H. *Foster Parenting Young Children.* New York: The Child Welfare League, 1974.

FELLIN, PHILLIP; TRIPODI, TONY; AND MEYER, HENRY J. *Exemplars of Social Research.* Itasca, Illinois: F. E. Peacock Publishers, 1969.

FERSH, ROBERT J. "Food Stamps: Program at the Crossroads." *Public Welfare* 39 (Spring 1981): 9–14.

FIELD, MARTHA HEINEMAN. "Social Casework Practice During the Psychiatric Deluge." *Social Service Review* 54 (December 1980): 482–507.

FINK, ARLENE, AND KOSECOFF, JACQUELINE. *An Evaluation Primer.* Beverly Hills, California: Sage Publications, 1980.

FISCHER, JOEL. "The Social Work Revolution." *Social Work* 26 (May 1981): 199–207.

FLEMING, JENNIFER BAKER. *Stopping Wife Abuse.* New York: Doubleday, 1979.

FOLKS, HOMER, *The Care of Destitute, Neglected, and Delinquent Children.* Washington, D.C.: National Association of Social Workers, 1978.

FONTANA, VINCENT J. *Somewhere A Child is Crying: Maltreatment—Causes and Prevention.* New York: Macmillan Publishing Co., 1973.

FORCESE, DENNIS P., AND RICHER, STEPHEN. *Stages of Social Research: Contemporary Perspectives.* Englewood Cliffs, New Jersey: Prentice-Hall, 1970.

FORTUNE, ANNE E. "Communication in Task-Centered Treatment." *Social Work* 24 (September 1979): 390–396.

————. "Communication Processes in Social Work Practice." *Social Service Review* 55 (March 1981): 93–128.

FOWLER, WILLIAM. *Infant and Child Care; A Guide to Education in Group Settings.* Boston: Allyn and Bacon, Inc., 1980.

FRAIBERG, SELMA. *Every Child's Birthright: In Defense of Mothering.* New York: Basic Books, 1977.

FRACOME, COLIN. "Abortion Policy in Britain and the United States." *Social Work* 25 (January 1980): 5–11.

FRANKEL, LAWRENCE, AND RICHARD, BETTY BYRD. *Be Alive As Long As You Live.* New York: Lippincott and Crowell, 1980.

FREDERICKSEN, HAZEL, AND MULLIGAN, R. A. *The Child and His Welfare.* San Francisco: W. H. Freeman and Company, 1972.

FRIEDLANDER, WALTER A., AND APTE, ROBERT Z. *Introduction to Social Welfare,* 5th ed. Englewood Cliffs, New Jersey: Prentice-Hall, 1980.

GANTER, GRACE, AND YEAKEL, MARGARET. *Human Behavior and the Social Environment: A Perspective for Social Work Practice.* New York: Columbia University Press, 1980.

GARBARINO, JAMES. "Meeting the Needs of Mistreated Youths." *Social Work* 25 (March 1980): 122–126.

————, AND STOCKING, S. HOLLY. *Protecting Children From Abuse and Neglect.* San Francisco: Jossey-Bass, 1980.

GARRICK, MICHAEL A., MOORE, WILLIAM L. "Uniform Assessments and Standards of Social and Health Care Services." *Social Service Review* 53 (September 1979): 343–357.

GARVIN, CHARLES D.; SMITH, AUDREY D.; AND REID, WILLIAM J. *The Work Incentive Experience.* Montclair, New Jersey: Allenheld, Osmun and Company, 1979.

GAYMON, DONALD. "Underutilization in Affirmative Action Programs: What Is It and What Can We Do About It?" *Personnel Journal* 58 (July 1979): 456–459.

GEISER, ROBERT L. *Hidden Victims: The Sexual Abuse of Children.* Boston: Beacon Press, 1979.

——. *The Illusion of Caring: Children in Foster Care.* Boston: Beacon Press, 1973.

GERBNER, GEORGE; ROSS, CATHERINE J.; AND ZIGLER, EDWARD. *Child Abuse: An Agenda for Action.* New York: Oxford University Press, 1980.

GERMAIN, CAREL B. "The Ecological Approach to People-Environment Transactions." *Social Casework* 62 (June 1981): 323–331.

——. *The Life Model of Social Work Practice.* New York: Columbia University Press, 1980.

——. "People and Ideas in the History of Social Work Practice." *Social Casework* 61 (June 1980): 323–331.

——. *Social Work Practice: People and Environments.* New York: Columbia University Press, 1979.

GETZEL, GEORGE S. "Social Work With Family Caregivers to the Aged." *Social Casework* 62 (April 1981): 201–209.

GIL, DAVID G. *Child Abuse and Violence.* New York: AMS Press, 1979.

——. *Violence Against Children: Physical Child Abuse in the United States.* Cambridge, Massachusetts: Harvard University Press, 1970.

GILBERT, NEIL. "The Design of Community Planning Structures." *Social Service Review* 53 (December 1979): 644–654.

——, MILLER, HENRY, AND SPECHT, HARRY. *An Introduction to Social Work Practice.* Englewood Cliffs, New Jersey: Prentice-Hall, 1980.

——, AND SPECHT, HARRY. *Handbook of the Social Services.* Englewood Cliffs, New Jersey: Prentice-Hall, 1981.

GINSBERG, LEON H. "Roles for Social Workers in the Manpower Field." *Social Work* 20 (January 1975): 29–32.

——. *Social Work in Rural Communities.* New York: Council on Social Work Education, 1976.

——. "Changing Public Attitudes About Public Welfare Clients and Services Through Research." *Policy Studies Journal,* 10, (March 1982): 581–591.

GINZBERG, ELI. *Employing the Unemployed.* New York: Basic Books, 1980.

GIOVANNONI, JEANNE M., AND BECERRA, ROSINA M. *Defining Child Abuse.* New York: The Free Press, 1979.

GOLAN, NAOMI. *Treatment in Crisis Situations.* New York: The Free Press, 1978.

GOLDSTEIN, JOSEPH; FREUD, ANNA; AND SOLNIT, ALBERT J. *Before the Best Interests of the Child.* New York: The Free Press, 1979.

GOTTESMAN, ROBERTA. *The Child and the Law.* St. Paul, Minnesota: West Publishing Company, 1981.

GOULD, KETAYUN. "Family Planning and Abortion Policy in the United States." *Social Service Review* 53 (September 1979): 452–463.

GREENBLATT, MICHAEL. *Public Welfare: Notes From Underground.* Cambridge, Massachusetts: Schenkman Publishing Company, 1979.

GREENFIELD, LAWRENCE; ANDERSON, JOHN S.; AND FRIEDMAN, DANIEL J. "Developing a Quality Assurance Document for Monitoring Local Office AFDC Payments Administration." *Administration in Social Work* 4 (Spring 1980): 21–32.

_____, AND KOHL, JOHN P. "National Origin Discrimination and the New EEOC Guidelines." *Personnel Journal* 60 (August 1981): 634–636.

GREENSTONE, J. DAVID. "Dorothea Dix and Jane Addams: From Transcendentalism to Pragmatism in American Social Reform." *Social Service Review* 53 (December 1979): 527–559.

GRUBER, ALAN R. *Children in Foster Care: Destitute, Neglected, Betrayed.* New York: Human Sciences Press, 1978.

GUMMER, BURTON. "A Framework for Curriculum Planning in Social Welfare Administration." *Administration in Social Work* 3 (Winter 1979): 385–396.

_____. "Is the Social Worker in Public Welfare an Endangered Species?" *Public Welfare* 37 (Fall 1979): 12–21.

_____. "On Helping and Helplessness: The Structure of Discretion in the American Welfare System." *Social Service Review* 53 (June 1979): 214–228.

_____. "Social Work, Caring, and Human Resource Development." In National Conference on Social Welfare, *The Social Welfare Forum, 1980*, pp. 92–103. New York: Columbia University Press, 1981.

HAEUSER, ADRIENNE AHLGREN, AND SCHWARTZ, FLORENCE S. "Developing Social Work Skills for Work with Volunteers." *Social Casework* 61 (December 1980): 595–601.

HALL, GERTRUDE H., AND MATHIASEN, GENEVA. *Guide to Development of Protective Service for Older People.* Springfield, Illinois: Charles C. Thomas, 1973.

_____, AND MATHIASEN, GENEVA. *Overcoming Barriers to Protective Services for the Aged.* New York: National Council on the Aging, 1968.

HALLMAN, HOWARD W. *Community Based Employment Problems.* Baltimore: Johns Hopkins University Press, 1980.

HAMMER, TOVE HELLAND. "Affirmative Action Programs: Have We Forgotten the First-Line Supervisor?" *Personnel Journal* 58 (June 1979): 348–389.

HANDLER, JOEL F. *Protecting the Social Service Client: Legal and Structural Controls on Official Discretion.* New York: Academic Press, 1979.

HANNAH, GERALD T.; CHRISTIAN, WALTER P.; AND CLARK, HEWITT B. *Preservation of Client Rights.* Riverside, New Jersey: The Free Press, 1980.

HARBERT, ANITA S., AND GINSBERG, LEON H. *Human Services for Older Adults: Concepts and Skills.* Belmont, California: Wadsworth Publishing Company, 1979.

HARTFORD, MARGARET E. *Groups in Social Work: Application of Small Group Theory and Research to Social Work Practice.* New York: Columbia University Press, 1972.

HARTMAN, ANN. "The Family: A Central Focus for Practice." *Social Work* 26 (January 1981): 7–13.

HAWLEY, NANCY P., AND BROWN, ELIZABETH. "Children of Alcoholics; The Use of Group Treatment" *Social Casework* 62 (January 1981): 40–46.

HAYES, JIM; HEALD, ANN; MAGEE, GAIL; CHAU, NGUYEN VAN; RUSTIN, BAYARD; SHEARER, COLLEEN; AND VAN ARSDALE, PETER W. "Help for the Indochinese: How Much Is Too Much?" *Public Welfare* 38 (Summer 1980): 4–9, 59–64.

HAYSLIP, BERT; RITTER, MARY LOU; OLTMAN, RUTH; AND MCDONNELL, CONNIE. "Home Care Services and the Rural Elderly." *The Gerontologist* 20 (April 1980): 192–199.

HEFFERNAN, W. JOSEPH. *Introduction to Social Welfare Policy.* Itasca, Illinois: F. E. Peacock, 1979.

HELFER, RAY E., AND KEMPE, C. HENRY. *The Battered Child.* Chicago: The University of Chicago Press, 1968.

———. *Child Abuse and Neglect: The Family and the Community.* Cambridge, Massachusetts: Ballinger Publishing Company, 1976.

HENDERSON, GEORGE. *Understanding and Counseling Ethnic Minorities.* Springfield, Illinois: Charles C. Thomas, 1979.

HERRMANN, KENNETH. *I Hope My Daddy Dies, Mister.* Ardmore: Dorrance and Company, 1975.

———. *I'm Nobody's Child.* Ardmore, Whitmore Publishing Company, 1982.

HICKEY, TOM, AND DOUGLASS, RICHARD L. "Neglect and Abuse of Older Family Members: Professionals' Perspectives and Case Experiences." *The Gerontologist* 21 (April 1981): 171–176.

HOBBS, CHARLES D. *The Welfare Industry.* Washington, D.C.: The Heritage Foundation, 1978.

HOLLIS, FLORENCE, "On Revisiting Social Work." *Social Casework* 61 (January 1980): 3–10.

HORNBY, HELAINE. "Foster Care and the Power of the State: Understanding The Client's Perspective. *Children Today* 10 (March–April 1981): 2–5.

HOSEK, JAMES R. *The AFDC-Unemployed Fathers Program and Welfare Reform.* Santa Monica, California: Rand Corporation, 1979.

HOYMAN, MICHELE. "Interpreting the New Sexual Harrassment Guidelines." *Personnel Journal* 59 (December 1980): 996–1000.

HUTCHINSON, DOROTHY. *Cherish the Child: Dilemmas of Placement.* Metuchen, New Jersey: The Scarecrow Press, 1972.

———. *In Quest of Foster Parents: A Point of View on Homefinding.* New York: Columbia University Press, 1943.

HYDE, A. C., AND SHAFRITZ, J. M. *Program Evaluation in the Public Sector.* New York: Praeger Publishers, 1979.

IACCARINO, SANDRA. "Privileged Communication in Social Work" *Social Casework* 61 (June 1980): 367–371.

JENKINS, SHIRLEY, AND NORMAN, ELAINE. *Filial Deprivation and Foster Care.* New York: Columbia University Press, 1972.

———, AND SAUBER, MIGNON. *Paths to Child Placement: Family Situations Prior to Foster Care.* New York: Community Council of Greater New York, 1966.

JEWETT, CLAUDIA L. *Adopting the Older Child.* Harvard, Massachusetts: Harvard Common Press, 1978.

JOFFE, CAROLE. "Abortion Work: Strains, Coping Strategies, Policy Implications." *Social Work* 24 (November 1979): 485–490.

JOHNSON, H. WAYNE. *Rural Human Services: A Book of Readings.* Itasca, Illinois: F. E. Peacock, 1980.

JONES, JOAN M., AND MCNEELY, R. L. "Maternal Deprivation and Learned Helplessness in Child Neglect." In National Conference on Social Welfare, *The*

Social Welfare Forum, 1980, pp. 154–164. New York: Columbia University Press, 1980.

JONES, MARTHA. "Preparing the School-Age Child for Adoption." *Child Welfare* 63 (January 1979): 27–36.

JORDAN, BILL. *Helping in Social Work.* Boston: Routledge and Kegan Paul, 1979.

JOSEPH, SISTER M. VINCENTIA, AND CONRAD, SISTER ANN PATRICK. "A Parish Neighborhood Model for Social Work Practice." *Social Casework* 61 (September 1980); 423–432.

JUSTICE, BLAIR. *The Broken Taboo: Sex in the Family.* New York: Human Sciences Press, 1979.

———, AND JUSTICE, RITA. *The Abusing Family.* New York: Human Sciences Press, 1976.

KADUSHIN, ALFRED. *Adopting Older Children.* New York: Columbia University Press, 1970.

———. *Child Welfare Services: A Sourcebook.* New York: Macmillan Company, 1970.

KAGLE, JILL DONER. "Evaluating Social Work Practice." *Social Work* 24 (July 1979): 292–296.

KAHN, ALFRED J. *Planning Community Services for Children in Trouble.* New York: Columbia University Press, 1963.

———, AND KAMERMAN, SHEILA B. *Social Services in International Perspective: The Emergence of the Sixth System.* Washington, D.C.: U.S. Government Printing Office, 1976.

KAMERMAN, SHEILA B., AND KAHN, ALFRED J. *Family Policy: Government and Families in Fourteen Countries.* New York: Columbia University Press, 1978.

———. *Social Services in the United States: Policies and Programs.* Philadelphia: Temple University Press, 1976.

KATZ, SANFORD N. *When Parents Fail: The Law's Response to Family Breakdown.* Boston: Beacon Press, 1971.

KEMPE, C. HENRY, AND HELFER, RAY E. *Helping the Battered Child and His Family.* Philadelphia: J. B. Lippincott Company, 1972.

KEMPE, RUTH S., AND KEMPE, C. HENRY. *Child Abuse.* Cambridge, Massachusetts: Harvard University Press, 1978.

KENDALL, KATHERINE A. *Reflections on Social Work Education: 1950–1978.* New York: International Association of Schools of Social Work, 1978.

KENISTON, KENNETH, AND THE CARNEGIE COUNCIL ON CHILDREN. *All Our Children: The American Family Under Pressure.* New York: Harcourt Brace Jovanovich, 1977.

KLEIN, ALAN F. *Effective Groupwork: An Introduction to Principle and Method.* New York: Association Press, 1972.

———. *Social Work Through Group Process.* Albany, New York: State University of New York, 1970.

KLEINKAUF, CECILIA. "A Guide to Giving Legislative Testimony." *Social Work* 26 (July 1981): 297–305.

KLIBANOFF, SUSAN, AND KLIBANOFF, ELTON. *Let's Talk About Adoption.* Boston: Little, Brown and Company, 1973.

KLINE, DRAZA, AND OVERSTREET, HELEN-MARY FORBUSH. *Foster Care of Children: Nurture and Treatment.* New York: Columbia University Press, 1972.

KONOPKA, GISELA. *Group Work in the Institution: A Modern Challenge.* New York: Whiteside, Inc., 1954.

———. *Social Group Work: A Helping Process.* Englewood Cliffs, New Jersey: Prentice-Hall, 1972.

KORN, RICHARD R. *Juvenile Delinquency.* New York: Thomas Y. Crowell, 1968.

KOTZ, NICK, AND KOTZ, MARY L. *A Passion for Equality: George Wiley and the Movement.* New York: W. W. Norton, 1977.

KRAUSE, HARRY D. *Child Support in America: The Legal Perspective.* Charlottesville, Virginia: The Michie Company, 1981.

KRUGER, LOIS: MOORE, DORI; SCHMIDT, PARTICIA; AND WIENS, RONNA. "Group Work with Abusive Parents." *Social Work* 24 (July 1979): 337–338.

LANGLEY, ROGER, AND LEVY, RICHARD C. *Wife Beating: The Silent Crisis.* New York: E. P. Dutton, 1977.

LARSEN, JOANN, AND MITCHELL, CRAIG T. "Task-Centered, Strength-Oriented Group Work with Delinquents." *Social Casework* 61 (March 1980): 154–163.

LAUFFER, ARMAND. *Social Planning at the Community Level.* Englewood Cliffs, New Jersey: Prentice-Hall, 1978.

LEHMANN, VIRGINIA, AND MATHIASEN, GENEVA. *Guardianship and Protective Services for Older People.* New York: National Council on Aging Press, 1963.

LEIBY, JAMES. *A History of Social Welfare and Social Work in the United States.* New York: Columbia University Press, 1978.

LEVITAN, SAR A., AND BELOUS, RICHARD S. *More Than Subsistence: Minimum Wages for the Working Poor.* Baltimore: Johns Hopkins University Press, 1979.

LEVY, CHARLES S. "The Ethics of Management." *Administration in Social Work* 3 (Fall 1979): 277–288.

———. "Personal Motivation as a Criterion in Evaluating Social Work Practice." *Social Casework* 61 (November 1980): 541–547.

LEWIS, HELEN M. "Social Impact of Environmental Research." *Human Services in the Rural Environment* 5 (March/April 1980): 12–16.

LIEBERMAN, MORTON A., AND BORMAN, LEONARD D. *Self-Help Groups for Coping with Crisis.* San Francisco: Jossey-Bass, 1980.

LIFTON, BETTY JEAN. *Lost and Found: The Adoption Experience.* New York: The Dial Press, 1979.

———. *Twice Born: Memoirs of an Adopted Daughter.* New York: McGraw-Hill, 1975.

LIGHTMAN, ERNIE S. "What Happens When Recipients Unionize: A Canadian Experience." *Public Welfare* 38 (Spring 1980): 22–28.

LOEWENSTEIN, SOPHIE FREUD. "Inner and Outer Space in Social Casework." *Social Casework* 60 (January 1979): 19–29.

LOHMANN, ROGER A. *Breaking Even: Financial Management in Human Service Organizations.* Philadelphia: Temple University Press, 1980.

———, AND WOLVOVSKY, JAY. "Natural Language Processing and Computer Use in Social Work." *Administration in Social Work* 3 (Winter 1979): 409–422.

LONGRES, JOHN F., AND MCLEOD, EILEEN. "Consciousness Raising and Social Work Practice." *Social Casework* 61 (May 1980): 267–276.

LYNN, LAWRENCE, E., JR. *The State and Human Services: Organizational Change in a Political Context.* Cambridge, Massachusetts: MIT Press, 1980.

MCAFEE, R. BRUCE. "Performance Appraisal: Whose Function." *Personnel Journal* 60 (April 1981): 298–299.

McCann, Charles W., and Cutler, Jane Park. "Ethics and the Alleged Unethical." *Social Work* 24 (January 1979): 5–8.

McCullough, M. K., and Ely, P. J. *Social Work with Groups.* New York: Humanities Press, 1968.

McCurdy, William B. *Program Evaluation: A Conceptual Tool Kit for Human Service Delivery Managers.* New York: Family Service Association, 1980.

MacDonald, Maurice. "Food Stamps: An Analytical History." *Social Service Review* 51 (December 1977): 642–658.

_____. *Food, Stamps, and Income Maintenance.* New York: Academic Press, 1977.

McDonald, T. P., and Piliavin, Irving. "Separation of Services and Income Maintenance: The Workers' Perspective." *Social Work* 25 (July 1980): 264–267.

McFadden, Emily Jean. "Fostering the Battered and Abused Child." *Children Today* 9 (March–April 1980): 13–15.

McNamara, Joan. *The Adoption Adviser.* New York: Hawthorne Books, 1975.

McNeil, John S., and McBride, Mary L. "Group Therapy with Abusive Parents." *Social Casework* 60 (January 1979): 36–42.

McShane, Claudette. "Community Services for Battered Women." *Social Work* 24 (January 1979): 34–39.

Maas, Henry S. *Social Service Research: Reviews of Studies.* New York: National Association of Social Workers, 1978.

Macarov, David. *Work and Welfare: The Unholy Alliance.* Beverly Hills, California: Sage Publications, 1980.

Magel, Don, and Price, Cheryl. "Innovations in Rural Service Delivery." *Human Services in the Rural Environment* 1 (September/October 1979): 20–28.

Magill, Robert S. *Community Decision Making for Social Welfare: Federalism, City Government, and the Poor.* New York: Human Sciences Press, 1979.

Mahaffey, Maryann, and Hanks, John (Eds.). *Practical Politics: Social Work and Political Responsibility.* Silver Spring, Maryland: National Association of Social Workers, 1982.

Malloy, James M. *The Politics of Social Security in Brazil.* Pittsburgh, Pennsylvania: University of Pittsburgh Press, 1979.

Manela, Roger, and Lauffer, Armand. *Health Needs of Children.* Beverly Hills, California: Sage Publications, 1979.

Martin, Harold P. *The Abused Child: A Multidisciplinary Approach to Developmental Issues and Treatment.* Cambridge, Massachusetts: Ballinger Publishing Company, 1976.

Martin, John M., and Fitzpatrick, Joseph P. *Delinquent Behavior: A Redefinition of the Problem.* New York: Random House, 1965.

Martinez-Brawley, Emilia E. *Pioneer Efforts in Rural Social Welfare: Firsthand Views Since 1908.* University Park, Pennsylvania: Pennsylvania State University Press, 1980.

_____. "Rural Social Work Research: An Inventory" *Human Services in the Rural Environment* 5 (November/December 1980): 9–16.

Maslow, Abraham H. *Farther Reaches of Human Nature.* New York: Viking Press, 1971.

Mathews, R. Mark, and Fawcett, Stephen B. *Matching Clients and Services: Information and Referral.* Beverly Hills, California: Sage Publications, 1980.

May, Edgar. "Fifty Years of Looking Ahead." *Public Welfare* 38 (Fall 1980): 9–14.

Maybanks, Sheila, and Bryce, Marvin. *Home-Based Services for Children and*

Families: Policy, Practice, and Research. Springfield, Illinois: Charles C. Thomas, 1979.

MAYER, MORRIS FRITZ; RICHMAN, LEON H.; AND BALCERZAK, EDWIN A. *Group Care of Children: Crossroads and Transitions.* New York: Child Welfare League, 1977.

MENDELSON, JUNE E., AND DOMOLKY, SERENA. "The Courts and Elective Abortions under Medicaid." *Social Service Review* 54 (March 1980): 124–134.

MESA-LAGO, CARMELO. *Social Security in Latin America: Pressure Groups, Stratification, and Inequality.* Pittsburgh, Pennsylvania: University of Pittsburgh Press, 1979.

MEYER, CAROL H. "Social Work Purpose: Status by Choice or Coercion?" *Social Work* 26 (January 1981): 69–75.

————. "What Directions for Direct Practice?" *Social Work* 24 (July 1979): 267–272.

MILLER, DOROTHY L.; HOFFMAN, FRED; AND TURNER, DENIS. "A Perspective on the Indian Child Welfare Act." *Social Casework* 61 (October 1980): 468–471.

MILNER, MURRAY, JR. *Unequal Care: A Case Study of Interorganizational Relations in Health Care.* New York: Columbia University Press, 1980.

MONK, ABRAHAM. "Social Work with the Aged: Principles of Practice." *Social Work* 26 (January 1981): 61–68.

MORALES, ARMANDO. "Social Work with Third-World People." *Social Work* 26 (January 1981): 45–51.

MORELL, BONNIE BROWN. "Deinstitutionalization: Those Left Behind." *Social Work* 24 (November 1979): 528–532.

MORGAN, BETTY. "Four Pennies to My Name: What It's Like on Welfare." *Public Welfare* 37 (Spring 1979): 13–22.

MORRIS, LYNNE CLEMMONS, AND MORRIS, JUDSON HENRY, JR. "Preparing Human Service Workers for Practice in Boom Communities." *Human Services in the Rural Environment* 6 (1981): 22–28.

MORRIS, ROBERT. *Social Policy of the American Welfare State: An Introduction to Policy Analysis.* New York: Harper and Row, 1979.

MUNSON, CARLTON E. "Symbolic Interaction Theory for Small Group Treatment." *Social Casework* 62 (March 1981): 167–174.

MUNSON, LAWRENCE S. "Performance Standards: Do Training Directors Practice What They Teach?" *Personnel Journal* 59 (May 1980): 365–367.

MURDACH, ALLISON D. "Bargaining and Persuasion with Nonvoluntary Clients." *Social Work* 25 (November 1980): 458–463.

MURRAY, CHARLES A., AND COX, LOUIS A., JR. *Beyond Probation: Juvenile Corrections and the Chronic Delinquent.* Beverly Hills: Sage Publications, 1979.

NAGEL, STUART S., AND NEEF, MARION. *Policy Analysis in Social Science Research.* Beverly Hills, California: Sage Publications, 1979.

NAPARSTEK, ARTHUR J. "Community Empowerment; The Critical Role of Neighborhoods." In National Conference on Social Welfare, *The Social Welfare Forum, 1980,* pp. 53–64. New York: Columbia University Press, 1981.

NARDONE, MARYANN. "Characteristics Predicting Community Care for Mentally Impaired Older Persons." *The Gerontologist* 20 (December 1980): 661–668.

NEELY, CAROLYN T. "A New Emphasis in Rural Welfare." *Social Work* 24 (July 1979): 335–336.

NEELY, RICHARD. *How Courts Govern America.* New Haven, Connecticut: Yale University Press, 1981.

NELSEN, JUDITH C. *Community Theory and Social Work Practice.* Chicago: University of Chicago Press, 1980.

_____. "Support: A Necessary Condition for Change." *Social Work* 25 (September 1980): 388–393.

NELSON, GARY. "Social Services to the Urban and Rural Aged: The Experience of Area Agencies on Aging." *The Gerontologist* 20 (April 1980): 200–207.

NEUBER, KEITH A. *Needs Assessment: A Model for Community Planning.* Beverly Hills, California: Sage Publications, 1980.

NORTHEN, HELEN. *Social Work with Groups.* New York: Columbia University Press, 1969.

O'CONNELL, BRIAN. "The Independent Sector and Voluntary Action." In National Conference on Social Welfare, *The Social Welfare Forum, 1980,* pp. 39–52. New York: Columbia University Press, 1981.

PALMER, JOHN L., AND PECHMAN, JOSEPH A. *Welfare in Rural Areas: The North Carolina-Iowa Income Maintenance Experiment.* Washington, D.C.: The Brookings Institution, 1978.

PARKINSON, GARY C. "Cooperation Between Police and Social Workers: Hidden Issues." *Social Work* 25 (January 1980): 12–17.

PARRY, NOEL; RUSTIN, MICHAEL; AND SATYAMURTI, CAROLE. *Social Work, Welfare and the State.* Beverly Hills, California: Sage Publications, 1980.

PELTON, LEROY H. *The Social Context of Child Abuse and Neglect.* New York: Human Sciences, Press, 1980.

PERLMAN, HELEN HARRIS. *Relationship: The Heart of Helping People.* Chicago: University of Chicago Press, 1979.

PERLMUTTER, FELICE DAVIDSON. *A Design for Social Work Practice.* New York: Columbia University Press, 1974.

PERLMUTTER, FELICE, AND SLAVIN, SIMON. *Leadership in Social Administration.* Philadelphia: Temple University Press, 1980.

PETERSON, ROGER. "Social Class, Social Learning, and Wife Abuse." *Social Service Review* 54 (September 1980): 390–406.

PETTY, M. M., AND BRUNING, NEALIA S. "Relationships Between Employee Training and Error Rates in Public Welfare Programs." *Administration in Social Work* 4 (Spring 1980): 33–42.

PICCARD, BETTY J. *An Introduction to Social Work: A Primer.* Homewood Illinois: Dorsey Press, 1980.

PIERCE, LOIS H., AND HAUCK, VICTOR B. "A Model for Establishing Community-Based Foster Group Home." *Child Welfare* 60 (July/August 1981): 475–482.

PIKE, VICTOR, DOWNS, SUSAN; EMLEN, ARTHUR; DOWNS, GLEN; AND CASE, DENISE. *Permanent Planning for Children in Foster Care: A Handbook for Social Workers.* Washington, D.C.: U.S. Department of Health, Education, and Welfare, 1977.

PINCUS, ALLEN, AND MINAHAN, ANNE. *Social Work Practice: Model and Method.* Itasca: F. E. Peacock, 1973.

PINDERHUGHES, ELAINE B. "Teaching Empathy in Cross-Cultural Social Work." *Social Work* 24 (July 1979): 312–316.

PIPPIN, JAMES A. *Developing Casework Skills*. Beverly Hills, California: Sage Publications, 1981.

PIVEN, FRANCES FOX, AND CLOWARD, RICHARD A. *Regulating the Poor: The Functions of Public Relief*. New York: Pantheon Books, 1971.

POLANSKY, NORMAN A. *Child Neglect: Understanding and Reaching the Parent*. New York: Child Welfare League, 1972.

POLIVKA, LARRY; ECCLES, PATSY; AND MILLER, EUGENIA T. "Removal of Status Offenders From the Juvenile Justice System: The Florida Experience." *Child Welfare* 63 (March 1979): 177–185.

POOLE, DENNIS L. *Rural Social Welfare: Educators and Practitioners*. New York: Praeger Publishing Company, 1981.

POPPLE, PHILIP R. "Social Work Practice in Business and Industry, 1875–1930." *Social Service Review* 55 (June 1981): 257–269.

PROCHASKA, JANICE, AND COYLE, JANE R. "Choosing Parenthood: A Needed Family Life Education Group." *Social Casework* 60 (May 1979): 289–295.

PROTTAS, JEFFREY MANDITCH. *People-Processing: The Street-Level Bureaucrat in Public Service Bureaucracies*. Lexington, Massachusetts: D. C. Heath, 1979.

PURYEAR, DOUGLAS A. *Helping People in Crisis*. San Francisco: Jossey-Bass, 1980.

RADIN, NORMA. "Assessing the Effectiveness of School Social Workers." *Social Work* 24 (March 1979): 132–137.

RAPPAPORT, BRUCE M. "Family Planning: Helping Men Ask for Help." *Public Welfare* 39 (Spring 1981): 22–27.

RATHBONE-MCCUAN, ELOISE. "Elderly Victims of Family Violence and Neglect." *Social Casework* 61 (May 1980): 296–304.

RAYMOND, LOUISE. *Adoption and After*. New York: Harper and Row, 1955.

REAMER, FREDERIC G. "Ethical Content in Social Work." *Social Casework* 61 (November 1980): 531–540.

———. "Fundamental Ethical Issues in Social Work: An Essay Review." *Social Service Review* 53 (June 1979): 229–243.

REID, WILLIAM J. *The Task-Centered System*. New York: Columbia University Press, 1978.

———, AND BEARD, CHRISTINE. "An Evaluation of In-Service Training in a Public Welfare Setting." *Administration in Social Work* 4 (Spring 1980): 71–85.

———, AND EPSTEIN, LAURA. *Task-Centered Practice*. New York: Columbia University Press, 1977.

REIN, MARTIN, AND WHITE, SHELDON H. "Knowledge for Practice." *Social Service Review* 55 (March 1981): 1–41.

RESNICK, HERMAN, AND PATTI, RINO J. *Change from Within: Humanizing Social Welfare Organizations*. Philadelphia: Temple University Press, 1980.

RHODES, SONYA L. "The Personality of the Worker: An Unexplored Dimension in Treatment." *Social Casework* 60 (May 1979): 259–264.

———. "Trends in Child Development Research Important to Day Care Policy." *Social Service Review* 53 (June 1979): 285–294.

RICHMOND, MARY E. *Social Diagnosis*. New York: Russell Sage Foundation, 1917.

———. *What is Social Case Work?* New York: Russell Sage Foundation, 1922.

RICKARD, SCOTT T. "Effective Staff Selection." *Personnel Journal* 60 (June 1981): 475–478.

ROBERTS, ALBERT R. *Sheltering Battered Women: A National Study and Guide to Services.* New York: Springer Publishing Company, 1980.

ROHE, WILLIAM M., AND GATES, LAUREN B. "Neighborhood Planning: Promise and Product." *The Urban and Social Change Review* 14 (Winter 1981): 26–32.

RONDELL, FLORENCE, AND MURRAY, ANNE-MARIE. *New Dimensions in Adoption.* New York: Crown Publishers, 1974.

ROSS, BERNARD, AND SHIREMAN, CHARLES. *Social Work Practice and Social Justice.* Washington, D.C.: National Association of Social Workers, 1973.

ROSS, MURRAY G., AND HENDRY, CHARLES G. *New Understandings of Leadership: A Survey and Application of Research.* New York: Association Press, 1957.

———, AND LAPPIN, B. W. *Community Organization: Theory, Principles, and Practice,* 2nd ed. New York: Harper & Row, 1967.

ROTH, WILLIAM. "The Energy Crisis and Social Work." *Social Work* 25 (July 1980): 317–318.

ROTHMAN, JACK. *Social R & D: Research and Development in the Human Services.* Englewood Cliffs, New Jersey: Prentice-Hall, 1980.

———. *Using Research in Organizations: A Guide to Successful Application.* Beverly Hills, California: Sage Publications, 1980.

RUSSELL, THOMAS H., AND SILBERMAN, JAYE M. "Improving the Delivery of Specialized Foster Care Services." *Social Casework* 60 (July 1979): 402–407.

SABLE, PAT. "Differentiating Between Attachment and Dependency in Theory and Practice." *Social Casework* 60 (March 1979): 138–144.

SAFFORD, FLORENCE. "A Program for Families of the Mentally Impaired Elderly." *The Gerontologist* 20 (December 1980); 656–660.

SALAMON, LESTER M. *Welfare: The Elusive Concept—Where We Are, How We Got There, and What's Ahead.* New York: Praeger Publishers, 1978.

SCANLON, PAULINE L. "A Gestalt Approach to Insight-Oriented Treatment." *Social Casework* 61 (September 1980): 407–415.

SCHENK, QUENTIN F. *Welfare, Society, and the Helping Professions.* New York: Macmillan Publishing Co., 1981.

SCHINKE, STEVEN PAUL. "Evaluating Social Work Practice: A Conceptual Model and Example." *Social Casework* 60 (April 1979): 195–200.

SCHODEK, KAY. "Adjuncts to Social Casework in the 1980's." *Social Casework* 62 (April 1981): 195–200.

SCHOECH, DICK. "A Microcomputer Based Human Service Information System." *Administration in Social Work* 3 (Winter, 1979): 423–440.

SCHOSSLER, LEONARD J. "Child Support Enforcement: An Assessment of IV-D's First Four Years." *Public Welfare* 37 (Fall 1979): 22–32.

SCHULBERG, HERBERT C., AND BAKER, FRANK. *Program Evaluation in the Health Fields,* Vol. 2. New York: Human Sciences Press, 1979.

SEABURY, BRETT A. "Communication Problems in Social Work Practice." *Social Work* 25 (January 1980): 40–44.

———. "Negotiating Sound Contracts with Clients." *Public Welfare* 37 (Spring 1979): 33–38.

SEGALMAN, RALPH, AND BASU, ASOKE. *Poverty in America: The Welfare Dilemma.* Westport, Connecticut: Greenwood Press, 1981.

SHULMAN, LAWRENCE. *The Skills of Helping Individuals and Groups.* Itasca, Illinois: F. E. Peacock Publishers, 1979.

SHYNE, ANN W. *Child Welfare Perspectives: Selected Papers of Joseph H. Reid*. New York: Child Welfare League of America, 1979.

SILBERMAN, CHARLES E. *Criminal Violence, Criminal Justice*. New York: Random House, 1978.

SILVERMAN, PHYLLIS ROLFE. *Mutual Help Groups: Organization and Development*. Beverly Hills, California: Sage Publications, 1981.

SIMONS, RONALD L., AND AIGNER, STEPHEN M. "Facilitating an Eclectic Use of Practice Theory." *Social Casework* 60 (April 1979): 201–208.

SIPORIN, MAX. "Marriage and Family Therapy in Social Work." *Social Casework* 61 (January 1980): 11–21.

SLAVIN, PETER. "Day Care in West Virginia: A Distinctive Approach." *Public Welfare* 37 (Fall 1979): 40–51.

SMALLEY, RUTH E. *Theory for Social Work Practice*. New York: Columbia University Press, 1967.

SMITH, B. BABINGTON, AND FARRELL, B. A. *Training in Small Groups: A Study of Five Methods*. Elmsford, New York: Pergamon Press, 1979.

SMITH, DOROTHY. *In Our Own Interest: A Handbook for the Citizen Lobbyist in State Legislatures*. Seattle: Madrona Publishers, 1979.

SMITH, VIRGINIA W. "How Interest Groups Influence Legislators." *Social Work* 24 (May 1979): 234–240.

SOROSKY, ARTHUR D.; BARAN, ANNETTE; AND PANNOR, REUBEN. *The Adoption Triangle: The Effects of the Sealed Record on Adoptees, Birth Parents, and Adoptive Parents*. New York: Anchor Press, 1978.

SOSIN, MICHAEL. "Social Welfare and Organizational Society." *Social Service Review* 53 (September 1979): 392–405.

———. "Social Work Advocacy and the Implementation of Legal Mandates." *Social Casework* 60 (May 1979): 265–273.

SPIEGEL, ALLEN D. *Curing and Caring: A Review of the Factors Affecting the Quality and Acceptability of Health Care*. New York: Spectrum Publications, 1980.

———. *The Medicaid Experience*. Germantown, Maryland: Aspen Systems Corporation, 1979.

———. *Medical Technology, Health Care and the Consumer*. New York: Human Sciences Press, 1981.

SPINDLER, ARTHUR. *Public Welfare*. New York: Human Sciences Press, 1979.

SPIRO, SHIMON E. *Issues and Explorations in Social Work Education*. Tel Aviv: Israeli Association of Schools of Social Work, 1978.

STEIN, THEODORE J. *Social Work Practice in Child Welfare*. Englewood Cliffs, New Jersey: Prentice-Hall, 1981.

STEINER, GILBERT Y. *Social Insecurity: The Politics of Welfare*. Chicago: Rand McNally, 1966.

———. *The State of Welfare*. Washington, D. C.: The Brookings Institution, 1971.

STEINER, JOSEPH R., GROSS, GERALD M. "Underlying Agendas in the New Social Work Code of Ethics." In National Conference on Social Welfare, *The Social Welfare Forum, 1980*, pp. 207–218. New York: Columbia University Press, 1981.

STEMPLER, BENJAMIN L., AND STEMPLER, HANI. "Extending the Client Connection: Using Homemaker-Caseworker Teams." *Social Casework* 62 (March 1981): 149–158.

STERN, LEWIS M. "Response to Vietnamese Refugees: Surveys of Public Opinion." *Social Work* 26 (July 1981): 306–312.

STONE, HELEN D. *Foster Care in Question: A National Reassessment by Twenty-One Experts.* New York: Child Welfare League, 1970.

———, AND HUNZEKER, JEANNE M. *Education for Foster Family Care: Models and Methods for Foster Parents and Social Workers.* New York: Child Welfare League, 1974.

STREAN, HERBERT S. *Psychoanalytic Theory and Social Work Practice.* New York: The Free Press, 1979.

STREET, DAVID; MARTIN, GEORGE T., JR.; AND GORDON, LAURA KRAMER. *The Welfare Industry: Functionaries and Recipients in Public Aid.* Beverly Hills, California: Sage Publications, 1979.

STRETCH, JOHN J. "Seven Key Managerial Functions of Sound Fiscal Budgeting: An Internal Management and External Accountability Perspective." *Administration in Social Work* 3 (Winter 1979): 441–452.

———. "What Human Services Managers Need to Know about Basic Budgeting Strategies." *Administration in Social Work* 4 (Spring 1980); 87–98.

SUNDEL, SANDRA STONE, AND SUNDEL, MARTIN. *Be Assertive: A Practical Guide for Human Services Workers.* Beverly Hills, California: Sage Publications, 1980.

SUSSMAN, ALAN, AND COHEN, STEPHAN J. *Reporting Child Abuse and Neglect: Guidelines for Legislation.* Cambridge, Massachusetts: Ballinger Publishing Company, 1975.

TAMBOR, MILTON. "The Social Worker as Worker: A Union Perspective." *Administration in Social Work* 3 (Fall 1979) 289–300.

TAYLOR, WILLIAM L., AND CANGEMI, JOSEPH P. "Employee Theft and Organizational Climate." *Personnel Journal* 58 (October 1979): 686–688.

TEITELBAUM, LEE E., AND GOUGH, AIDAN R. *Beyond Control: Status Offenders in the Juvenile Court.* Cambridge, Massachusetts: Ballinger Publishing Company, 1977.

THURSZ, DANIEL, AND VIGILANTE, JOSEPH L. *Metting Human Needs: An Overview of Nine Countries.* Beverly Hills, California: Sage Publications, 1975.

———, AND VIGILANTE, JOSEPH L. *Meeting Human Needs: Additional Perspectives from Thirteen Countries.* Beverly Hills, California: Sage Publications, 1977.

———, AND VIGILANTE, JOSEPH L. *Reaching People: The Structure of Neighborhood Services.* Beverly Hills, California: Sage Publications, 1978.

TILLEMA, RICHARD G. "Starting Over in a New Land: Resettling a Refugee Family." *Public Welfare* 39 (Winter 1981); 35–42.

TIMM, JOAN THROWER. "Group Care of Children and the Development of Moral Judgment." *Child Welfare* 59 (June 1980); 323–334.

TIMMS, NOEL. *Social Welfare: Why and How?* Boston: Routledge and Kegal Paul, 1981.

TITMUSS, RICHARD M. *Commitment to Welfare.* New York: Pantheon Books, 1968.

TOSELAND, RONALD. "Increasing Access: Outreach Methods in Social Work Practice." *Social Casework* 62 (April 1981): 227–234.

TRADER, HARRIET PEAT. "Welfare Policies and Black Families." *Social Work* 24 (November 1979); 548–552.

TRATTNER, WALTER I. *From Poor Law to Welfare State: A History of Social Welfare in America,* 2nd ed. New York: Macmillan Publishing Co., 1979.

TREGOR, HARVEY. "Police-Social Work Cooperation: Problems and Issues." *Social Casework* 62 (September 1981): 426–433.

TRIPODI, TONY, AND EPSTEIN, IRWIN. *Research Techniques for Clinical Social Workers.* New York: Columbia University Press, 1980.

———; FELLIN, PHILLIP; EPSTEIN, IRWIN; AND LIND, ROGER. *Social Workers at Work: An Introduction to Social Work Practice.* Itasca, Illinois: F. E. Peacock, 1972.

TROHANIS, PASCAL LOUIS. "Developing Community Acceptance of Programs for Children." *Child Welfare* 59 (June 1980); 365–373.

TUCKER, DAVID J. "Coordination and Citizen Participation." *Social Service Review* 54 (March 1980); 13–30.

TURNER, FRANCIS J. *Psychosocial Therapy: A Social Work Perspective. New York: The Free Press, 1978.*

———. *Social Work Treatment: Interlocking Theoretical Approaches,* 2nd ed. New York: The Free Press, 1979.

TURNER, JOHN B., *Encyclopedia of Social Work,* 17th ed. Washington, D.C.: National Association of Social Workers, 1977.

U.S. DEPARTMENT OF HEALTH, EDUCATION AND WELFARE. *Characteristics of General Assistance in the United States 1978.* Washington, D.C.: U.S. Government Printing Office, 1979.

———. *Model State Subsidized Adoption Act and Regulations.* Washington, D.C.: U.S. Department of Health, Education, and Welfare, 1976.

———. *Public Assistance Recipients and Cash Payments by State and County February 1979.* Washington, D.C.: U.S. Government Printing Office, 1980.

———. *Subsidized Adoption in America.* Washington, D.C.: U.S. Department of Health, Education, and Welfare, 1976.

U.S. DEPARTMENT OF HEALTH AND HUMAN SERVICES. *Characteristics of State Plans for Aid to Families with Dependent Children under The Social Security Act Title IV-A.* Washington, D.C.: U.S. Government Printing Office, 1980, 1981.

———. *1977 Recipient Characteristics Study, Aid to Families with Dependent Children, Part I, Demographic and Program Statistics.* Washington, D.C.: U.S. Government Printing Office, 1980.

———. *1977 Recipient Characteristics Study, Aid to Families with Dependent Children, Part II, Financial Circumstances of AFDC Families.* Washington, D.C.: U.S. Government Printing Office, 1980.

———. *Research Tables Based on Characteristics of State Plans for Aid to Families with Dependent Children.* Washington, D.C.: U.S. Government Printing Office, 1980.

———. *Social Security Programs Throughout the World 1979.* Washington, D.C.: U.S. Government Printing Office, 1980.

———. *Social Services U.S.A.* Washington, D.C.: U.S. Government Printing Office, 1979.

UNITED STATES SENATE SPECIAL COMMITTEE ON AGING. *Protective Services for the Elderly: A Working Paper.* Washington, D.C.: U.S. Government Printing Office, 1977.

VINYARD, DALE. "White House Conference and the Aged." *Social Service Review* 53 (December 1979): 655–671.

VLADECK, BRUCE C. *Unloving Care: The Nursing Home Tragedy.* New York: Basic Books, 1980.

VOROS, GERALD J., AND ALVAREZ, PAUL. *What Happens in Public Relations.* New York: American Management Association, 1981.

WALKER, LENORE E. *The Battered Woman.* New York. Harper and Row, 1979.

WALLACE, BARBARA. "Devising Survival Strategies for Cities and People" (Interview with Anthony Downs). *Public Welfare* 37 (Winter 1979): 23–30.

WALLACE, MARQUIS EARL. "A Framework for Self-Supervision in Social Work Practice." *Social Casework* 62 (May 1981): 293–304.

WALLACH, ARTHUR E. "System Changes Begin in the Training Department." *Personnel Journal* 58 (December 1979): 846–848.

WALZ, THOMAS H. "The Art of Humanizing a Welfare Department." In National Conference on Social Welfare. *The Social Welfare Forum, 1980,* pp. 65–76. New York: Columbia University Press, 1981.

WARD, MARGARET. "Parental Bonding in Older-Child Adoptions." *Child Welfare* 60 (January 1981): 24–34.

_____. "The Relationship Between Parents and Caseworker in Adoption." *Social Casework* 60 (February 1979): 96–103.

WARREN, ROLAND L. *The Community in America,* 2nd ed. Chicago: Rand McNally, 1972.

_____. *Perspectives on the American Community: A Book of Readings,* 2nd ed. Chicago: Rand McNally, 1973.

WATTS, ANN D. "Planners' Perceptions of Rural/Small Town Issues." *Human Services in the Rural Environment* 5 (September/October 1980): 15–21.

WEINER, MARCELLA B., BROK, ALBERT J. AND SNADOWSKY, ALVIN M. *Working with the Aged: Practical Approaches in the Institution and Community.* Englewood Cliffs, New Jersey: Prentice-Hall, 1978.

WEISS, CAROL H. *Using Social Research in Public Policy Making.* Lexington, Massachusetts: Lexington Books, 1977.

WEISSBOURD, BERNICE, AND GRIMM, CAROL. "Family Focus: Supporting Families in the Community." *Children Today* 10 (March–April 1981): 6–11.

WHITE, MARY S. "The Role of Parent-Child Visiting in Permanency Planning for Children." In National Conference on Social Welfare, *The Social Welfare Forum,* 1980, pp. 165–176. New York: Columbia University Press, 1981.

WHITTAKER, JAMES K. *Caring for Troubled Children.* San Francisco: Jossey-Bass, 1979.

_____, AND TRIESCHMAN, ALBERT E. *Children Away From Home: A Sourcebook of Residential Treatment.* Chicago: Aldine Atherton, 1972.

WIJNBERG, MARION H., AND COLCA, LOUIS. "Facing Up to the Diversity in Rural Practice: A Curriculum Model." *Journal of Education for Social Work* 17 (Spring 1981): 91–97.

WILENSKY, HAROLD L., AND LEBEAUX, CHARLES N. *Industrial Society and Social Welfare.* 17 (Spring 1981): 91–97.

WILTSE, KERMIT T. "Foster Care in the 1970's: A Decade of Change." *Children Today* 8 (May–June 1979): 10–14.

WITKIN, STANLEY L.; SHAPIRO, CONSTANCE H.; AND MCCALL, MARGARET. "How to Evaluate Public Welfare Training." *Public Welfare* 38 (Summer 1980): 28–41.

WOLK, JAMES L. "Are Social Workers Politically Active?" *Social Work* 26 (July 1981): 283–288.

WOODEN, KENNETH. *The Children of Jonestown.* New York: McGraw-Hill, 1981.

WOODSWORTH, DAVID E. *Social Security and National Policy: Sweden, Yugoslavia, Japan.* Montreal: McGill-Queens University Press, 1977.

WRIGHT, SONIA R. *Quantitative Methods and Statistics: A Guide to Social Research.* Beverly Hills, California: Sage Publications, 1979.

WYCOFF, EDGAR B. "Canons of Communication." *Personnel Journal* 60 (March 1981): 207–211.

WYERS, NORMAN L. "Whatever Happened to the Income Maintenance Line Worker?" *Social Work* 25 (July 1980): 259–263.

YAGER, ED. "When New Hires Don't Make the Grade (The Case for Assessment Centers)." *Personnel Journal* 59 (May 1980): 387–390.

YANKEY, JOHN A., AND COULTON, CLAUDIA J. "Promoting Contributions to Organizational Goals: Alternative Models." *Administration in Social Work* 3 (Spring 1979): 45–56.

YOUNG, MARJORIE HOPE. "Social Work Under Apartheid." *Social Work* 25 (July 1980): 309–313.

YOUNGHUSBAND, EILEEN. *Social Work in Britain: 1950–1975.* London: George Allen and Unwin, 1978.

ZASTROW, CHARLES H. *Introduction to Social Welfare Institutions: Social Problems, Services, and Current Issues.* Homewood, Illinois: Dorsey Press, 1980.

——. *The Practice of Social Work.* Homewood, Illinois: Dorsey Press, 1980.

ZENTNER, MONNA. "The Paranoid Client." *Social Casework* 61 (March 1980): 138–145.

Index